Woodsmoke

Compiled by
Richard and Linda Jamison

First Printing: July 1997

International Standard Book Number:
0-88290-611-9

Horizon Publishers' Catalog and Order Number:
1241

Printed and distributed
in the United States of America by

**Horizon
Publishers
& Distributors, Incorporated**

Mailing Address:
P.O. Box 490
Bountiful, Utah 84011-0490

Street Address:
50 South 500 West
Bountiful, Utah 84010

Local Phone: (801) 295-9451
WATS (toll free): 1 (800) 453-0812
FAX: (801) 295-0196

Internet: www.horizonpublishers.com

Other Woodsmoke Products

∙ ∙

Other Books in the Woodsmoke series

The Best of Woodsmoke

"Touching Time"—*Richard Jamison*; The Use of Pitch—*Richard Jamison*; The Wickiup—*Jim Riggs*; Water Location—*Richard Jamison*; Dangerous Animal Altercations—Quick Rabbit Bows—*Richard Jamison*; Surviving a Blizzard With Only a Blanket—*Larry J. Wells*; Surviving Winter Hazards—*Larry J. Wells*; Nature's Yeast—*Linda Jamison*; The Hot Coal Bed—*Larry D. Olsen*; Deadfall Trapping—*Larry D. Olsen*; Pine Needle Bed in the Woods—*Ernest Wilkinson*; The Stone Axe—*Paul Hellweg*; Primitive Fishing—*Richard Jamison*; The Art of Making Arrowheads—*Paul Hellweg*; Troubleshooting Bow and Drill Fires—*Richard Jamison*; The Primitive Hand Drill Firemaking Technique—*Ron "Gus" Gustaveson*; Complete Use of the Deer—*Jim Riggs*; Wilderness Cordage—*Richard Jamison*; Surviving Mentally—*Gary Wisdom*; Basics of Keeping Warm—*Richard Jamison*.

Primitive Outdoor Skills

The Primitive Life Style—*Linda Jamison*; Easy-to-make Stone Tools—*Paul Hellweg*; Swamp Craft—*Richard Jamison*; A Trapper's Viewpoint—*Ernest Wilkinson*; Ancient Steam-pit Cooking—*Rich Johnson*; The Arrow—*Richard Jamison*; The Survival of Purpose—*Larry Dean Olsen*; Sagebrush: The Ancient Survival Kit—*Jim Riggs*; A Plea to Those Who Would Be Self-sufficient—*Larry Dean Olsen*; Bulrush Weaving: East Sand-cast Pots—*Linda Jamison*; Snow Caves the Easy Way—*Richard Jamison*; "Touching Time"—*Richard Jamison*; The Sweat Lodge—*Jim Riggs*; Insect Food—*Linda Jamison*; The Horno: An Outdoor Oven—*Margaret Wilkinson*; The Digging Stick—*Linda Jamison*; 101 Uses of a Snake Bag—*Jim Riggs*; Animal Field Care—*Ernest Wilkinson*; The Hot Draft Bed—*Richard Jamison*.

Instructional Video Series

Each video is packed with interesting primitive how-to's and potentially life-saving knowledge of ancient living skills geared for both the novice and experienced outdoor sports person.

Fire I.

Hand-drill fire making technique with featured expert, Jim Riggs. Beginning with the collection of materials, each step is thoroughly explained in an easy-to-follow process. 30 min.

Fire II.

Bow-drill fire making technique with featured expert, Richard Jamison. From materials through proper form, this is a comprehensive how-to anyone can imitate successfully. 30 min.

Fire III.

Fire saw, fire plow, fire thong, and fire piston fire making techniques with featured expert, Mel Deweese. The four unusual methods are thoroughly demonstrated and adaptable materials discussed. 30 min.

Shelters

How to find and construct natural shelters. Host Richard Jamison discusses and demonstrates the materials and elements necessary to build or locate shelter. Step-by-step instruction is presented for constructing the versatile wickiup shelter. 30 min.

Primitive Cooking

Pit cooking, stone oven baking, spit cooking, skewering, and cooking in the ashes. Host Richard Jamison explains how to build effective cooking fires for specific types of cooking and demonstrates five unique methods of outdoor cooking. 30 min.

Primitive Pottery

Coil and scrape hand-built technique with featured expert Wayne Brian. Beginning with the geological strata where clay is found, the film includes material preparation, modeling a vessel and an outdoor firing. 60 min.

To Order these products, contact:

Horizon Publishers

50 South 500 West P.O. Box 490
Bountiful, Ut 84011-0490
(801) 295-9451 WATS 1-800-451-0812

Woodsmoke—Dept. WS

P.O. Box 1384
Sandy, Ut 84091

Table of Contents

Introduction i

Acknowledgments ii

Contributors' Biographies iii

Our Human Family 1

The Ultimate Weapon .15

Old Finnish Hunting and Fishing Techniques 25

Primitive Process Pottery 35

Stone Survival Tools 53

Yucca 61

Make Your Own Hide Glue 77

Traditional Basketry Materials 85

Tracking Skills 99

The Primal Gourmet 109

Whole-Shoot Willow Baskets 121

A Paleo Prescription 137

Barking Up the Right Tree 149

The Remarkable Fire Piston 163

An Introduction to the Atlatl 177

Badgerstone 191

Pine Needle Basketry 199

"Rocking On" with the Paiute Deadfall 209

Philosophy of a Caveman 225

Living with Nature 231

References 247

Index 254

Introduction

I t has only been in the last few hundred years that we humans have become disconnected with our life force. And as a consequence, our perception of our place in nature has deteriorated to the point that we are systematically destroying our environment and ourselves. Yet, ironically, by taking a step back in time, it is possible to take an immense step forward in understanding.

While we do not believe it is possible to return completely to the old ways, we do believe that once a person experiences the excitement of creating fire by ancient methods, molds a piece of the earth into a functional vessel of beauty, builds shelter using what nature provides, or experiences first-hand any of the life skills of our ancient ancestors, he or she will understand the vital alliance we all have with our past and our environment.

Since its inception in 1977, it has been the intent of Woodsmoke to instill, through education, a sense of appreciation and responsibility in men and women and young people—creating an awareness of the relationship of humankind to Mother Earth. We have endeavored to do this through workshops, field sessions, on film and in print. Thus, we believe woodsmoke can truly erase the fumes of civilization.

Acknowledgments

Woodsmoke is and has always been a combined effort of many, and so this book is dedicated to our "abo" friends and trail companions—practitioners who have devoted themselves to a lifetime of study, experimenting and living the old ways, and have generously shared their findings with others. To our contributors and all who fit this description, thank you. You have helped convey understanding and meaning to our lives.

Richard and Linda Jamison

Contributors' Biographies

....

Turkka Aaltonen

Turkka is a long-time Woodsmoke associate, survivalist and a published freelance writer in his native Finland. Turkka is the director of the Finnish Survival Guild, which conducts training workshops and expeditions in that country. He has written four books on outdoor subjects and publishes a quarterly booklet titled *Survival News*, which contains how-to information on primitive and technical outdoor skills.

Donald Fisher

Donald first became interested in aboriginal lifestyles as a student of Paul Hellweg at California State University. The two became friends and have collaborated on many projects during the past fifteen years. Don now teaches primitive skills, including stoneworking, lithics and brain tanning at colleges, universities and museums near his home in Indianapolis, Indiana.

Paul Hellweg

Paul is a past contributor to early *Woodsmoke Journal* issues as well as the books *The Best of Woodsmoke* and *Primitive Outdoor Skills*. He serves as an Assistant Professor on the faculty of California State University Northridge, where he teaches classes in backpacking, mountaineering, wilderness survival and basic flintknapping. An excellent flintknapper, Paul studied under the master, Don Crabtree. Paul is the author of the book *Flintknapping, the Art of Making Stone Tools* and eight other books including three climbing guides and several reference books.

Linda J. Jamison

Linda has participated in many primitive expeditions, both as a student and as an instructor. She has conducted field trips and lectured on wild plant identification and use at the University of Southern Colorado, University of Colorado, Pikes Peak Community College and to many clubs and organizations during the past twenty years. She was a director of Highland Survival School and editor of *Woodsmoke Journal* for six years. An English major, Linda currently writes film scripts and proposals in addition to being a published freelance writer of outdoor educational material. She was the executive producer of the Woodsmoke video series.

Richard L. Jamison

Richard is a noted expert who has received national recognition for his skill in primitive craftmanship and knowledge of aboriginal (prehistoric) skills. He is an accomplished, award-winning outdoor photographer (having majored in art with emphasis on photography at Weber State University in Utah) and a published writer. In 1973, Richard produced and filmed a series of outdoor educational films that was used by other instructors in schools throughout the United States and Europe. As director of Anasazi Expeditions, Richard conducted numerous primitive expeditions over the past twenty years, accumulating an impressive "trail time." He was publisher of *Woodsmoke Journal* for six years and compiled two books which are distributed nationally—*The Best of Woodsmoke* and *Primitive Outdoor Skills*. In 1992, he produced and hosted a series of six *Woodsmoke* outdoor educational videos which are marketed nationally, primarily to schools and libraries. He is currently a production designer/ art director in the motion picture industry, specializing in large-format (IMAX).

Peg Mathewson

Peg is a graduate student of the University of California, Berkeley, majoring in Ethnobotany, Art, and Anthropology of Native America. The daughter of two professors of Anthropology, she has been exposed to her chosen field all her life and has studied with traditional California basket weavers for eight years. Peg teaches primitive skills in the San Francisco area and in Oregon and has attended many primitive expeditions both as a student and instructor. In addition to her skill as a basketmaker, she is an outstanding craftsperson in many areas of the aboriginal lifestyle.

Larry Dean Olsen

Larry is the author of the best-selling book, *Outdoor Survival Skills* and the originator of the award-winning "480" 30-day survival trek at Brigham Young University. He has been a pioneer in instigating primitive survival courses as an effective rehabilitation program in the United States. Larry has lectured and taught primitive survival throughout the nation and is currently Chairman of the Board of "Anasazi," a program for troubled youth that emphasizes the primitive lifestyle as a means to build self-esteem.

Jim Riggs

Jim has a degree in anthropology and conducted aboriginal life skill courses and workshops for sixteen years at the Malheur Field Station in

Oregon. He is a member of the Board of Directors of the Society of Primitive Technology and is a regular contributor to the *Bulletin of Primitive Technology*. An expert craftsman, he has contributed many replicas to the High Desert Museum in Oregon. Jim is also a talented writer, photographer and illustrator; he is the author of *Blue Mountain Buckskin* as well as many published magazine articles and was the primitive skills trainer for the popular film *Clan of the Cave Bear*. Jim currently resides near Wallowa, Oregon.

Steve Watts

Steve directs the Southeastern Native American Studies program at the Schiele Museum of Natural History in Gastonia, North Carolina and is a founding board member of the Society of Primitive Technology. Steve's interests range from Upper Paleolithic Europe to the aboriginal peoples of Africa and the Pacific. He teaches aboriginal skills courses throughout the United States. His replicas of prehistoric tools and weapons are on display or in experimental use at more than a dozen museums in the Southeast and Gulf regions. Steve received his undergraduate degree from Appalachian State University and a master's degree from Duke University.

David Wescott

Dave was a pioneer in primitive outdoor education and is a superb craftsman and seasoned outdoorsman. He was a student of Larry Dean Olsen's early Youth Leadership-480 survival program and earned a degree in Youth Leadership from Brigham Young University. Subsequently, Dave worked with Outward Bound and now owns and operates Boulder Outdoor Survival School (BOSS), a well-respected organization that has been in existence for many years to give people of all ages a chance to develop their self-confidence and outdoor skills. BOSS sponsors the annual "Rabbit Stick" primitive skills conference in Rexburg, Idaho. Dave is the editor of the *Bulletin of Primitive Technology* and a founding board member of the Society of Primitive Technology.

Tamara Wilder and Steven Edholm

Tamara and Steven have been experimenting with primitive living skills for about 5 years, much of which time was spent living in semi-primitive conditions. This time has given them a clear concept of how people might have lived before modern times. Their main occupations are tanning buckskin using the wet-scrape, brain tan method and instructing others in skills such as brain tanning and uses of the deer, cordage and net making, firemaking, flintknapping, basketry and plant uses. Tamara and Steven were originally exposed to the art of basketry by Margaret (Peg) Mathewson and have spent countless hours gathering materials and weaving baskets. Their basketwork is featured in an Imax film titled *Tresure of the Gods*, which is shown in the Zion Canyon Theater near Zion National Park in southern Utah. Each year Tamara and Steven take part in the Rabbit Stick Primitive Skills Conference in addition to teaching courses on the "old ways" for the Santa Cruz Mountain Natural History Association and the Miwok Archeological Preserve of Marin, California.

Ernest Wilkinson

Ernest is an expert on animal behavior and an authority on winter survival techniques. He is a member of the Outdoor Writer's Association and has authored many magazine articles on outdoor subjects as well as a book, *Snow Caves for Fun and Survival*. Ernie is also a professional wildlife photographer. Until recently, he and his wife, Margaret, raised mountain lions, badgers, wolves and other animals for filming. He was principal photographer for the film *Cougar Country*, which featured his own mountain lion, Tabby. A series of seven videos have recently been produced using his unique footage of wild animals. Ernie currently works as a taxidermist, government trapper, guide and survival instructor in Monte Vista, Colorado.

Margaret Wilkinson

Margaret is a woman of many talents with an impressive knowledge of the outdoors. She and her husband, Ernest, have lived and worked all their lives in the mountains that surround their home and business in Monte Vista, Colorado. Together, they conduct an annual primitive skills encampment which is attended by people from all over the United States and Europe. Margaret is a wild plant expert and operates a medicinal herb shop and conducts classes and workshops on a variety of outdoor educational subjects. She also designs and sews leather garments for customers throughout the country in conjunction with their taxidermy business.

Woodsmoke

Linda Jamison

Our Human Family
Understanding Our Ancient Ancestors

● ●

What can a people so removed from our world teach us?
And does it matter that our conception of our ancient
ancestors is correct? I think it matters a great deal. We
can't even begin to tackle constructively the multiple,
interlocking problems threatening our species and our
planet today without some grasp of who and what we are,
how we got that way and what does or does not work for us.

The same age-old questions have plagued humanity since we were first capable of cognitive thinking: "Who are we, where did we come from and where are we going?" I maintain that some of the answers to those questions lie in our ancient past. By studying who we were, we can learn who we are. In learning about our early cousins—their environment, their moral structure, their lifestyle—we will make genealogical attachments. Then we can take the decisive step toward experiencing that lifestyle, and having experienced it, we will be qualified to speculate on the reasons for their failures and successes and convey those lessons to our modern world.

I have been on the ancient trail. It was a learning experience that changed my life forever. I remember seeing things for the first time-familiar things, but from a different perspective. I saw a fire up close because I was on my knees blowing for all I was worth to turn a small glowing coal to flame. I saw water with my nose buried in a small pool as

I slurped up as much as I could hold to tide me over to the next water source. I saw little creatures swimming in the bottom of those pools. I saw the stars without the interference of city lights and smog. I saw food as something to give me energy and stamina, not simply something to occupy my time and satisfy my cravings. I saw animal life as a lesson instead of an intrusion. I saw relationships in terms of giving and sharing and teaching. I saw life as valuable...all life.

Still we are not, nor will we ever be, a Stone Age people again. I knew a young man whose greatest dream was to "become an Indian." He was an Anglo, but he so admired the natural lifestyle and skills that were a way of life for many Native Americans that he truly believed that if he emulated their lifestyle he would become an Indian. Of course no amount of wanting could have made him an Indian. But he could not conceive of the fact that his own ancestors were an ancient people who also lived their lives in accordance with the laws of nature, long before the inhabitants of this continent.

My own Neolithic ancestors were skilled makers of axes, several types of flint knives, stone tools, utensils of bone and simple forms of pottery for cooking and storage. They lived in squat houses, built with half their structure below the surface of the earth, lined with dry-stone wall construction and a fire pit in the center for warmth and light. In early times they lived primarily in family groups referred to as tribes, headed by a chief who was loyally respected as "the law." They were buried in a crouched position, along with an assortment of weapons and possessions, in pits dug in the earth and lined with stone and either roofed with slabs or covered with heaps of stones. They were Highland Scots.

Had my friend understood the contributions of his own culture, he would have had pride and admiration for his ancestors' achievements. And if he could have understood his relationship to all humanity he might have learned that he is part of the Native American culture through the vast family of humankind. There appears to be a resurgence of people like my friend, people who are driven by the desire to return to their beginnings. This is a good and settling thing. Although some Native Americans are able to learn valuable lessons from their great-grandfathers, for the most part the culture is fast disappearing.

Yet many Native Americans can offer valuable insight into the thoughts and ways of more ancient people. Without their insight there would be only two sources of information as to how early people lived: one provided by archaeologists who dig up the material things that humans made and used; and another from what has been written about present-day tribes, bands, and villages of uncivilized people. However, a Plains Indian medicine bundle viewed simply as an archaeological object would relate little compared to how much an ethnologist can discover by talking to a living Native American of that heritage.

    The clues to what we really want to understand—the way of life and the humanity of our various ancestors—aren't directly preserved, but inferred from the material things that they made. Much of the evidence is missing, and archaeologists often disagree over the meaning of the evidence that has survived.

    For instance, a tribe of western Australian aborigines, the Pitjendadjara, carry on a religious and moral life of great intensity, but they make and use so few and such perishable material objects that, were these people introduced to us only through archaeology, we would barely know that they had existed and we would know nothing of their moral life. They make only five tools: a spear, an atlatl, a wooden carrying dish, a stone slab on which to grind food and a digging stick. They perform their rituals to ask for abundance of animal and plant food, and they follow a morality of personal relations with dignity and conscience.[1]

    Once, my husband Richard and I spent a week in Comb Wash, one of our favorite canyons south of Blanding, Utah. The main purpose of the trip, aside from physical and mental revival, was to collect grey and red clay for pottery. On the first day we each carved a walking stick from carefully selected willows growing near our campsite. We peeled the bark off in a few places to effect a design, and carved our initials and the date on the bare wood. Then the tip was fire-hardened in the ashes of our campfire.

    Every day we walked several miles up and down the red and white sandstone canyons looking for likely clay sources. On each excursion we collected new "treasures." Richard found a perfect hammerstone and used it to cleave flakes from some of the large jasper nodules that were abundant in the stream bed. But the sharp edges of the blanks (slender flakes of stone to use for chipping arrowheads) cut his shirt pockets and weighted down his day pack. So that evening I made a sturdy, basket-like carrying sack from yucca leaves. It had a long strap and was designed specifically for collecting rocks.

    By hiking the canyons and stream beds I could search for smooth pottery-polishing stones, and I collected many. We also found several deer antlers that had been dropped the year before and brought them back to use for tools.

    At the time we collected them, all of these materials were indeed useful items of significant value. In fact, we could hardly wait to show each other our prize of the day: the smoothest polishing stone, or the perfect splinter of flint. And, by the time we were ready to leave the area, we had several containers of clay, pottery (some fired and some in various stages of completion), minerals for paint, sand to use for temper, thin yucca leaves for paint brushes, a bundle of sunflower stalks for atlatl darts, a tin can full of pine pitch for attaching arrow points to darts, a quantity of cedar bark to twist into rope and a few dozen (perfectly straight) dead yucca stalks for hand-drill fires. All this in addition to our walking sticks, the yucca bag, chunks of jasper and a day-pack full of multi-shaped and various-sized polishing stones.

Yet none of these items, so essential in primitive life, are necessary in the modern world; just as many "necessities" of the modern world lose value in the natural world where there are no electric outlets. Primitive people, like the Pitjendadjara, learned to condense their belongings to what was necessary and valuable. It made moving easier, but it also eliminated some of the petty jealousies and hoarding we see manifest in modern societies, where feeling deprived of whatever others have accumulated causes violence, and even killing.

It has been our experience that when materialism in the form of hoarding rears its ugly head on the trail, the students instinctively chastise the guilty party, usually by shunning, to bring him or her into compliance with the moral code of the group.

If we could travel back in time to a Neanderthal settlement of fifty thousand years ago, we would most certainly meet a more hospitable reception and face less danger than a Neanderthal would in any large American city. On the other hand, the culture-shock experienced by Neanderthals transported to the late twentieth century would be violent indeed. They would be horrified by the noise, filth, cruelty, exploitation, alienation and other conditions of modern life, especially as it is lived amidst roads and buildings constructed of dead and spiritless materials inflicted upon us by technology.

I often compare life in the city to a drive with the car windows up. We manage to arrive where we set out to go, but the experience is glazed by the closed window. We need to open our windows, let our hair blow in the breeze, get out and look at what we are passing by, touch it and feel it. Experience life. Many people say that the hardest part of a primitive living experience is coming back to civilization. It's true. I go to the desert to rejuvenate, to become grounded when life in the city becomes too stressful or cluttered, and as I meld back into the modern world it seems that the flaws of our society are glaring.

Our Beginnings
According to current belief, human evolution on this planet covers roughly 15 million years. During that time our bodies and minds were changing drastically, we were evolving, adapting to our environment.

Scientists agree that the African savanna was the cradle of early humanity. But what was so special about the African savanna? The landscape was one of rolling woodland, open plains and occasional high mountain ranges. Like an inverted bowl, flat coastal plains rose steeply to an interior plateau between 1,200 and 4,000 feet above sea level to form the highlands. Two million years ago, several species of the genus Homo (man: comprising all manlike creatures that ever walked on their hind legs) existed side-by-side in the lush Garden of Eden that is now Africa, until a shakedown left only a single species. It didn't happen overnight, but it was on this highland plateau that Homo sapiens (thinking man) first appeared more than 250,000 years ago. It is this ancient ancestor with whom we shall attempt to relate.

Then, between 700,000 and 900,000 years ago, the first small bands of modern people migrated north from Africa, together with the many types of animals they hunted. (As Pliny the Elder aptly put it, "Always something new out of Africa.") And it now appears that another evolutionary crisis occurred within the last 60,000 years and that all of us, all five billion of us, are descended from the survivor of that crisis. A statistician somewhere calculated that this primeval Eve was our 10,000th great-grandmother.[2]

During the last 35,000 or so years before written history, adaptation changed to adaptability. When we began to express and separate our inner and outer worlds through the use of symbols (language), we had adapted, by something that happened in our brain, to limitless adaptability. We could now shape and define our world and communicate knowledge to others of our kind, we could express what we felt, we could project ourselves into tomorrow's situations and we could remember what happened yesterday, and derive lessons from the experience. We could devise tools and thereby improve our situation. We continued to grow and improve as was, and is, human nature. In all this, the key is adaptability.

One of the core things that separates the human world and the animal world is that animals dwell in a kind of instinctive present. By contrast, as a result of our adaptability, we alter history. Alone among all creatures on earth, mankind has a sense of destiny.

The principle of adaptability has taken us from the Old Stone Age to the Computer Age, from silica chips to silicon chips, from crossing the Bering Strait to landing on the moon. As a result, it is no longer our nature to live instinctively. Except for a few scattered pockets of people living primitive lifestyles in isolated areas of the world, that particular phase of our evolution disappeared millenniums ago. That is why it is so important for us, as modern day practitioners of early life skills, to study and re-learn the skills that were an inherent part of the lives of our ancient ancestors.

We cannot walk into the wilderness and expect our DNA to take over and save us from an unfamiliar environment.

Although we cannot observe our ancestors directly, or look for thoughts lost 100,000 years ago, especially when there are no written records, we can use common sense to figure out what kinds of behavior would have been useful or productive to early communities and families. Across the long march of time love and loyalty, trust and sharing, agreement on the rules and a strong sense of belonging are what worked just as they work in modern tribal communities. The greed, exploitation, selfishness, callousness and aggression which propel current movers and shakers would have been suicidal in a tribal context, as they are today, in the long run.

What can a people so removed from our world teach us? And does it matter that our conception of our ancient ancestors is correct? I think it matters a great deal. We can't even begin to tackle constructively the multiple, interlocking problems threatening our species and our planet today without some grasp of who and what we are, how we got that way and what does or does not work for us.

Neanderthal
Let's begin by taking a look at Homo sapiens, the Neanderthal.

Today, we take for granted cultural differences among people in different areas. Every modern human population has its characteristic house style, implements and art. For instance, if you were shown chopsticks, a bottle of Coors beer, and a boomerang and asked to associate one object each with China, Colorado and Australia, you would have no trouble. No such cultural variation is apparent for Neanderthals. Even tools from 40,000 look essentially the same as tools from 100,000 years ago. They lacked innovation. For a people that had no writing or other way of transmitting information and a life expectancy of only thirty-five years, it stands to reason that their technological progress would stagnate. Yet, they were the first people to use fire on a regular, everyday basis. Nearly all Neanderthal caves have small areas of ash and charcoal indicating a simple fireplace.

Neanderthals looked much the same no matter where they came from. Neanderthal women stood about five feet tall, and the men five feet six inches, according to anthropologist Erik Trinkaus of the University of New Mexico. They were heavily built, with large, powerful bones and muscles. Their weight was at least twenty pounds heavier than a modern person of comparable height. Although they walked basically as we do, they moved irregularly—as Trinkaus puts it, "more like a halfback doing broken field running than like a sprinter."

A Neanderthal's handshake would have been bone-crushing. They had big faces, prominent brow ridges and their lower jaws sloped backwards, leaving very little chin. In adult Neanderthals, the front teeth were worn down from using their teeth as a third hand, like a vise. By the time they were in their thirties, their teeth were often worn to the roots.

Cartoons depict a Neanderthal male, club in hand, dragging his female by the hair, an attitude that portrays early man as savage and crude, yet more and more material has come to light suggesting the opposite. As busy as they must have been, Neanderthals seemingly made time for kindness. They placed flowers, such as thistle and hollyhock in graves, indicting a possible belief in a life beyond the present, and they cared for their elderly. One fossil from the Shanidar cave in Iraq was a physical wreck, with a clubfoot and withered arm. Yet, the fellow survived to 30, implying that Neanderthals had a well-developed social conscience and cared for those who probably contributed little to the economy of the group. In fact, many skeletons of older Neanderthals show signs of severe impairment such as withered arms, healed but incapacitating broken bones, tooth loss and severe osteoarthritis. Only care by younger clan members could have enabled the older members of the group to stay alive.[3]

Hunters and gatherers usually live in small isloated roving bands. In fact, until the rise of civilization, man lived in communities so small that every adult knew everyone else. These communities were intimate and people came to have the same ways of doing things. They mated with and lived almost entirely with others like themselves. They remained in that community and had a strong sense of solidarity. These communities had no writing, but we know about their life because it is the same as most contemporary uncivilized communities.

In a small, intimate community all people were known as individuals. Men and women were seen as persons, not as parts of mechanical operations, the way we see so many of those around us today. Also, the groupings of people within the primitive community depended on status and role, not on mere practical usefulness. There were fathers, mothers, older people and spiritual leaders; each kind of person was accorded prestige.

The original human society was one of kinship, and cooperation was essential to secure food and shelter and for defense against foes, human and otherwise. But the essential order of society, the glue which held people together, was morality. Each pre-civilized society was held together by largely undeclared but continually realized ethical concepts.

People did the kind of things they did, not because somebody just thought it up, or ordered them to do it, but because it seemed to flow from the very necessity of existence. The reasons given after the thing was done, in the form of dress or ceremony, asserted the rightness of the choice. We can, with good reason, assume that 50,000 years ago mankind had developed a variety of moral orders, each expressed in some local tradition, and comparable to what we find among aborigines today. Their tradition was made up of an accumulation of experience.

Richard and I, and others who have experienced the aboriginal lifestyle, know that an interesting thing happens when a group of strangers converge and end up relying on each other for life's necessities. Immediately, leaders emerge. But, like Neanderthal, appearances are deceiving—those with innate leadership ability are seldom obvious at first. In modern life, the leader is often the bully or the person who has more of what everyone else wants. Thus, he or she uses it to buy popularity. But bullying techniques, brashness and brute force do not set anyone apart on the trail, except as a bore.

It usually happens as we strike out for our first campsite. Although he or she seldom takes the lead, one of the group will take notice of a straggler and offer encouragement. Once settled into a daily routine, they are often the first to ask questions and to try their hand at new skills. If they fail, they continue relentlessly until they achieve their objective. But most of all, once they have accomplished a thing, they help others, and delight in their excitement. By caring and helpful serving, the new leader inadvertently earns the respect of the majority of the group, and becomes "chief." Other kinds of leaders also emerge. Some are more adept at a particular skill than anyone else, and thus respected for their ability.

Teaching basketry has always been my job on the trail because it is something I enjoy and do reasonably well. I am pleased to think that my contribution adds to the overall success of the experience. But, on one particular trip, I was quickly replaced by a young girl—the most timid of the group. After watching the basket-making demonstration, she collected her materials and retired to a secluded rock overhang. At the evening campfire she emerged with a beautifully crafted piece of art. We were all astounded at her skill and asked if she had received previous training. She had not. As a result of her natural talent she gained the respect of everyone. Her advice was sought instead of mine, and she was drawn into the circle. It was a growing experience for her, and a humbling one for me.

In ancient settlements there were no full-time specialists because in hunter-gatherer communities there simply was not enough food to go around unless every member of the group contributed to the supply. And in the primitive societies of the present day there are rarely full-time specialists. So we can assume that in the early condition of humanity what men did was customarily different from what women did, but what one man did was much like what another man did. There were men with special skills at activities carried on by all men and the same was true of women.

At any one time the members of a primitive community may be doing notably different things: the women looking for edible roots while the men hunt meat; some men out on a hunting party while others at home perform a rite for its success. Yet, all of these activities merge to a purpose and express a view of duty that all share. This life style is attested to in every isolated, undisturbed primitive society we observe today and has been the case on every trip I have attended.

It is interesting, however, that studies of modern hunter-gatherers show that most of a family's calories come from plant food gathered by women. Men catch rats and other small game that they don't mention in their heroic campfire stories. Occasionally they get a large animal, which does indeed contribute significantly to everyone's protein intake, but it's only in the Arctic, where little plant food is available, that big-game becomes the dominant food source. Humans didn't reach the Arctic until around 30,000 years ago.[4]

I personally doubt that hunting was the driving force behind early societies. For most of our history we were not mighty hunters. In fact, it was the hunting-gathering way of life that allowed us to evolve over hundreds of thousands of years. In this, women were partners and their gathering was more dependable than the men's hunting, making their contribution vital.

Still, the mystique of "Man the Hunter" is so rooted in us that it is hard to abandon our belief in its long-standing importance. Consequently, on our modern-day abo treks, although everyone is instructed in all of the life skills, when it comes to actually functioning as a cohesive unit, the men set traps and clean and skin the animals (stuff I don't want to do anyway), while the women collect plants and make pottery. We build our own shelter, often cooperatively, collect bark for bedding, cook collectively and clean up our own areas. If someone happens to make extra ash cakes, he might offer to trade for cordage or some other item of perceived similar value. Pottery is a big commodity for trading and can exact a fish or rabbit or sleeping mat in exchange. Everyone shares.

The Big Merge
During a relatively short span of about 100,000 years, Neanderthals spread across Europe, the Middle East and western and central Asia. Their cousins, other Homo sapiens, were found as far away as China and South Africa.

Some magic element was added about 60,000 years ago that produced innovative, fully modern people who proceeded to spread westward into Europe, quickly supplanting the Neanderthals. Presumably, they also spread east into Asia and Indonesia, displacing the earlier people there, about whom we know little.

Anthropologists disagree about what happened when early modern humans met Neanderthals. As recently as 35,000 years ago there were still Neanderthals in western Europe. But when the anatomically modern people appeared in Europe, suddenly so did sculpture, musical instruments, lamps, trade, and innovation. Within a few thousand years the Neanderthals were gone.

In one theory, modern humans stormed into Europe about 40,000 years ago and either beat Neanderthals to scarce resources or actually exterminated them. And a new kind of genetic analysis shows that no Neanderthal mitochondrial genes, which reside outside cell nuclei, remain in modern humans.

That genetic work remains controversial and archeological findings in caves in Qafzeh near Nazareth, Israel and Kebara, near Mount Carmel, show both Neanderthals and early modern humans living together peacefully. For thousands of generations the Neanderthals match (either by originality or imitation) their more modern cousins advance for advance. Perhaps they intermarried, the best of each merging to produce the hybrid who would eventually conquer the planet.[5]

By contrast, Neanderthals who remained isolated in western Europe apparently reached a dead end. Some researchers speculate that they were technologically and socially backward. Perhaps they didn't have as fine a division of labor, or maybe they had more babies and could not move on when climate changes sent herds of animals (food) in search of better weather. Or perhaps Neanderthals were simply unable to keep a fire burning when they moved. Any of these factors could have given early modern humans enough of an edge to leave Neanderthals in the evolutionary dust.

Some scientists feel that environmental changes caused the demise of Neanderthal; however, Neanderthals actually thrived during the Ice Age. It is more likely that they met the same fate as other cultures when a numerous people with more advanced technology invade the lands of a much less numerous people with less advanced technology: for instance, the displacement that occurred when European colonists invaded North America and Australia or when the Bantus invaded lands of the southern African Bushmen.

How is this different from what we read about in our newspapers every day? Someone once said that a society that is unwilling to learn from its past is destined to repeat it. Is it any wonder that my friend wanted to be an Indian? The Native American tradition teaches respect for life, be it human or otherwise, and a sense of oneness with the earth which gave us life. It was what my friend perceived as a grounded way of thinking and living that he longed to become a part of. An honorable quest.

Cro-Magnon

Where there had previously been Neanderthals, there were suddenly (about 35,000 years ago) anatomically modern people known as Cro-Magnons. (This happened at different times in different parts of the world.) Should one of these ladies or gentlemen stroll down Broadway in modern attire they would not stand out from the crowd in any way.

The tools of Cro-Magnon people suggest innovation, and were developed rather rapidly, and in succession, according to Paleolithic standards. Although tools continued to be made of stone, they were now thin blades struck off a larger stone. Standardized bone and antler tools appeared for the first time, as did compound tools of several parts tied or glued together, such as spear points set in shafts or ax heads hafted to handles. Cro-Magnons had needles for sewing clothing, awls, mortars and pestles, rope and cordage used for nets or snares, fish hooks and net sinkers.[6]

Finally, man legitimately became the Big Game Hunter. This was made possible by sophisticated weapons that could kill dangerous animals from a distance. Bagging some of the larger animals must have required communal hunting methods based on detailed knowledge of each species' behavior. Cro-Magnon sites are much more numerous than Neanderthal sites, implying greater success at obtaining food.

Cro-Magnon people are also well-known for their art. Best known are the rock paintings in caves like those in Lascaux, France, with stunning polychrome pictures of now-extinct animals. But equally impressive are the bas-reliefs, necklaces and pendants, fired-clay effigies and musical instruments ranging from flutes to rattles. Once they had something they could spare, Cro-Magnons began to trade.

Unlike Neanderthals, some Cro-Magnons lived past the age of sixty. The additional twenty years probably played a big role in their advancement. Accustomed as we are to getting our news on a daily basis from the television or newspaper, it is hard to appreciate how important even one or two old people were in a preliterate society. For instance, just one old person could mean the difference between life and death for a whole society if they had lived through the ravages of plague and learned which herbs were successful in treating the illness.

By 8,000 B.C., human populations were found on all the world's continents, with the possible exception of Greenland. There were people in widely scattered parts of the habitable earth, though not very many in any one place and not very many altogether. No city had yet been built anywhere.

When the warming climate melted the glaciers and raised the seas, encroaching forests drove the great grazing animals, the chief prey of the Cro-Magnon, north, some to extinction. Something new and profound would eventually sweep across Europe and the rest of the world—agriculture. Then, as a consequence of having time for leisure and social contact—civilization.

The passage from pre-civilized to civilized life meant great change, both materially and in the way humans functioned as a group. The primitive and pre-civilized communities of today are held together essentially by common understandings as to the ultimate nature and purpose of life. The pre-civilized society was like the present-day primitive society in those characteristics—isolation, smallness, homogeneity, persistence in the common effort to make a way of life under relatively stable circumstances. "The morale of a folk society—its power to act consistently over periods of time and to meet crises effectively—is not dependent upon discipline exerted by force or upon devotion to some single principle of action, but to the concurrence and consistency of many or all of the actions and conceptions which make up the whole round of life."[7]

Not surprisingly, researchers have found few indications of warfare among the clans of the late Ice Age. Violent conflicts came later, when man built permanent agricultural settlements and came to regard the land he lived on as his property, and his alone. By then, Cro-Magnons had evolved into the Gauls, the Celts, the Mesopotamians and all the other tribes that founded great civilizations and went on to fight each other for centuries in Asia and Europe, as well as in the New World. As one anthropologist puts it, "In the light of twentieth century human behavior we should be careful of whom we call brutish."

Still, it is difficult, if not impossible, for most people to relate in any way with a people so far removed from their own experience as our Paleolithic ancestors. Until 1856, when the first clue to human ancestry was found in a limestone quarry in the Neander Valley near Dusseldorf, we had no idea of the vast age of the earth, or of the long history of humanity.[8] Virtually everyone assumed that mankind had always had the same form as modern humans. It is not surprising, then, that no one was prepared for a primitive "skeleton in the closet."

A few years ago, Richard and I shared the experience of returning to our ancestral homeland, Scotland. Neither of us had been there previously, but we both sensed a strong feeling of being home. In the short time we were there, we formed a oneness with the land, the past and traditions of our early ancestors. Because of that trip, we better understand why many black Americans are choosing to take African names and wear their traditional dress, and why Mexican Americans want to preserve their language and culture even as they blend into the hodgepodge of American society. And we understand more of what native Americans feel for their native lands.

Of course the native American has a connection to this land. They are in fact, native North Americans! Many Indians still build their traditional shelters, hogans and sometimes pueblos, alongside modern structures. They construct sweat lodges and dance and celebrate in traditional ways. By doing this they stay in touch with who they are and what they are about.

The rest of us, anyone whose Neolithic ancestors did not originate on this continent, tend to move from city to city, from house to house with little attachment. But then, there is nothing aesthetic about a high-rise apartment in the midst of a teeming metropolis.

But is it possible to be "in" a society and not be of it? The great "back to nature" movement in the '60s, although somewhat misdirected, was part of an instinctive craving to get ourselves into balance with our ancient DNA—to live close to the earth, to dig in the dirt, to become a kinder, gentler people. Sadly, materialism overcame the natural yearnings, and we have now actually lost ground (even the voice of the movement, *Mother Earth News*, disappeared for a time!).

I am not alone in believing that if it is at all possible to bring sanity back to our civilization, it must be accomplished through an awareness of who we are and what we should be about. It must be accomplished by returning to our beginnings and connecting to one another for strength and support. We are, after all, part of a universal family. We must stop trying to force ideas and ideals on one another and learn to appreciate and love our fellow humans for their inherent goodness. I am not naive enough to expect that we will return to a Garden of Eden where there is no malice or conflict. That has always and will always exist. Nor is it possible in this busy age of computers and high finance to leave everything familiar and move to an isolated nook, as much as we would like to do so. But I do believe that if we re-learn the skills of our ancient past, and by doing so become reunited with our natural world and natural selves, we may be able to rescue humanity—not civilization, but humanity.

Who would have imagined that in the past 130 years, the short time during which we have been aware that ancient Homo sapiens existed, we would experience a great need to re-learn their ways of life as a means to rescue ourselves from ourselves. Many elders of the native American cultures are preaching for a return to tradition but it is not exclusively their tradition. It is the tradition of us all. We can and should listen to and study what they are saying, and apply it in our lives to whatever degree possible. If each person does something, an ever-growing world awareness truly can alter the collective consciousness.

To Ralph Waldo Emerson's question, "Why should we grope among the dry bones of the past?" we can answer, "Because our ancient cousins knew a few basic things about life and living that we have forgotten and will have to re-learn if we are to have any future at all, let alone a future that will allow us to evolve further and realize our as yet undreamed-of human potential."

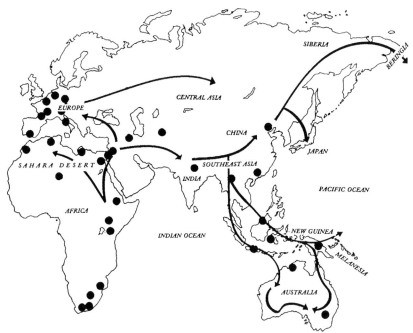

MAN'S WORLD IN ICE AGE TIMES (beginning with Homo sapiens (archaic) about 250,000 years ago) extended from the crown of Eurasia to the Cape of Good Hope, and from England across Siberia. Later Homo sapiens (modern 10,000-35,000 years ago and Neanderthal 32,000-125,000 years ago) spread farther—peopling northern Europe and Siberia and by about 50,000 years ago moving on to Australia by sea and later across the Bering Strait to the Western Hemisphere.

Source(s): *Epic of Man*, Courtlandt Canby, ed. (New York: Time Incorporated, 1961) pp. 15-16.
Brian M. Fagan, *The Journey From Eden* (London: Thames and Hudson, Ltd., 1990) p. 235.

Steve Watts

The Ultimate Weapon
The Southeastern Indian Rivercane Blowgun

● ●

In the summer of 1954 I stood wide-eyed in the cool shade

of the big trees and watched an unnamed Cherokee man

shoot a thistle fletched dart from a rivercane blowgun.

It sped from the muzzle in a blur, and before I could

blink or think or try to understand, it was there–stuck

firmly in a softwood log target.

To the Cherokee man, I was just another nameless seven-year-old boy. I was one of hundreds, or perhaps thousands, of seven-year-old boys who had witnessed his demonstration that summer on the Qualla Boundary in the Great Smoky Mountains of North Carolina. But to me, he was a magician. With a few sticks and a tuft of dried plant fibers he had opened a door.

A man, a boy and a rivercane blowgun—tied up tightly forever in a bundle of childhood memories.

The Legacy

To the historic Cherokee, Creek, Houma, Catawba, Yuchi, Choctaw, Seminole, Natchez, Chitimacha, Biloxi and other native peoples of the North American Southeast, the blowgun was an important and valued hunting weapon in the pursuit of small game. To the Catawba, Choctaw and Cherokee, it remains to this day a symbol of traditional values and cultural pride.[1]

Old guns are carefully curated and even venerated—being passed down through extended families generation after generation. Recently, I was privileged to inspect (and shoot!) a 150 year-old Cherokee gun. The patina of its surface (literally golden) was surpassed only by the glass-like

15

smoothness of its bore—the result of the passage of countless numbers of darts through its interior. Its owner had just recently obtained it. It was the blowgun that he had shot as a young boy under the tutelage of a man who hunted with it regularly in the 1920s and '30s.[2] To the new owner, it represents not only a piece of the Cherokee spirit and passion, but the memory of a valued teacher and friend as well.

Contemporary traditional Choctaws and Cherokees highly prize the blowgun's use as well as its survival. Blowgun competitions are fierce at annual fall and summer fairs and gatherings. Shooting long rounds of competition (often lasting several days and involving hundreds of shots at distances up to 60 feet), blowgun champions take great pride in their accomplishments. Their shooting skills and the craftsmanship of their guns and darts are common topics of conversation and debate.

Though few today rely on the blowgun as a means of providing meat for the table, Southeastern traditionalists are very conscious of the blowgun as a cultural trait—almost a standard. Some, such as the Catawba, who no longer manufacture blowguns on a regular basis still cling to it as a treasured tribal symbol. Others, such as the Waccamaw, who have no record of blowgun use in their written history, see it as essentially "Southeastern" and purchase guns of Cherokee manufacture for use, display and demonstration. Its importance as a living tradition, connecting the present with the aboriginal past, can hardly be overstated.

The Lineage
The prehistoric tradition of the blowgun in the Southeast is unclear. Some doubt the blowgun's antiquity in the region. Archaeology has not yet provided us with a pre-contact example. The fragility of the materials used in the manufacture of blowguns and darts makes their survival in the archaeological record difficult at best. Perhaps some southern cave or wet site will someday yield a prehistoric specimen. Accidental or intentional burning in the past could provide us with a charred fragment. There are questions yet to be asked. For instance, how would a charred rivercane blowgun fragment differ in attributes from a charred cane fragment used in wattle wall construction, or bench seats in a burned house, or free-standing cane within or near an occupation site burned in a clearing operation?

Kroeber (1948) believed the blowgun to be a late introduction from South America. Some have argued that its presence in the earliest historic accounts speaks of more ancient roots.

Whenever and however the rivercane blowgun came to the Southeast, it was firmly entrenched as an important part of the small game hunting arsenal by the Historic Period:

"The derivation of the blowgun in the Southeast remains for the present, after all, an open question. To my mind the case in favor of its being a diffused trait from South America is no stronger than that for its local invention." NASH 1963

"(The Choctaw) are very skilful in the use of the blowgun...when they see something which they want to hit they blow it, and they often kill small birds." BOSSU 1768

"The young savages...blow it so expertly as seldom to miss a mark fifteen or twenty yards off and that so violently as to kill squirrels and birds therewith." ROMANS 1775

"(The Cherokee children) at eight or ten years old, are very expert at killing small animals and birds with a sarbacan, or hollow cane, through which they blow a small dart, whose weakness obliges them to shoot at the eye of the larger sort of prey, which they seldom miss." TIMBERLAKE 1765.

"This (the Yuchi blowgun) was almost exclusively used for bringing down small animals, squirrels and birds." SPECK 1909.

"With other peoples of the Southeast the Catawba shared the trait of using the blowgun or blowpipe exclusively for the purposes of hunting small animals and birds. It has had a desultory survival down to the present generation of older men, and is known by the designation wa'sa pu'he, 'cane blowing,' or 'dart blowing.'" SPECK 1938.

Historic Manufacturing Techniques

Although elderberry stems are sometimes used in the manufacture of blowguns by the Houmas of Louisiana, it is rivercane (Arundinaria gigantea) that is most often associated with the traditional weapon made by most southern native peoples. It is the material of choice both from a utilitarian and a cultural point of view. Called swamp cane in the western southeast (Choctaws, Chitimachas, etc.) and rivercane in the eastern southeast (Cherokees, Creeks, Catawbas, etc.) Arundinaria is found growing most often in bottomlands along rivers and streams.

Rivercane habitats are threatened in the Carolinas and other parts of the southeast. The rich bottoms are perfect for agriculture as well as rivercane. Consequently, cane has been driven to the edge of fields and streams by more than 200 years of cultivation. This is of much concern to blowgun makers in the area. Cherokee craftsmen often travel long distances to obtain proper blowgun cane. Trips to Alabama, Georgia and Kentucky from their North Carolina mountain homes are not unusual. The search for good blowgun cane is ongoing, and a Cherokee maker— no matter where he travels—is ever on the lookout.

Much of the rivercane in the southeast has hybridized with bamboo, an Asian import.[3] This crossing results in shorter lengths of sections between the joints and deeper flutes at the branch junctions. These attributes, along with the tendency of bamboo to split when drying, have made bamboo itself an unsatisfactory substitute for the native material. Traditional blowgun makers seek out the long-section canes of the pure stock.

Second-year growth is chosen for blowgun making. First-year growth rivercane is weak and never seems to dry out firmly enough to produce a good gun. Craftsmen scan the canebrakes for plants of their favorite diameters and lengths. Some are chosen for serious hunting or competition, and some for sale to tourists. Yet, the traditional blowgun maker chooses each cane carefully, scorning those who clear-cut a patch and use canes of mixed or inferior quality.

All of the known accounts of blowgun manufacture that we have from the Historic Period refer to the use of metal tools for hollowing and smoothing the weapon's bore. It must be remembered that European contact in the North American Southeast began more than four hundred years ago with the Spanish invasions. Access to metal tools, no doubt, quickly altered aboriginal blowgun manufacturing techniques.

Once the cane has been cut, bundled and allowed to dry, the blowgun maker begins the process of straightening. A cane that looks as straight as an arrow in the field will reveal all kinds of kinks, curves and wiggles when later examined. Fortunately, rivercane responds well to the heat straightening techniques that are commonly used with wood. The blank (the cane cut to length) is heated over flames or coals and bent at the crooked places over the maker's knee or the edge of a log, stump or rock.

According to Lossiah (1980),[4] there are two straightenings which must occur: curves in the sections between the joints, and bends which occur at the joints. At-the-joint bends require more care as the cane is likely to snap at this juncture if too much pressure or too little heat are applied. Straightening can be a frustrating process. An experienced blowgun maker can straighten a blank in a matter of minutes. Less experienced folks can spend hours working to straighten without undoing sections already dealt with.

Once the blank is straightened, it is time to turn attention to the blowgun's interior. The joints must be removed and the walls of the joints reamed flush with the interior of the already hollow sections between the joints. It is this reaming process which is critical to making a good blowgun. Failure to adequately reduce the interior joint walls will result in an excessively slowed dart or, even worse, a stuck one.

The historic method for penetrating the joint walls most often involves the use of a heated metal rod. An experienced blowgun maker

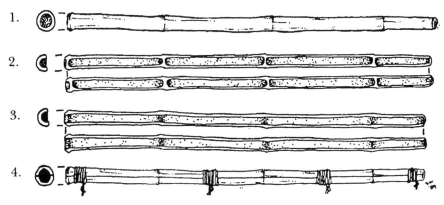

*1. A well-seasoned piece of rivercane is chosen and straightened, then cut in
length (4-8 feet). 2. The blank is split in two equal halves. 3. The joint walls
are cut away. 4. The two halves are glued back together and bound with
cordage.*

will have several different diameters of metal rods on hand to accommodate various cane sizes. The more joint wall material that can be removed
in this boring/burning process, the less remains for the next step of
reaming. Yet, too large a diameter rod can burn through a wall or split
the blank at the narrower muzzle end.

   For reaming, the traditional Historic-era tool is the homemade rasp.
This consists of a slender piece of split hardwood—hickory or locust—at
least half the length of the intended blowgun. Once sized and smoothed
so as to work freely back-and-forth within the cane's interior, the last few
inches inside the forward end are wrapped with a roughened piece of
metal. Strips of tin cans with small holes punched to create many sharp
edges (like the common kitchen cheese grater) are often used for this. It
is truly remarkable how well these homemade rasps get the job done,
quickly removing the remaining joint walls inside the gun. Once reamed,
the interior is smoothed further by sanding or burnishing with a
hardwood rod to remove any remaining splinters or rough spots which
may catch or slow a dart. Truly well-made blowguns exhibit polished
interiors which become even smoother with the passage of time and many
darts.

   Trimming and smoothing the mouthpiece and muzzle ends complete
the blowgun. Exteriors may be polished at this stage, and on rare
occasions, decorated by sooting patterns of rings or spirals. Even less
common is the practice of sooting the whole exterior surface—resulting
in a totally black blowgun.[5]

Blowguns may vary in length from as short as three feet to as long as ten feet or more for serious hunting or competition. Longer guns provide more accuracy—all other things being equal. Yet, longer guns are much more difficult to manufacture. Five to seven foot guns are very common. The Choctaw even distinguish between five to six foot guns for nighttime hunting in the brier patch and eight to nine foot guns for daytime hunting on open ground (Nash 1963).

Before leaving this consideration of historic techniques, it must be remembered that this is an ever-evolving craft among contemporary Cherokees, Choctaws and others. Even though the blowgun is an important symbol of their past, it is also alive within the culture of the present. And, even though the simple hand tools described above are considered traditional at this point (and completely adequate to get the job done), many present-day native craftsmen employ modern substitutes. The commercial round wood rasp is sometimes substituted for the punched tin variety. Drill bits attached to long metal rods are sometimes used for boring instead of the older burning method. And, sandpaper often substitutes for a hardwood burnishing tool. The techniques change but the blowgun remains.

A Proposed Aboriginal Method of Construction

For those wishing to understand how southeastern rivercane blowguns may have been manufactured prehistorically or for those seeking to manufacture such a weapon themselves using only aboriginal-style tools and techniques, questions remain. How the boring and reaming operations were accomplished prior to the introduction of metal tools is still a matter of speculation. Various suggestions and traditions have been offered. The Choctaw believe that the joints were knocked out using a sharpened piece of cane of a smaller diameter, and the remaining joint wall fragments were reamed using a stone point/drill hafted to a long shaft (Nash 1963). The Catawba version cites the same knocking out method followed by rasping with sand and a hardwood shaft.[6] Either of these methods, or yet other methods not here noted, may result in the successful manufacture of a serviceable weapon.

I have tested one possible method and offer it below. In short, it involves a splitting and rejoining technique. This approach corresponds to South American Indian methods and is alluded to in at least one historic Creek reference: "The blowgun was made of a cane stalk about as long as a man is tall. To remove the pith it was sometimes necessary to section the cane, then bind it together again (Speck 1907)." Does this sketchy Creek account reflect a personal or tribal idiosyncrasy, or is it an echo of a widespread technology which predates the iron rod?

To begin, rivercane is gathered, bundled and allowed to dry. Cane can be harvested and cut to length with unmodified stone flake knives or with more formalized bifaces. Choose a length between four and seven feet for your first attempt. Once dry (give it at least a month if possible), the blank must be straightened using heat as in the historic technique.

Rivercane tapers in diameter from the bottom to the top. The mouthpiece end (the larger diameter end) is trimmed up and smoothed. It is best to locate the mouthpiece directly on or near a joint for strength.

The muzzle end is likewise trimmed and smoothed. This end should have an inside diameter near to the diameter of your thumb. Trimming the ends can be accomplished using unmodified stone flakes and smoothed using a fine sanding/grinding stone. A smooth mouthpiece allows for comfort and a tight, no-leak seal with the shooter's lips. A smooth muzzle end insures speedy release of the dart from the end of the gun.

Next, the blank is split from end to end beginning at the smaller muzzle end. Splitting is relatively easy if care is taken. A flake makes a cut in the direct center of the muzzle end to begin the split. The flake itself, or a thin sliver of hardwood, is then pushed down the length of the blank. This splitting results in two halves, exposing the inner joint walls in cross-section.

The interior wall halves are then cut away using flakes or bifaces and the remnant material ground smooth using a properly sized grinding stone. No grinding or smoothing of the walls between joint sections is required.

All that now remains is to rejoin the two halves. Hide glue, pitch or beeswax can be used. The important thing is to insure an air-tight seal between the two halves from mouthpiece to muzzle. Once the chosen adhesive is in place and the seams properly joined, the blowgun is bound at points along its length using buckskin, rawhide or lengths of plant fiber cordage. South American Indians often wrap the entire gun with bark after rejoining.[7] A final interior treatment is the passage of a hardwood shaft with a buckskin swab attached through the gun several times to insure the removal of any adhesive which may have seeped to the inside.

This is but one possible aboriginal-style method of blowgun manufacture. There are, of course, many others. One craftsman I know, for instance, accomplished the successful construction of a blowgun by knocking out the joint walls with a hardwood shaft and then reaming the interior with a rasp made of a long cattail shoot with quartz sand attached to the working end with hide glue. I sure didn't think it would work, but it did.[8]

The Darts

Of course, no consideration of blowguns can be complete without giving attention to the ammunition—the darts. The Southeastern Indian blowgun dart is a rather large affair when compared to those used by their South American cousins. Unlike South America, no poison was used in blowgun hunting, so the Southeastern dart must carry a little more heft to complete the task of shock and penetration. It works in many ways like a small arrow. In fact, the Catawba word for arrow and dart are the same: "wa" (Speck 1938).

The shafts of these darts were historically constructed of a variety of materials. The most common were split out pieces of hardwood, eight to ten inches in length, up to 3/8 inch in diameter, shaved to a round cross-section and pointed on one end (Speck 1938).

Black locust is the wood of choice among Cherokee today. Chitimacha dart shafts were sometimes constructed from a rivercane splinter which, after being subjected to heat, was twisted into a corkscrew shape. The Choctaw also manufactured such shafts (Nash 1963). Longer shaft lengths have been found. There are Cherokee darts in collections which exceed twenty-one inches in length.[9]

Likewise, the fletchings found on these darts are made from a variety of natural materials. The fletching material must fill the inner cavity of the gun so as to catch the air and send the dart on its way. Yet, it must be of a material that is flexible enough to expand at the large mouthpiece end and contract at the small muzzle end of the blowgun. It must be fairly durable, yet light enough so as not to slow the dart's flight once it has left the gun.

Although cotton was preferred as a fletching material among the Gulf Coast tribes, and feathers and fur were used by the Catawba, the fletching of choice among the Cherokees and others was, and is, thistle (Carduus L.) This plant, viewed by most today as a pest, is still found growing along roadsides and in open fields throughout the South. The flower heads are gathered in the late summer and early fall by craftsmen and stored for a winter of dart making. Once dry, the thistle down (soft inner fibers of the flower) are removed and they alone are used for fletching.

Thistle flowers allowed to dry at will open up and send their fibers flying in all directions. To prevent this, dart makers wedge the freshly cut flower heads between two strips of hardwood or within the cleft created by splitting a piece of rivercane. In this way, the thistle can be stored, allowing one flower head at a time to be removed and the fibers processed. Proper cleaning and manipulation of these fibers is crucial to successful dart making. It is a craft that can only be learned by much trial and error and is best learned first-hand from an experienced dart maker.

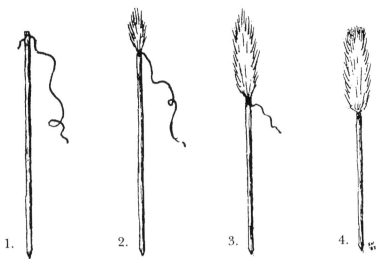

1. Whittle and smooth hardwood shaft—8-12" long and up to 1/8" in diameter. Insert thread into split cut in butt end. 2. Begin wrapping thistle down to shaft in spiral of overlapping layers. 3. Cover 2-4" of shaft with down—ending with a few wraps around the shaft and an overhand knot. 4. Completed dart—blunt cut or burn end of thistle down even with butt end of shaft.

A split is made in the blunt end of the dart shaft and a length of fine thread is inserted. A few twists of the shaft bind the thread in place without a knot. Today most dart makers use cotton thread. The Cherokees say that in the past milkweed or stinging nettle cordage was used.[10] The free end of the string is held in the teeth. A bundle of prepared thistle down is held in one hand, fanned out into a row between the thumb and index finger. The other hand holds the shaft, and with its upper end lying on the index finger with the down, it is simultaneously rotated clockwise and moved up and in toward the base of the thumb.

The result of this is that thistle fibers are caught at their base between the string and the shaft, creating a continuous spiral of attached fibers. When completed, the fletching appears to be a uniform gathering of down, the string being hidden.

Once two to four inches of fletching has been applied, the end of the string is wrapped several times to catch the base of the last fibers and an overhand knot is tied. The fibers on the upper end are trimmed or burned flush with the blunt end of the shaft. The completed dart is then spun between the palms, fluffing it out and releasing any unattached down.

If this sounds like some kind of impossible magic trick requiring more hands than most of us have, then you've come close to the feeling a beginning dart maker has as he attempts to juggle shaft, string and thistle. At the same time one is doing this, he or she is trying to judge just how much down to feed into the process, in what concentrations so as to wind up with a fletching that is full enough to do the job, but not so large as to cause the dart to become stuck in the blowgun's bore.

It is the skilled dart maker who, through much experience, consistently matches the caliber of his dart with his gun. To watch a master Cherokee craftsman roll darts at a rate of one every couple of minutes is to experience the elegance of primitive technology in action.

In the fall of 1554, a very young Catawba boy stood wide-eyed in the cool shade of the big trees on the edge of an open field and watched a hunter shoot a thistle-fletched dart from a rivercane blowgun.

It sped from the muzzle in a blur, and before the boy could blink or think or try to understand, it was there—stuck firmly in the chest of a rabbit now lying still in a patch of blue-stemmed grass.

To the hunter, this boy was not just any boy. This was his son. The only son who would carry on the practice of making and using this blowgun. The only one who would be entrusted to pass on this craft and teach his son who would follow.

To the boy, this man was a magician. With a few sticks and a tuft of dried plant fibers he had opened a door as only a father can do. A father, a son and a rivercane blowgun—tied up tightly forever in a bundle of survival and living tradition.

The author heat straightening the blowgun blank. Bends both at and between the joints must be straightened before interior work begins. (Photo: Michael Eldredge)

Proper shooting technique: both hands are held at the mouthpiece end in such a way as to make an airtight seal. The exhale which sends the dart on its way is short and forceful. (Photo: Steve Watts)

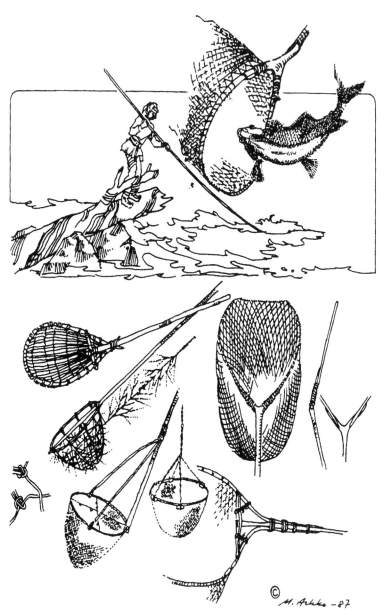

Ancient fishermen used landing nets to get salmon and whitefish during the spawning season. Many Lapps, Finns and other Arctic folk still use this method.

Turkka Aaltonen

Old Finnish Hunting and Fishing Techniques

●●●●●●●●●●●●●●●●●●●●●●●●●●●●●●

It is important for every survivalist in the Arctic to learn

to snare ptarmigan, that's why we teach it every winter in

the Finnish Army and Air Force survival training. If you

can snare ptarmigans, you can use the same method for

grouse and other woodland birds.

The ancestors of the Lapps who came to Finland and Scandinavia following the last Ice Age, about 10,000 years ago, were reindeer and seal hunters and fishermen. At this time nature was rich with game and fish.

Finland was first inhabited about 9,500 B.C., the people of that time followed the enormous droves of wild reindeer when they came north. Signs of their presence are still evident near the Central Volga and Ural Mountains. The Finns were really the last of the primitive cultures.

The closest ancestry to today's Finns are Carelians, Estonians and distant relations among Hungarians. In Russia and Siberia there are still many small groups of Finns living under Russian rule.

The climate and flora are very similar in Scandinavia and Western Siberia and there are similarities in North America as well. For this reason the way of life, occupations, and some folklore is often similar.

The basic weapons for ancient Finns were the hunting spear, bow and arrows, axe and knife. Because they had the bow, there is no proof that early Finns used the atlatl. At that time they also used spears, harpoons and leisters (multi-forked spears). Our hunting spear was a pointed weapon, not meant for throwing. The oldest spearheads were made of bone tubes like those of the shin bone of elk or wild reindeer. If the hunter put some sharp points on both sides of this bone spearhead, it became a very effective weapon for big game or the large brown bear. Used without the shaft, the spearhead became a dagger or knife.

Finnish hunters traveled by skis, carrying a hunting spear which served twofold as a ski pole. Old skis were unpaired. the left ski was long and heavy while the right ski was short and light for kicking speed. Very often some fur was attached under the right ski for friction.

Hunting spears were used in Finland from the Stone Age to the 1800s. Some old bear hunters tried flintlock rifles, but the climate often caused their gunpowder to be damp. Bears don't wait for you to dry out gunpowder, and the hunters learned that it is better to use cold steel—sturdy hunting spears. We still have many brown bears in Finland. In the old days it was considered a sacred animal—son of the forest gods.

The oldest hunting bows were longbows made of a single staff of juniper or yew. After the stick longbow period, Finns began to build bows with a combination of woods. These bows were about 160-170 centimeters long. No one know for sure how strong they were, although they probably gauged forty to seventy pounds of pull. The archer pulled the bow in the mongolian style, like Ishi.[1]

The basic construction was like that of all oriental bows. The Finns used two or three different tree species and glue made from perch skin. The finished bow was coated with a tight tape made from birch bark. The

---

[1]Ishi was the last survivor of the northern California Yana culture. He is considered the last north American 'wild' Indian to wander into civilization from a Stone Age existence. His first contact was August 29, 1911–from that time until his death in December, 1914, his every movement was meticulously studied by anthropologists.

The peculiarities of Ishi's shooting were, first, that he preferred to shoot from a crouching position. He held the bow diagonally across the front of the body, the face of the bow higher than the other limb and to the left. The string was drawn at cheek level.

Ishi's method of arrow release was seemingly a Yana variant of the Mongolian or Asiatic release, which is one of the five common classes of arrow releases worldwide, but one not otherwise reported for native America. It has been speculated that this technique was brought from Asia when Ishi's people migrated to this continent thousands of years ago.

The Mongolian release is used for shooting the composite bow with the aid of a thumb ring, since it is the flexed thumb which accomplishes the pull, the fingers being used only to guide and support the arrow. Ishi used no thumb guard or ring, and his bow was a simple, not a composite one. Ishi drew the bow with the flexed right thumb as in the classic Mongolian release. The Yana variation was in one finger position: the tip of the middle finger was placed lightly against the thumbnail to steady and strengthen its hold.

belly of the bow was made of pine or spruce and the backside was always made of birch. Sometimes the tips were made from the limbs of the bird cherry tree (Prunus padus). All parts were glued with fish skin glue. The string was made from sinew, or in later times, from nettle fibers.

The material for the arrow shaft was the straight wood of the pine tree. Arrows for the longbow were made by whittling, but crossbow arrows were made on a primitive lathe. Hawk and sea eagle feathers were used for fletching.

All bowhunters, including Finns, had special arrows for different animals: birds, fish and also a whistling arrow to frighten flying mallards back to the water. Wild ducks think that the whistling arrow is a diving eagle or goshawk. It is much easier to shoot mallards with a bow and arrow when they are on the surface of the water.

The crossbow displaced the longbow around 1500. Nobility and the military already had firearms by this time, but they were forbidden to ordinary folks. At this time Finns suffered under heavy Swedish exploitation, and only the wilderness and its freedom gave them the ability to survive. In the far north they still use the crossbow and special blunt-tipped arrows for squirrel hunting. These blunt-tipped arrows are made on primitive hand-lathes.

Wild reindeer were hunted in many ways; pitfalls and traps were used most often. Hunters knew that the annual migratory route of the reindeer was always the same so Finns built long fences with gates, and in every gate was a pitfall or trap. The long fence was located in a narrow area between two lakes. Like native North Americans, ancient Finnish hunters used the entire reindeer—nothing was wasted.

About one thousand years ago Finnish fur traders were very rich and had great influence. The red fox was very popular at that time, and the fur hunters killed them in all possible ways. One popular method which seems crude and even cruel by today's standards, was the use of pawboards-made from a tree trunk with an axe. In the middle of the pawboard was a spike for bait, such as a hare's head. On both sides of the spike were long narrow slits. When the fox leapt up for the bait, it's front leg became wedged in the slit. The whole trap is about 180 centimeters high.

During the fur trade era, squirrel fur was very popular in Europe. In fact, squirrel was so important to fur traders that the name for squirrel fur is "raha", which means money in today's Finnish language.

Squirrels were hunted with traps and snares, but those methods are almost all forbidden for hunting in Europe today, with the exception of Ptarmigan, which you can legally hunt with snares in the winter. But, you must be a native inhabitant of one of the three northern territories of

During the winter, ptarmigan eat the buds of the Arctic birch, so it is easy to catch them by setting snares near the branches. The loops are about the size of a large man's fist, with small twigs to hold the loop open. (Illustration by Martti Arkko)

Finland to do so. Catching ptarmigan with snares is one of the last connections to the old hunting traditions.

Ptarmigan is not a very big bird, only about the size of a fat male pigeon. But snaring ptarmigan is easy to learn and very productive. In olden times, Arctic people survived on the dark, tasty meat. Today some people hunt ptarmigan to sell to restaurants, but in many families it is used as a staple food. In any case, it is delicious and gourmets love to eat it.

It is important for every survivalist in the Arctic to learn to snare ptarmigan, that's why we teach it every winter in our Army and Air Force survival training. If you can snare ptarmigans, you can use the same method for grouse and other woodland birds.

Before the introduction of shotguns about 300 years ago, nets were very popular for hunting birds especially along the Finnish sea coast. (If you ask Finnish bird hunters what they think about the southern European method of catching birds, they are all adamantly against it.)

The old hunters used nettle string, human and horse hair and string made of flax fiber for their snares. Today thin brass or steel wire is used. You must check your snares each day or ravens and other predators will do it for you.

Early Finnish hunters could check only four hundred to six hundred snares a day, but modern hunters can cover more ground on snowmobiles. Although the winter daylight is very short in Lapland, a good hunter can make a living with two thousand snares, but most hunters can only handle about one thousand snares a day.

When our ancestors first came to Finland all of their fishing methods were designed for lakes and rivers. But Finland has over 2000 kilometers (1240 miles) of sea coast, so they made some changes in their fishing gear adapting to coastal fishing. An alert ethnographer can still see that the origins of our fishing tackle are from inland waters. And some of the same fishing methods are still used today.

Primitive fishermen eagerly anticipated the tidewater, even though some small low-water ponds gave them small fishes, mussels, crabs and edible algae (in the Baltic Sea areas there is no tide at all). With 9,500 years of experience, fishing is very popular in Finland, both as an occupation and as a national sport that is carried on all year.

The second best time for primitive fishing is spawning time. During spawning, it is easy to catch large amounts of fish. Fish nets are very effective for this work. The oldest fish net was found in Finland in 1914. It is more than 8,000 years old and is made of the inner bark fiber of the willow (Salix caprea). The net was made for catching salmon and other large fish. The cordage was quite thick compared to modern nylon or monofilament line. It is a wonder that this old net could catch fish at all. But the old nets were active nets like seines. The fishermen surrounded the fish and drove them onto the beaches with the nets. Modern net fishing is passive. The nets are invisible so the fish swim straight into them and get stuck by their gills or fins.

I tested one very old, traditional way of fishing with a seine made of leafy twigs during spawning time. To make it, you top two small trees, such as birches, and lay them horizontally level. After that you tie bunches of leafy twigs to the stems to make a wall. With this you can surround fish and force them to the beach, or catch them safely with a leister.

During spawning, all species of salmon move from the sea into the rivers to find their original spawning ground. During this time it is possible to use a landing net to catch salmon and whitefish as they swim up-river. The rapids are the best places to do this, and fishermen who use a long-handled landing net try to find rapids where there are some submerged rocks on the river bottom. Behind these stones is turbulence where fish can rest during their journey. Knowing these places makes fishing with a landing net easy.

Old landing nets were built from thin sticks, birch roots and eventually, nettle fibers. The handle is about 5-6 meters long. If you like to catch whitefish, you should use a net bag with a diameter of about 50 centimeters, for salmon 80 centimeters. When the net bag is dry it will only weigh about 1 kilogram, but when wet it is so heavy you can scarcely maneuver it.

Smelts are also a good species of fish to catch with a landing net. Fishing for smelt in this manner is very popular near my home in Pori, Finland, with hundreds of fishermen coming every April. And if you visit Stockholm, Sweden in April you can see people fishing for smelt with landing nets while they are standing on the bridge right in the middle of the city.

Another effective method of obtaining fish is to knock them out through the ice. In the early winter when the ice is just starting to form, it is clear and transparent for a few days, yet thick enough to walk on. During that time we use a big, heavy axe or wooden hammer to knock fish unconscious through the ice. Our ancestors used stone clubs to hit fish under the ice. No one really knows why the fish rise to the top of the ice, perhaps they are just curious or maybe it is the light or oxygenation that draws them. Burbots (Lota lota, a member of the cod family) are easiest to knock out and sometimes you can get pikes and ides (Idus idus), too. It takes about two or three minutes for the fish to recover after a strong hit to the head, so you must hurry and break the ice and grab the fish before it wakes up. You can sometimes catch a lot of fish this way, but the time during which the ice is clear is very short and it doesn't happen every year because occasionally it snows at the time when the lakes are freezing.

Fishermen once used a trotline for winter fishing under the ice. The lines were not very long, ranging from ten to twenty-five meters, depending on how deep the water was. The basic line was made of pine root or birch bark rope; hemp or flax was used during the Bronze Age (1500-500 B.C.). The short lines that are connected to the basic line with slip knots were made of nettle or willow fiber. Horse hair was used after domestic animals were brought to Finland during the Bronze Age. Roaches or small fish such as perch were used as bait and gorges inserted inside. The gorge is the predecessor of all fish hooks and fishermen once made them from wood, bone, antler and stone. We use birch or wood from the bird cherry tree. It would be advisable for all fishing enthusiasts and scientists to try using gorges so they will understand the ancient fishing methods better. Metal hooks are very new to fishing—the first metal hooks were made from copper or tin, which was easy to shape.

In the winter, ice was a problem for primitive people fishing with a trotline. How do you get the line to sink? You need a special tool to make holes in the ice. A very effective tool is made from the shinbone of elk or wild reindeer. We just tested this primitive tool in our Army survival camp for instructors. It took about twenty minutes of hard work to go through 40 centimeters of thick ice, and this tool sharpens itself while you are

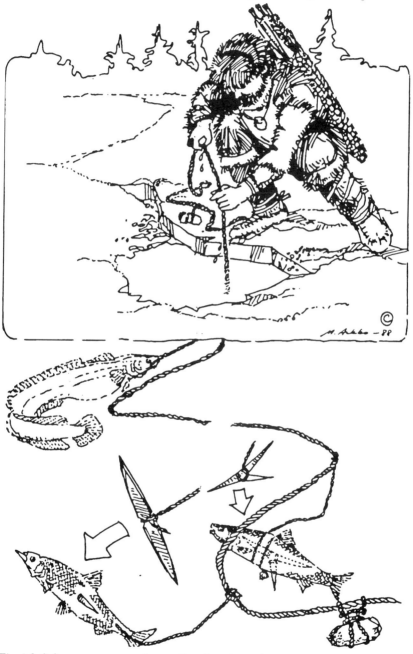

Finnish fishermen once used a trotline for winter fishing under the ice. The lines were not very long, ranging from about ten to twenty-five meters, depending on how deep the water was. (Illustration by Martti Arkko)

working with it. Just make a tool like a short-handled spear with a bone point.

Fishing with a pine-root trotline with juniper gorges is historically Finnish and some of the old fishermen still use it. When visiting my friend Martti Arkko at his wilderness studio last winter we used this method to get some burbots into our fish soup.

During the winter, the burbot is a common catch—it is not beautiful but tastes good. Burbot roe is also a great delicacy. In Siberia, our ancestors used burbot skin, tanned with human urine, for clothing and other gear.

Leistering with a big, birch-bark torch still keeps old and young Finns alike out late on many summer nights. In fact, using a leister from a boat to kill fish as they sleep was so effective that it was forbidden by law from 1902 until 1941. For modern people, leistering just one dark fall night without wind will furnish so much fish, and resulting new mental power, that it is easy to work until Christmas. Today, you can fish with a leister all year except from April to June, during spawning. Bow fishing is also allowed by law today.

During early spring days, you can shoot large, spawning pikes with a bow as they sun themselves in shallow water. Australian Aborigines do the same thing with atlatl and spears.

The first leister was only a tree branch, after that primitive fishermen

In earlier times, fishermen used birch bark fire claws and torches to light the path for night fishing.

Large kiddles, made of pine splinters provided a stable source of fish year round. Old Finns and other finno-ugrian folks made aspen dugout canoes for water travel.

made more barbs using wood, antlers, bone etc. In Finland we still use the traditional leisters for our nightly fishing sessions, but a birch bark torch is not used anymore, and iron fireclaws have been replaced by electricity.

A large fish trap, or kiddle, made of splinters or slats, is almost universal. The kiddle is well-known in Hungary, Central Volga, India and China and was also used by some North American Indian cultures. It is used at the seaside, on lakes and rivers. The oldest splinter kiddle known in Finland is from the Stone Age (9500-1500 B.C.). Seaside fishermen built a new kiddle every spring after the ice melted, but the lakeside ice moved so little that it did not break the kiddle and people could use the same fish trap for many years.

Pine is very easy to split into nice straight splinters about three to six centimeters wide and two to four centimeters long. Kiddle builders also need many piles of wood to make the trunk of the trap. No nails or iron are used in these traps, all bindings are made with birch switches. You can collect fish from kiddles all summer long. First come the pikes, followed by bream. When the perch comes, it brings autumn with it. The oldest written documents of splinter kiddles date to 1,300 years ago and also mention the rights of ownership to fishing waters. The oldest records of such laws in my neighborhood date to 1466.

Pearling is also a part of old Finnish hunting and fishing tradition, and was in its golden years from 1700 to 1850, during which the pearl mussel was fished almost to extinction. The pearl mussel needs salmon to be able to propagate because the mussel larvae lives its first year inside the gills of salmon. Pearl mussels have been protected by law since 1957, but my photographer friend, Rainer Nikkanen, had a special permit for an ethnographic study with photos and film of two old pearl fishing brothers. They opened 500 pearl mussels but found no pearls, it was a pity, but the film and photos were a success.

Finally, we will look at fishing with a tame otter. Fishing with a group of tamed cormorants was very popular in China many centuries ago. And some oriental fishermen still do it to demonstrate ancient fishing techniques for tourists.

At one time otter fur was eagerly procured for hats and collars because good otter skin was so strong it lasted a lifetime. Old Carelian Finns used otter traps and trapped them alive. Young otters were easy to tame, clever and playful, curious and trusting. In some places of North Carelia it was a great pleasure for children to take their tame otters for a winter fishing trip. You simply make a few holes in the ice and the otter does the rest.

By mid-winter, much of the oxygen is gone from the small lakes and the fish seek refuge together in the deepest corner of the lake. One boisterous otter can raise hell out there on the dark lake bottom. But they also fill the baskets full of fresh fish, and everyone (except the fish) is happy.

Children in North Carelia enjoyed taking their tame otters for a winter fishing trip. It is only necessary to make a hole in the ice, the otter will do the fishing.

Linda Jamison

Primitive
Process Pottery

• •

*Clay twists, bends and flattens. You can tear clay apart
and put it back together again. You can make coils by
rolling the clay between your palms. You can make balls
by rolling the clay in your hands, and you can make slabs
by mashing it flat. The clay's potential is, literally, in your
hands, so it is most important to listen to it's commands—
feel the rhythm, the pulse.*

During the past twenty years or more I have wandered among
many ancient pot shards in the Southwest without truly appreciating the
technology that produced them. Now I walk with renewed understanding
that each small shard represents the employment of a large and complex
body of technical knowledge concerning the properties of various clays,
their most advantageous combinations, the preparation of the materials,
structural necessities in the building of vessels and finally, firing to just the
precise degree of hardness.

Clay was mined from nearby (and sometimes not-so-nearby) deposits,
paints were manufactured from plants and minerals and frequently water
had to be transported over great distances to make the clays, slips and
paints. Not only were functional vessels produced, finished products of
stunning beauty were made with only the most rudimentary tools, and
neither the potter's wheel nor the kiln were used. In spite of this, during
the tenth through the sixteenth centuries, highly decorated pottery was
manufactured in quantities that would boggle the mind—and made with

such skill that many have survived the centuries, retaining all of their original beauty.

I was first introduced to primitive process pottery in 1979 by Samantha (Sam) Winborn. Sam is a talented craftsperson who, as with most modern-day abos, was eager to share her knowledge and skills with anyone who had a mind to learn.

I attended Sam's workshop at the second annual Rabbit Stick Rendezvous long enough to poke my thumbs into a little ball of clay and shape it into something recognizable, and long enough to determine that this was one art form I could get excited about. The most important thing I gleaned, though, is the conviction that clay is a medium which provides a linking of humanity and earth, because it truly comes alive when you take it to hand. It's a lump of soil that says "Make something of me."

Eleven years later I met Wayne Brian, a master primitive potter from Mesa, Arizona. I spent two days hanging around Wayne's camp pestering him with endless questions, and eventually bought two small effigy pots and a mountain goat canteen—once I held them in my hands I couldn't imagine parting with them. (Beauty is found not in things, but in the relationship among things, and I definitely related.) Thankfully, while prehistoric pottery is for museums and under-glass viewing of special collections, replicated primitive pottery is for the intimate enjoyment of the potter and the masses.

At this stage I do not believe I can create vessels as beautiful as Wayne's, but I believe that anyone willing to put forth the necessary effort can discover the relationship between the human spirit and the earth spirit. And that, in my opinion, is the ultimate reward.

The more I learn about collecting and processing "found clays" the more I marvel at the patience and skill of early people who produced superior pottery that is light, strong and watertight. It is truly one of the great scientific and artistic achievements of ancient technology.

History

We can only speculate how pottery first came to be, but we can be sure it was the result of a long evolution with many trials and failures. The most primitive vessels of early men and women were their hands—then leaves, bark, shells and sections of plants were inevitably used. Later, the hollowed-out shells of gourds and squash served as major containers for food, especially liquids. By means of these, early people could not only dip water, but transport it from place to place.

We do know that native American pottery has been around since prehistoric times and was manufactured by the sedentary peoples of the Southwest for at least two thousand years.

Three cultural groups, the Anasazi, Hohokam and Mogollon, share the distinction of being among the finest prehistoric artists to have lived on the face of the earth. And of all their known art forms, pottery has best survived the centuries and truly demonstrates the ability of these craftsmen and women. But to fully appreciate these ancient vessels, we must learn the manner in which they were made.

So before you embark on a pottery-making adventure, I encourage you to first visit museums, galleries and exhibitions featuring primitive pottery of various periods. If you can, visit a potter like Wayne, who replicates early cultures. Knowing what has been accomplished before and by others adds value and appreciation to the art, not to mention your own efforts.

Clay Sources and Collection

At long last, my early study of geology has meaning and purpose—in fact, I find almost as much enjoyment locating clay as I do making a pot. And every terrain is now a possible new source of clay, or minerals for temper or paint.

Clay is a soil that comes from sedimentary rock formed by the accumulation of materials at the earth's surface as a result of the geological processes going on there. It varies greatly in composition, so an understanding of geological strata and soil characteristics can be a great help when you search for local sources.

After millions of years of being acted upon by wind, frost, ice, water, snow, heat, cold and the gasses of the air, the rocks on the surface of the earth break down into various forms.

Plateau formations contain alternating weak and resistant rock layers and layers of clay and shale. Also, in areas where slumping (a landslide where rock masses tilt back as they slide from an escarpment) occurs, thick deposits of sedimentary rocks generally overlie clay or shale. Or you can look for natural flood plains where the valley floor is flattened and broadened by river erosion and floored with deposited sediments. In bends of the river the velocity of the water is slowed and the coarsest material comes to rest nearest the river bed, building up natural embankments or levees along the sides; behind these levees are the backswamps in which the finer sediments are deposited.

Also pay attention to erosion where there are hills and banks; most clays do not erode as quickly as other mineral and earth surfaces and so are exposed. Clay deposits can also occur in rocky areas—in fact, the clay used in Zuni pottery is a dark, bluish clay shale found in layers usually near the tops of the mesas.

When moist, clay holds a particular shape and becomes "plastic."

Deep cracks in the surface of dried soil is also an indication of a degree of this plasticity. Once you locate a likely source of clay, dig a foot or two into the deposit to get a true specimen, then wet a small amount about the size of a marble and roll it into a ball. Flatten the ball. If a sample is sticky and cracks when pressed flat, dig enough to give it a try. But remember, although clays are found widely scattered throughout the earth, some are useful for making pottery and some are not.

For instance, alluvial clay carried into lakes or valleys by rivers is not always good to use for pottery because a lot of organic matter is mixed with the clay. It is better to gather residual clay from fresh road cuts and eroded hills, or along the banks of stream beds. Residual clay was at one time sedimentary clay that has had thousands of years to improve through compaction.

There are three main impurities to watch for when digging for clay: iron pyrite (a sulfide sometimes known as fool's gold), limestone (calcite), and gypsum (a sulfate). If small white crystals appear on the surface of the raw material, it probably contains gypsum. Gypsum can cause scumming, a white film on red-firing clays. Gold colored particles are usually pyrite. Small pyrite particles cause black spots in reduction firing, larger particles can cause small pop-outs (small explosions that look like rock chips in a car window) during firing. Calcite acts as a bleach on red fired clay turning it a buff color. Large amounts of quartz in the form of sand or silt can also cause problems. Nevertheless, clay that is found having some of these impurities is still usable, depending on the amount of them in the clay.

With a little time and close observation, you will certainly find sources of workable clay—from there you will doubtless expand to experiment with color. Pure clay is white, but most that you find will be colored brown, green or red by iron compounds. Due to weathering, a clay may be one color on the surface, and another at deeper levels. However, if the clay is the same both on the surface and at the inner depth, it is probable that it will also fire true. Mixing clay is not recommended, although some potters do it. The most common colors in raw field clays are gray-green, dark brown, reds and gray, but it is almost impossible to determine the fired color of the clay as it is found on site.

Be aware, too, that the color of the clay alone is not always responsible for the fired color. Pots that are oxidized in firing will be brighter in color as a result of the oxygen that completely burns the fuel, opposed to the black or gray cast that results from soot, smoke, and reducing gases that exist in reduction firing.

It is helpful to label your clay samples. I have several buckets of red and gray clay specimens which have proved excellent for pottery, but unfortunately I did not note their location. I have since learned to tie a small tag to the handle of the clay bucket to indicate specific locations. For even better identification, after the specimen is processed I make a tile about half the size of a bathroom tile on which I also code the clay source. Then, on a piece of cardboard I trace an outline of the tile before it is dried and again when dry to measure the amount of shrinkage. After the tiles have been fired I measure the tile again for additional shrinking and note color changes. In this way I am able to weed out unsuitable clays from those that I want to use again.

Clay Preparation
After you collect your clay, the next step is to dry and clean it of large, obvious sticks and rocks, then crush or grind it. This was originally done with a special mano (grinding stone) on a metate (grinding surface).

One cleaning method used by the ancients was accomplished by winnowing the dry clay like wheat to oust small pebbles and fine gravel, either of which will ruin a pot if not removed. The larger impurities are, of course, picked out by hand.

Another way to prepare small clumps of clay is to put them in a container, such as an enameled basin, a bucket or large (fired) bowl, and add enough water to saturate them. Once the clay has been thoroughly softened with water you can remove the pebbles by squeezing and kneading it.

Next, fill the container with water, stir well and allow the clay to settle overnight, or until the sediments separate; the heavier elements descend to the bottom, the clay remains in the center of the container, and the water rises to the top. Discard the water and pour the clay into another container, taking care not to scoop up any of the debris that has settled in the bottom. Finally, you can either pour the clay into a canvas bag and hang it in a shady place to drain, or spread it on a flat surface and allow the moisture to evaporate until it is either suitable to work, or completely dry for storage. If you plan to use the clay right away, watch the drying process closely—if it dries a little too much, wet the bag. If it dries completely you will have to crush it and start again.

When you are ready to use your clay it must first be mixed with temper, then moistened and kneaded and wedged (slammed against a flat surface) to remove any air pockets that cause pop-outs during firing.

Crushed igneous (volcanic) rock and sand make good temper, as do pulverized pot shards because they have already been naturally fired at high temperatures. The purpose of adding tempering material is to counteract the tendency of pure clay to crack during the shrinkage that takes place as it dries and when it is fired. Clay with no temper will be apt to lose its adhesiveness and crack during drying and firing, while clay with too much temper will be short and brittle in working. If your pot cracks badly while drying it can be ground up and more temper added. If, on the other hand, your pot will not retain its shape while being molded, pull it down, add more dry clay to the paste and re-knead.

As my experience grows, I find that I can determine with some accuracy which clays contain enough temper in their natural state and those which require the addition of temper by simply rubbing the wet clay between my fingers to feel the grit. Another way to tell is to wash a portion of clay through a sieve and measure the amount of temper it contains.

The dry clay method consists of mixing the clay and temper while both ingredients are dry. There is no particular formula, although experience helps you judge the color of the resulting mixture—it is generally about one-fourth temper and three-fourths clay. When following the wet-clay procedure, add temper to the water-soaked clay until you arrive at the desired texture and color.

Next, knead the entire mass until the water is thoroughly absorbed—the consistency should be like putty, just dry enough to crack if pinched. Then divide the clay into chunks about the size of loaves of bread so they can be easily handled. Work the paste to a uniform consistency in exactly the same way you knead dough on a board or canvas, then wedge it by slamming it against a hard surface to remove air pockets. Finally, cover the clay with a piece of damp cloth to keep it moist until you are ready to use it.

Form

Before you begin to mold your pot, you should have some idea of its function. Your limitations are determined more by your skill in mixing the materials, building the vessel and firing it than by the inherent nature of the material; therefore, forms are dictated by the purposes for which they are designed. In hand-built pottery there is no limitation to the circular forms that are inevitable when pottery is turned on the wheel.

I fell in love with a small "horned toad" canteen that Wayne replicated from one he saw in a museum. It was flat and rounded with an opening on one end and carried by means of a tether around the neck. I'm sure the piece would have been less captivating, albeit still functional, if produced on a potters wheel.

There are only a few basic forms in Southwestern primitive pottery: equal height and width, tall and narrow and short and wide; yet there are many variations. So once a form is established for a general purpose, such as a bowl for eating, mixing or holding various items, you are free to develop that form.

Paraphernalia

Before you begin, collect several molds, scrapers, polishing stones, a board, a water container, mops, wiping rags, a sanding stone, paint and receptacles and brushes. You can gather your materials from nature as the ancients did, or you can substitute modern, craft-store conveniences that meet the same need, but there is a lot to be said for replicating an ancient tradition in the old ways. (I keep a basket of tools conveniently at hand to take with me when I travel, and I have even set up a pottery workshop in my motel room on occasion.)

In ancient times the molds, called pukis, were the bases of broken bowls or ollas (large jars). Pieces of pottery can be made especially for this purpose, or any open, globular mold can be used. Sprinkle a small amount of sand, temper material or wood ashes in the puki so the clay doesn't stick. A small piece of cotton cloth also works nicely.

Potsherds with edges sharpened on a piece of sandstone were formerly used as scrapers. Experienced potters have many scrapers of different shapes and sizes for different areas of the pot.

Very smooth, fine-grained weatherworn pebbles without any acute angles or sharp edges are used to put the final finish on the pottery. Like scrapers, several polishing stones of various sizes should be collected, including some larger ones that are more flat than spherical. Because they are distinctly the personal property of the potter, polishing stones historically (or pre-historically) often became heirlooms. The same is true today.

Traditionally, the potter sat on the ground with a flat board (or some other flat surface) on her lap on which the puki was continually turned as she worked. You may find, as I do, that sitting on the ground in this manner for a long period of time is difficult. I prefer a small table and chair. When I have completed several pieces, I place them in rows on a board to dry. This lessens the possibility of dropping them if they must be moved. (Flat-bottomed vessels can be built directly on boards.)

Always keep a small container filled with water at your side to moisten parts of the pot from time to time, and to clean your hands. When scrapers are not being used they can be kept in the water container.

Mops consist of a rag, a piece of leather or a soft rabbit's tail, attached to a stick to serve as a large paint brush for applying slips.

An apron, or any piece of cloth, can serve as a wiping rag for your hands. If you get clay on your clothing, simply let it dry and brush it off.

A small piece of sandstone is handy to sand and smooth the dry vessel.

Slips and paints that are ready for use can be kept in open glazed basins. Generally, large quantities of slips and paints are mixed at one time

To make a yucca paint brush, cut a thin leaf to about six inches, then pound the end to remove the pulp and thin the remaining fibers. (Photo: Richard Jamison)

and stored in these paint receptacles for later use. Allow the paint to dry before you store it.

Paint brushes made from the main ribs of yucca leaves are traditionally used to apply designs to the pottery. Cut a thin length about six inches long, then chew or pound it about one inch from the end of the leaf to remove the pulp and separate the fibers. Finally, trim off most of the chewed fibers to make a narrow brush. The number of fibers you leave will determine the fineness of the point; for very thin lines use a brush with only one or two fibers. The dry fibers will be stiff and brittle and must be handled with care, so when not in use, protect your yucca brushes in a receptacle that will cover the shredded ends until you are ready to use them again, then soften the ends by soaking them in water for two or three minutes.

Modeling
Clay twists, bends and flattens. You can tear clay apart and put it back together again. You can make coils by rolling the clay between your palms. You can make balls by rolling the clay in your hands, and you can make slabs by mashing it flat. The clay's potential is, literally, in your hands, so it is most important to listen to it's commands—feel the rhythm, the pulse.

In this way you will realize the potential in this latent lump of earth, potential for graceful contours and disciplined lines.

Coil and scrape technique

Be sure to keep the clay moist as you work. Begin by taking a bit of prepared clay slightly larger than your fist and rolling it into a ball. Press the ball into a pancake about one-half inch thick. If a crack appears, dip your fingers in water and smooth it out. If many cracks appear, you need to start over with fresh clay because cracks will ruin the vessel for any use. (Remember, clay with too much temper will crack easily.) Next, place your pancake into the puki and gently contour it to the mold.

From this point you will construct your vessel with coils. Start the coils by holding a small amount of clay in both hands and rolling it back and forth between your palms, working from the center to the ends. Then lay the rope flat and roll it evenly until it is about the length of the circumference of your pot. Dip your fingers into the water and moisten both the base and the coil before laying it in place to assure that each layer adheres to the next.

Continue to add coils according to the size and shape of your planned pot, smoothing both the inside and outside to meld one bit of clay into the other; or, the pinch marks can remain visible if you choose. A 'shingling' technique can also be used, resulting in a corrugated vessel—this was especially common among Anasazi groups. While the clay is still moist, the piece can be re-shaped and smoothed with a flat paddle by gently tapping the outside of the pot.

As the clay dries somewhat, it attains what is called a leather state and can be removed from the puki and thinned. (Large vessels should be allowed to dry about forty-eight hours.) Thinning is accomplished with a scraper and serves a twofold purpose; first, to thin the sides, thus reducing the weight of the finished piece, and second, to improve the surface of the vessel by removing marks left by the puki.

There are three steps to the scraping process: wetting, scraping and smoothing. First, soften the exterior surface by wiping it with a wet rag. When working on a large piece you may have to moisten the surface a second time, particularly in the area being worked. This step can be omitted when the pot only needs a small amount of scraping.

Now begin scraping near the shoulder of the pot and continue toward the base using short, quick strokes while turning the piece. Bowls are scraped to the very rim, but in ollas with a flaring lip the scraping continues only to the base of the flare. The interiors of vessels, even wide-mouthed bowls, are not scraped except to smooth and thin.

If scraping uproots an impurity, simply remove it and fill in the hole

Smooth both the inside and the outside with your thumb to obliterate the coils as each rope is added. (Photo: Richard Jamison)

with a pinch of soft clay, then smooth it over. If stress marks appear during the scraping process, remove them by redistributing the clay particles, moisten, then add bits of clay to the cracks. At this point you can add handles or decorations to your vessel by scoring the spot where you want to add on, spreading a layer of slip over both sides and pressing the clay together firmly. Hold it together gently for a minute until you are sure it will stick.

Once all the scraping is done your piece can be placed in a dry spot out of the sun to dry. Use care when drying your handiwork, as pottery dried too quickly in the direct sun often cracks. If you are interrupted before you complete your pot, cover it with a damp cloth or invert a large clay crock over it to prevent excessive drying.

When the pot is dry, use a piece of sandstone to smooth any rough or uneven spots, then soften the surface and interior with a wet cloth and rub it vigorously with your fingers to give it a uniform smooth texture. This process is the same as putting on a thin slip of paste. Also smooth the rim of the piece with great care using the wet cloth to even all the surfaces in preparation for the slip.

A polishing stone dipped in water is then used to smooth the exterior walls. Sometimes this is a mere smoothing, or the process can be continued to the point of giving an actual polish to the vessel.

Slips and polishing

Now the pot is ready for the slip—a liquid paint made from water and clay. Slip can be used as a base color and/or as a paint to supply the elements of polychrome designs. A slip is for the purpose of refinement, and therefore not necessary to making a useful and attractive piece of earthenware. It is a personal decision.

The materials used for slipping and polishing include the water-clay solution, mopping cloths or brushes and polishing stones. In prehistoric times slip was applied with a rabbit tail or animal fur mop. Slips can be watered-down clay from which the pot was made, or they might be from a different source. They can be thick or thin, colored or white. White slip, which is usually applied as a base for decorative work, is generally made from a fine, white, calcareous earth consisting mainly of carbonate of lime.

The slip is prepared in much the same way as the clay: it is dried thoroughly then ground and mixed with water to form a thin solution (slip the consistency of cream is preferred by some potters). Or, it can be dissolved in water in small lumps without the initial grinding. A sufficient amount is mixed with the water to give it the desired color.

Begin at the neck and rim and work down. At least two applications are made, covering the pot with uniform color.

The beautiful luster of burnished ware is the result of skillful polishing. Polishing is an exacting process begun while the slip is still damp. The first polishing strokes are done quickly, covering the whole piece. The next rubbing requires a little more pressure and overlaps the strokes. A thinner and longer stone can be used to polish the interior of the rim, but it is difficult if not impossible to polish the lower interior of the pot. Every inch of the slipped surface must be rubbed again and again. Once your piece has been burnished, be very careful of water, perspiration or other stains; these defects cannot be removed.

After the initial polishing, a thin coat of grease or oil can be applied with the fingers. The Southwest Indians often used turkey grease, but vegetable oil also works. The grease is allowed to soak into the surface for five to ten minutes, then the vessel is polished again. When the polishing is finally complete, wrap the pot in a soft cloth and store it until you are ready to fire.

Decoration

Decoration of pottery involves many aspects, including layout or adaptation of design. Painting is the most common decorative technique, but altered surfaces were also popular in prehistoric times.

Some common techniques included corrugated, wiped, tooled, punched, partially obliterated coils and flattened coils as well as combinations of these. Sometimes the coils used in making a vessel were simply left unobliterated (corrugated), or they were indented to produce a simple design. As a rule, cooking vessels were not decorated; color would have been lost completely on a cooking pot with its first blackening use. (The all-over corrugation popular with the Anasazi may have been for ease and security in handling the hot vessel.)

Another decorative technique known throughout the Southwest was modeling. Sometimes it was nothing more than forming a crude head and tail of a bird on a bowl or jar, or painting the wings and any other details which were represented. Or the handle of a pitcher might be formed in the shape of the body of an animal with all details painted on except the modeled head. Complete shaping of the entire figure of a human or animal may also be done to produce an effigy.

Painting

Painting was favored above all other styles of decoration and was greatly varied. For example, decorative treatment by spattering was common, performed, no doubt, by blowing paint through a hollow reed. Stippling, the application of a pattern of dots, was also popular.

Banded layouts are perhaps the most common painted decoration of all. A band is created by drawing two parallel lines. These lines can be vertical, creating square or rectangular areas; oblique, creating parallelograms; or horizontal, which make narrow bands. Designs can then be placed within each of these differently shaped areas. An important aspect of painted decoration in relation to form is where design will be placed, inside or outside a vessel.

It is often difficult to fit a pattern to the surface since the field is continuous. Therefore, the decoration of pottery requires not only a steady hand and coordination between hand and eye, but also great sensitivity to spatial values. Further, difficulty visualizing the design in relation to the surface is increased by the fact that you can't see the whole decorative field at one time.

Plan your design mentally before the work begins, then draw it on the vessel. Paint can be applied to a polished or an unpolished surface, but it must be done very carefully as a drip can ruin the polished surface.

Color

Certainly, great variation is possible in the employment of color. White, gray, cream, buff, orange, red and black have all been used as base colors at one time or another in the Southwest, and this by no means exhausts the possibilities afforded by the geological environment. White is generally used as the base and achieved with a slip to give an outer coating to the body of the vessel.

The most common vegetable paint used in the Southwest was obtained from a very common weed known as the Rocky Mountain bee plant (Cleome serrulata). Tansy mustard (Descurainia) was also used occasionally. In either case, the plants are gathered during April and May when the shoots are only six to ten inches high and still tender. They are covered with water and boiled in an open container; usually half a day is sufficient, but sometimes a whole day is required.

Once the liquid is boiled down to a thick syrup, it is drained from the pulp and placed in the sun to harden into a solid, black, rather sticky mass. When it is completely solid it can be stored for future use and will keep indefinitely. The longer it is kept the better black it produces. (If used during the first year, the resulting color will be slightly blue-black.) Guaco, as this organic paint is called, is prepared for use by breaking off a chunk of the dry, hardened mass and dissolving it in water.

Guaco can be used alone as a paint, or as a binder when mixed (about one-quarter guaco to three-quarters mineral paint) with finely pulverized minerals such as hematite and limonite, causing the paint to stick to the polished surface.

Mineral paints come from deposits formed at the earth's surface. They are, in effect, simply special kinds of sedimentary rocks. Table A is a summary of the chief characteristics of some common ore-minerals that can be used for paint.

It is important to remember that color in design is subject to many forces, both within the color itself and, frequently, in relation to the quantity and quality of the minerals or organic paints, the amount used,

Table A

Metal	Mineral	Composition	Color
Iron	Magnetite iron oxide	Fe_3O_4	Iron-black
Hematite	iron oxide	Fe_2O_3	Steel-grey Streak red
Limonite	hydrated iron oxide	$2Fe_2O_3.3H_2O$	Brown-yellow
Siderite	iron carbonate	$FeCO_3$	Brownish

the results of longer or shorter firing, and higher or lower firing temperatures.

Oxygen present when the pots are fired also influences the color of the final product. Where oxygen is present in sufficient amounts, pots will fire brown, orange, reddish or white, depending upon whether a brown-firing or white-firing clay is used. If the pots are covered by bark or other stifling material when fired, oxygen is kept out and the pottery turns gray or black, regardless of the clay used.

Firing

Firing is the last and most crucial step in pottery making. Ironically, pottery is both durable enough to last thousands of years, and yet so sensitive to change that insufficient heat may warp the pots, or an errant draft or too much heat in firing can break them. You can spend days shaping, drying, polishing, carving and decorating pots, only to chance losing one or all of them during the firing.

If flames from the fire lick at the sides of the pot, it will produce a smudged area called a fire cloud. Fire clouds are not necessarily undesirable features on a pot, depending on the intensity of the clouds and the personal preference of the potter. On plain ware they can be quite attractive, softly blending with the natural color of the clay. But on polychrome vessels, particularly those with decoration on the exterior, fire clouds may obscure the design.

To minimize your risks, choose a warm day with little or no wind and burn a bed of coals to pre-heat the area where the firing will take place. Place the finished pots around the perimeter of the fire to warm thoroughly. After a generous amount of coals has been prepared, spread them out with a stick and let them cool to white ashes. Next, place a rack of green sticks, several rocks or some large pieces of broken potsherds on the warmed area and carefully arrange the vessels on top. If you use rocks, be sure they are completely dry or they will explode when moisture in them expands from the heat. Finally, protect the vessels from ashes and flames by covering them with large potsherds.

Once the pottery is arranged, work quickly to construct a beehive of sheep dung, cow manure or other hot-burning fuel around and over the top of the pots until they are completely covered. Then surround the mound with a tepee of wood and set it on fire at the base.

During the firing, the molecular structure of the clay vitrifies, or fuses, in the soaring temperatures of the burning beehive, and bonds together into a hard, durable form.

After the flames subside, it may take four to five hours for the coals to return to atmospheric temperature. It is an exciting time because you will soon learn whether your firing was successful or not, but you must be particularly careful at this stage because if you expose a hot vessel to the cool air too soon it may crack. This is the moment of truth!

Certainly we can have only the greatest admiration for the first humans who took the mud from under their tired feet and fashioned it into beauty with their hands. True artistry is an inherent quality of potters of ancient times, as well as today. But to me, the greatest joy comes from delving into a bucket of clay up to my elbows, feeling the silky texture of the wet silt as I squish it through my fingers. The earthy smell of it takes me back to my childhood to relive the many hours I spent playing in mud, stirring dirt "batter" round and round to make imaginary cakes and pies. Thank you Mother, for allowing me to play in the mud!

Glossary of Pottery Terms

Carbonates—An organic compound; calcium, shell, limestone.

Found Clay—Clay from local sources; other than commercial clay.

Guaco—A paint medium derived from boiled plants, particularly "bee weed" (Cleome serrulata).

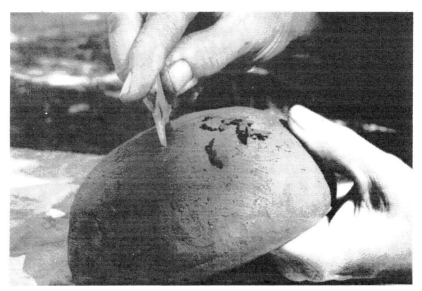

Once the clay has dried to a "leather" state it can be removed from the puki for scraping and thinning (Photo by Richard Jamison).

Mop on several layers of slip, working down. When the slip is a different color than the clay, add at least four coats. (Photo by Richard Jamison)

Hematite–A mineral. Red iron ore, used as a paint base.

Igneous Rock–Rocks formed by solidification of a molten magma, volcanic rock. Used for temper material.

Limonite–A mineral. Yellow iron ore, used as a paint base.

Manganese–A mineral. Black, used for paint.

Polychrome–Many-colored. Printed on a background of various colors. A vessel painted with two or more colors.

Puki–A bowl used as a base to support a vessel under construction.

Residual Clay–Clay found with parent rock.

Sedimentary Clay–Clay deposited by the action of water, also called alluvial clay.

Shard/Sherd–A broken fragment of a ceramic vessel.

Sinter–To become a cohesive mass when heated.

Slip–Clay in a liquid state used for a decoration or cement. Thin clay

Decorative techniques and designs such as these are adapted to their specific vessel forms. The two "ollas" at the top are plain ware, whereas the seed bowl to the right and the other bowls are painted. The bowl on the left has been decorated with a "punched" design and the one on the lower right is polished. (Photo by Linda Jamison)

painted over the surface of a vessel to color and/or create a smooth surface for polishing.

Spalling—Small chips and "popouts" that occur during firing, usually caused by carbonates in clay.

Temper—Material added to clay to reduce shrinkage.

Vitrify—To turn to glass under heat or fusion.

A small hand axe. (Photo: Paul Hellweg)

Paul Hellweg and Donald B. Fisher

Stone Survival Tools

• •

Almost any flake will suffice as an emergency survival tool; thus, you needn't worry about striking perfect flakes with every blow of your hammerstone.

Have you ever used a big rock to pound in a tent stake? Chucked a stone at a squawking raven or the neighbor's whining cat? Cut yourself on a piece of broken glass? Congratulations–for in an era of computers, space travel and telecommunications, you've just taken humankind back a couple of million years by proving the lasting effectiveness of stone tools.

For at least 2.5 million years, stone tools figured daily in primitive life, with uses ranging from hunting and gathering food to erecting shelters to making other tools from bone and wood. Stonework even played a part in ceremonial and religious practices.

Prehistoric stone-working skills are hardly lost or forgotten today. In our "modern" world we call it flintknapping, and although contemporary knappers don't often produce tools intended for everyday use, these stone objects can possess great utilitarian value. Can you use stone-age techniques to create substitutes for modern tools? Are there any basic stone-working techniques that don't require years of practice?

The answer on both counts is "yes." In a survival situation, or even just for fun, prehistoric techniques work as well for modern people as they did for our ancestors. In just a few hours you can acquire the skills to create stone survival tools, and the materials you need are certainly abundant. Naturally, mastering advanced stone-working skills requires more time and patience, but you can make at least half-a-million years' progress in a couple of afternoons.

53

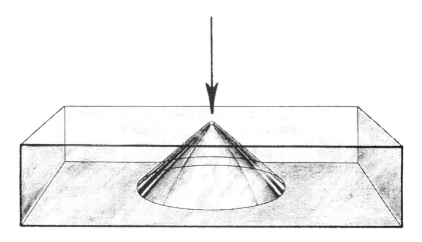

The principle of the "Hertzian Cone" or "Cone of Force": When you apply force vertically to a flat surface, the force will spread equally, forming a cone. (Illustration by Michael R. Seacord from Flintknapping: The Art of Making Stone Tools, *reprinted by permission of the author. (Canoga Park: Canyon Publishing Co., 1984)*

Basic Principles

In a survival situation, three tools are of basic importance: a knife, an axe, and an arrowhead–though admittedly the latter is of limited value if you don't already have a background in primitive archery techniques. All three can be made from stone with very little or no previous experience in flintknapping. But before you can make any of these, you must first understand basic stone-working concepts, and you must learn to choose the correct parent material for the kind of tool you wish to manufacture.

Instrumental to both is the "Hertzian Cone" or "Cone of Force" principle: when force is applied vertically to a flat surface, the force will spread equally, forming a cone. Think of a BB hitting a glass window. The spot where the BB strikes the glass results in a small, approximately one-sixteenth inch hole. But the side where it exits shows a larger hole, one-half inch or more in diameter. Viewed on edge, you can see the shape of the resultant cone (figure 1). Don't have a BB gun handy? Throw a rock in a calm body of water. From the point of impact, the force radiates equally in all directions.

The second concept necessary for successful stone-working comes with understanding the principle of conchoidal fracture. A conchoidal fracture looks like the inside half of a bivalve shell, and it results when you shear off a flake by striking a piece of useable stone. If stone will not fracture conchoidally, it is unsuitable for producing sharp-edged materials. Useable stone includes flint, obsidian, chert, jasper, agate, chalcedony, quartz, quartzite, and basalt–in essence almost any rock containing silica.

If you can't yet identify these kinds of rocks, just experiment by picking up a stone now and then, striking it with another, and noticing if the stone flakes. You will soon develop an eye for selecting likely material, even if you can't name it.

Striking Flakes
Merely striking a flake off a usable piece of stone is the quickest and easiest way to create a cutting tool. Assuming you use the correct type of stone, the resulting flake will taper off to a thin and sharp edge. A flake tool doesn't look too impressive, but it will work wonders at cutting soft materials: leather, cloth, meat, plants, and so forth.

Though some skill is required to consistently strike quality flakes, the basic technique is quite simple and is easily mastered. All that is required is an understanding of the previously discussed cone principles. By understanding the cone fracture principle, it is possible to visualize how flakes are removed in a direction different from the angle of applied force. Sound difficult? It isn't; just follow these three easy steps:

1.   Visualize a desirable flake.
2.   Imagine that flake as a cone section.
3.   The correct striking angle now becomes readily apparent (figure 2).

To strike flakes, use a hammerstone of sandstone, coarse-grained granite, or similar material. Hammerstones should be free of cracks to prevent breakage during use, and they should be of appropriate size to be easily wielded in one hand.

Almost any flake will suffice as an emergency survival tool; thus, you needn't worry about striking perfect flakes with every blow of your hammerstone. Instead, your main concern should be safety. A poorly placed hammerstone blow could shatter the parent stone, which you'll likely be holding in your hand. If the parent stone does shatter, pieces could fly in all directions. And if you're supporting the parent stone on a leg (as many knappers do), it's possible to drive a flake into your leg. Thus the following are minimum safety precautions: gloves, protective goggles, and a thick leather leg pad. When practicing stone-working techniques at home, always use these safety precautions. In a survival situation, however, protective devices are not likely to be available. In which case, proceed with extreme caution, always keeping in mind that there is potential danger.

Grinding an arrowhead on a sandstone slab. (Photo: Paul Hellweg)

simply abrade your raw material back and forth until a desired shape is achieved. Periodically rinse the grinding slab with water to wash away accumulating stone powder and thus speed up the abrading process.

Once your arrowhead has achieved its rough shape, sharpen its edges on the grinding slab in much the same manner that a knife is sharpened (abrading at about a 20° angle). Finally, give the arrowhead its finished shape by grinding away each corner of its base (using the edge of your grinding slab). The result is a functional and aesthetically pleasing stemmed arrowhead. Once you get the knack, you'll be able to create several in an hour. These arrowheads–along with a few blade knives and a sturdy hand axe–are all the stone tools you'll likely ever need.

Ethics

Any flintknapping activity, even the mere striking of a few flakes, has the potential to disrupt our nation's archaeological history. At some unforeseen future date, an archaeologist might discover the debris left over and mistake it for an aboriginal site. It is thus important that all debris be disposed of in a proper manner. If practicing at home, merely sweep up your residue materials and throw them out with the trash (it's difficult to imagine that a modern dump could ever be mistaken for an aboriginal site). If you plan to do a lot of practice at home, dig a waste pit in the back yard to accumulate all debris. When the time comes to close the pit, throw in a few coins to date the contents. If flintknapping in the field, dig a similar pit to hold all debris, and date it with a couple of coins before covering.

Artifacts created by modern knappers can also disrupt our archaeological heritage; after changing hands a few times they might someday be mistaken for original specimens. Artifacts should thus be signed and dated, either with pen and ink or through use of a small hand-held electric engraver (available inexpensively at most hardware stores).

Finally, when gathering stone-working materials, make certain that you are not disrupting an existing archaeological site. These few simple precautions will help preserve our archaeological heritage and will go a long way towards reducing potential friction between professional archaeologists and modern knappers.

Samples of arrowheads made by grinding: (left to right) sea shell, jade, and obsidian. (Photo: Paul Hellweg)

Yucca glauca (Small Soapweed, Spanish Bayonet) grows prolifically on the arid plains and in desert areas of the Rocky Mountains and in most of the Southwestern United States. (Photo by Richard Jamison)

Richard Jamison

Yucca
Nature's Self-Contained Possibles Bag
• •

An average yucca root is about seven to ten inches long and one to two inches in diameter and looks like a dried sweet potato (it may look like a sweet potato, but to be sure, it does not taste like one!). Recently a company marketed a shampoo called "Yucca Dew." Whether it actually contained any part of the yucca plant, I do not know.

Nature was truly in partnership with the early cultures. They learned, through much trial and error, to discover every imaginable function of the yucca, which lends itself to both utility and artistry in its diversity. Yucca is one of the many natural resources which was widely explored by prehistoric peoples, and can be similarly enjoyed today by anyone who will take the time to learn its secrets.

Identification
The yucca (all of its various species) is one of the most versatile plants growing in the Southwestern United States. It was used by early native American people every day in some form or another. Not only could it be harvested for food, but the fibers were utilized for cordage, baskets, sandals and clothing.

I doubt that I would be alone in admitting that I have pruned a few ornamental yucca leaves and stems when I was in a pinch for workshop materials. That being the case, I think it is worth noting here that you can find yucca almost anywhere in the United States, used in the landscaping of homes, businesses, and restaurants, including the exterior facades of many fast food establishments.

The two most familiar species of yucca are Yucca baccata (datil yucca, soapweed, Spanish bayonet) and Yucca glauca (small soapweed, Spanish bayonet). In its natural state, Yucca baccata grows all over the southwestern parts of the United States on dry plains and slopes. It can be found in the southern areas of the Rocky Mountains, west to California and south to Arizona and Texas. Yucca glauca can also be found in the Rocky Mountain area, on the eastern side of the Continental Divide, in Kansas and south to Texas and west to New Mexico.

Basically, the yuccas are easy to recognize. The plant primarily remains green all year, although some of the outer leaves may turn yellow or brown as they die to make room for more. Color may vary from bright green to blue green. Growth comes from the inside, or crown, of the plant. The leaves are densely clustered and grow from six to thirty inches in length, depending on the species. All yucca leaves are rigid but vary in shape from v to concave, and have a hard, sharp point at the end of the leaf.

In the spring of the year, a green stalk that looks a little like an asparagus emerges from the crown of the plant. Later, the young flowers start to develop, opening at the top of the stalk first. At full development, the flower stalk lengthens to support the large creamy white flowers. The yucca in blossom is very handsome, with its green spiked leaves and the lacy flowers adding beauty to the arid regions where it grows. It is during this stage that the plant is most attractive to photographers and painters and is often sought for book covers and calendars depicting the great Southwest.

Although flowers usually appear every year, fruit may not always develop. Yucca is pollinated exclusively by a small white yucca moth that stays in the flower during the day and at night carries the pollen from flower to flower. When it does develop, the banana-shaped, fleshy fruit of the Yucca baccata matures to about four to six inches long. This plant was important to the early people of the Southwest because of its abundance as a food source. Yucca glauca fruit is much smaller, developing pods only about one and a half to two inches long.

Besides size, the easiest method of telling Yucca baccata and Yucca glauca apart is the fruiting stage. Yucca baccata fruits become fleshy at maturity and the seeds remain until the pulp decays. The fruit of the Yucca glauca is dry when ripe, splitting and allowing the mature seeds to fall out.

Hereafter I will refer to both species simply as yucca since they are interchangeable for all practical purposes except as a food source—the fruit of Yucca baccata being more palatable, although the fruit of Yucca glauca is also suitable for eating if collected when immature.

The mature fruit of <u>Yucca glauca</u> grow in clusters on the tall stalks that support from two of three to a dozen of the fleshy pods. (Photo by Richard Jamison)

Note: The agave, (Agave sp.) or century plant, is not a member of the yucca family, but resembles yucca in many respects. In fact, it is often mistaken for a large yucca while the true yucca is mistakenly referred to as a small agave. The agaves were utilized by the Indians extensively in the southwest for food, fiber and beverages in the same manner as the yuccas, and so deserve consideration in the same context. Agaves grow further west than most species of yucca and can be found particularly in the vicinity of the Grand Canyon in Arizona and west to California. The leaves are much wider (up to two inches) than those of the Yucca baccata or Yucca glauca, and the stem or center stalk is much taller (eight to nine feet). The flowers grow in groups of two to six.

Uses
Most people consider plants to be either flowers or weeds. To botanists they are divided and sub-divided into various species. But to the aborigine they fell into four categories: edible, poisonous, medicinal, or constructive, and many plants fall into two, three or sometimes all of these categories. To get the most out of any plant we must also think in these terms. Not surprisingly, the yucca falls into three categories: edible, medicinal and constructive.

Fiber
The dictionary defines fiber as "any substance that can be separated into threads or thread-like structures for spinning, weaving, etc.; a thread-like root."

We know, of course, that fiber is found in many plants, including the yucca, and before you can put these fibers to use you have to extract them from the pulp of the plant.

The best time to collect yucca leaves for fiber is in summer or fall when the stalk has completed its growth and the leaves have reached their maximum length. The safest way I have found to remove the spiny yucca leaves from the crown is to place my foot at the base of the plant and push it over. This gives me access to cut off the pieces I need. The long, wide leaves are found on the outside of the plant and the shorter ones on the inside, so it is actually easier to collect the mature longer leaves.

Yucca, and its many related species, are unique in that the fiber from narrow splits of the leaves can be used with no special preparation. When using the whole split or unsplit leaf be very careful because not only the tips, but also the edges of the leaves, are very sharp. Simply remove the point and lay the leaf on a flat surface, preferably a log, and cut it into strips about a quarter inch wide. These strips are very strong and can be used as short ties or twined, braided, or twisted together for cordage. Long pieces

Long, silky yucca threads are the result of the retting process which is caused by soaking the leaves long enough for the pulp to decay and separate from the fiber. (Photo by Richard Jamison)

of yucca of this type have been found in early Pueblo dwellings where they were used to secure crossbeams.

The fleshy part of the leaf can be scraped to expose the fibers which are then extracted for further use, or the leaves can be retted (soaked) to allow the fleshy parts to separate naturally from the fibers. Prehistoric people used a stone scraper to remove the pulp from the yucca leaf, or this could have been accomplished by pulling the leaf between the teeth. I use the edge of my knife at a 90 degree angle, and with the yucca leaf on my knee, I draw it under the blade, adding pressure to scrape off the fleshy part, leaving just the bare fibers—it is usually necessary to scrape several times to remove all the pulpy material.

I don't generally recommend pounding the plant because it breaks down the fiber, but if you simply must pound it, be sure to use a wide flat object such as a piece of log or a large wooden mallet. And, since the idea is to keep the fibers as long as possible, be careful not to break them in the process. Remember, cordage made with long pieces of fiber is stronger than that made with several short ones spliced together.

If you want fine, silky fiber threads, you can soak the leaves after they are scraped (or pounded gently with a mallet). Soaking causes the green matter to decay and separate from the fibers. This process is called retting.

How To Make Cordage

Cording is the process of preparing the fibers of various plants for weaving, basketry and other uses. It precedes and is believed to be the forerunner of basketmaking, although cording differs slightly from both basketmaking and weaving.

To make cordage from yucca fibers:

▲ Separate the fibers and lay them out uniformly. The yucca leaf is larger at the bottom than at the top, so the fibers are thicker at the base.

▲ Roll a long length of fiber down your leg with your open palm until it is round and reasonably uniform in size.

▲ Bend the resulting string about two-thirds in half–or leave one end about one-third longer than the other.

▲ The small loop in the bend is your starting point and should be held between the left thumb and forefinger (if you are right-handed).

▲ You now have two loose ends hanging from the loop. Hold the

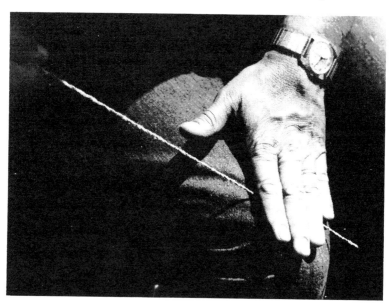

Roll the long fibers with the palm of the hand on the thigh until the strand is uniform. (photo by Linda Jamison)

Fold the twisted top strand counter-clockwise over the untwisted strand while holding the loop secure in the left hand. (Photo by Linda Jamison)

twist secure, and twirl the top piece clockwise between the right thumb and forefingers.

▲ Then fold the strand you have just twisted toward you, or counter-clockwise, and repeat the procedure with the opposite strand, moving the fingers on the left hand toward each new twist to hold it secure.

▲ When you reach about three inches from the end of your shortest strand, lay a new piece alongside the short end, overlapping it to give a strong splice, and roll the two together.

▲ Continue the twisting and folding until the desired length is reached.

Your cordage will not unravel because of the clock-wise, counter-clockwise twist which actually tightens against itself.

The strength of the cord will depend on the thickness of the strand and the quality of your materials; two or three strands of cordage may be twisted together in the same manner for more strength.

Hint: Be sure that your splices are not at the same point, or opposite in your cordage, as this will weaken the strand. Making uniform strands will insure against weak spots.

Early people understood the process of retting, and it is still done in industry today, using chemicals to speed the process.

To separate the pulp from the fiber, immerse the leaves totally in water for several days, agitating them occasionally, but be careful not to soak them too long or the fibers will be damaged in the process.

Cordage

Many of the early uses of cordage are known. Lacking the modern conveniences we have today–nuts, bolts, screws, nails, tape–primitive people tied their world together.

They tied their arrowheads to shafts, tied their game onto their waistbands for easy carrying, tied branches and logs together for shelter against the elements, tied babies in carriers and then to the mother. They also tied their clothing together, and made clotheslines for hanging up their belongings. They made breechclouts, ornamental hair bindings, various sorts of straps, braids for the foundation of fur and feather cord, thread for mending, and sometimes combined yucca cordage with other materials for greater strength.

As my children grew up, they were introduced to aboriginal skills early, and making yucca cordage provided a good learning experience. Once, while on a road trip, we stopped and gathered some yucca leaves and I taught them to make cordage, then we played a game to see who could make the longest piece first. It also taught a history lesson: the history of the early people of this and other lands.

Cording also has definite therapeutic value in stressful situations. It takes little or no concentration, yet is productive. Cording allows the mind to rest while productive, often the very process which helps an individual make correct decisions about future actions. And, there is satisfaction in seeing the complete metamorphosis as plant fibers become a useful item by your own hand.

The actual process of cording is far more difficult to explain than it is to do. By my own measure, a person becomes an expert corder upon completing 25 feet or more of cordage. Netting containing many miles of cordage has been found by archaeologists in cave dwellings.

Although yucca cordage is very strong, I don't recommend it for bowstring, nor is rope generally made from yucca fiber, but several cords of yucca braided together will result in a very strong strand.

Fur cord and feather cord mixed with yucca fiber was made and used by prehistoric Southwestern people. To make fur cordage, rabbit skins or the skins of other small, fur-bearing animals are cut into narrow strips which are then joined; these are wrapped over or twined together with yucca cordage.

Feather cordage is made by stripping the feathers down the midrib, then twisting the half piece spirally with yucca cordage. In early times, turkey wing and tail feathers were used. Fur and feather cordage can then be woven into warm blankets for sleeping, robes, sandals and other items.

Basketry

In the days before pottery, early peoples were gleaners and named Basketmakers because of their expertise in this form of art, which requires an intimate knowledge of fiber as well as manual skill. Then, in addition to knowing what to use, one must know where and when and how to collect it. So discovery of the yucca, as well as the herbs to color the fibers, must have been a trial-and-error procedure, requiring countless years and endless effort.

There are hundreds of legends about basketry and its origin, but basketmaking probably began with the weaving of nets. In early days, gourds were used to carry water. They were clumsy to handle, difficult to transport and fragile. Eventually water receptacles were baskets, water-proofed on the inside with pitch (pinon gum).

Obviously, the materials used for the basketry by any culture is largely determined by the environment, and in the Southwest yucca was plentiful and widely used in basketry for gathering, for cooking utensils, for sieves, and bowls, as well as for ceremonial and other uses.

In primitive times, coiled baskets were made using a thick bundle of yucca leaves as a filler with the outer wrapping made from long splits of fiber from the same plant. Sometimes the yucca fiber was first twined into cordage, then woven into a functional form.

Yucca leaves can be cut any time for basketry. If you want a yellow-green color use the mature leaves; if you want a bright green basket, use fresh, young leaves. The heart leaves provide white fibers.

Weaving

Since sheep were not introduced to the New World until after 1540, and cotton was not believed to have been cultivated in the Southwest until about 500-700 A.D. (later for some locations where there was not enough water for cultivation), yucca was the primary material used by early people of the Southwest in textile weaving because of its wide distribution and great abundance.

Sometimes yucca fiber was used alone for weaving and sometimes it was used in conjunction with other materials such as dogbane (Apocynum, also called Indian hemp), human and animal hair, feathers and fur pieces and eventually cotton. There was also great variety in the preparation of the material, from whole yucca leaves to fine cordage. Whole or partial leaves of yucca were used for mats, some sandals, and other items, while retted fibers were used in the finer products.

Probably the oldest of all forms of weaving are braiding, netting, and looping. These finger weaving methods involve single or multiple threads. In addition to braided belts, a variety of articles were made in the prehistoric Southwest by this process, including braided shoe-socks, apron bands, slings and small bags.

Nets of various sizes made from yucca-fiber cordage knotted together were used for large and small bags, traps to set over rodent holes, and to facilitate carrying clay jars or other containers. Large nets were used for catching birds and rabbits.

Frames were necessary for some of the finer weaving. The most simple was a loop of string from which warp (lengthwise) threads were hung. Next in simplicity was a weaving frame made from two sticks with warps strung between them, or a frame with warps secured at the top and bottom. These small frames were suitable for making small pieces like sandals, belts, bands and bags. For larger items, like mats, robes and the fur and feather blankets, two upright posts supported a cross-bar with warps thrown over the bar, and hanging free at the bottom.

Tump straps, a band that fits around the forehead with strong cords attached to suspend burdens and distribute the weight for easier carrying, were common in the prehistoric Southwest. They were often made from finely woven yucca fibers with a finished loop at each end through which heavy cords were threaded for fastening burdens. Cruder straps were also made by sewing two or three yucca leaves together, fraying their ends, then twining or wrapping them in such a way as to make loops.

Aprons were made from yucca cordage during Basketmaker times and have a long history in the Southwest. The most simple construction was yucca cords bent over a yucca waist cord, and fastened with plain twining. A mass of yucca cordage hanging from the woven belt formed the body of the apron. More elaborate aprons were produced from a combination of yucca and human or animal hair cordage, often decorated with very intricate designs. The basic form was a narrow belt which reached part way, or sometimes all the way around the waist with cordage filling if it was short, and with hanging fringes, generally in the front only. Sometimes aprons were made of bundles of cordage, secured at one point and a string run through to hold it in place. Breechclouts (a string belt worn about the buttocks) also had a wide distribution in the early Southwest.

Blankets, ponchos and shirts appeared in later periods and were often made on a loom with cotton thread mixed with some yucca fiber for added strength.

Shoe-socks or leggings and arrow quivers were also made, usually from scraps of larger pieces of fabric, but in later Pueblo periods, from cotton and wool. However, some have been found that included yucca string wound with feathers or twisted in with animal hair, affirming the fact that yucca fiber was regularly used in later prehistoric periods. Occasionally, feather cord was used in combination with yucca only at points in the sock where there is more pressure from the foot, thus making a softer pad.

Needle and thread

Not only does the yucca provide material for fabric clothing, it can also produce a needle and thread with which to stitch it together.

Once, on the trail, a student accidentally kicked my jacket close to the fire where a hole burned in the sleeve, and the down insulation escaped. I made a needle and thread from a yucca leaf by scraping off the pulp to the pointed end and thinning the fibers with my knife. I easily repaired the hole, and the emergency stitching lasted nicely for the remainder of the trip.

It's easy to make a few of these emergency sewing kits ahead of time just to have on hand. Simply trim the yucca leaf up to the pointed end so it is only about a quarter inch wide, then plane off the pulp with a knife or sharp stone. Soak it in water for a couple of days, agitating the water occasionally to separate the pulp from the fiber, dry it, and you have a needle with long, silky threads already attached.

Sandals

Animal skin sandals were made first by prehistoric people, possibly with yucca ties, but this eventually evolved into all-fiber elements of whole or corded yucca leaves. On the trail we often make the fast and efficient yucca "caterpillar" sandal. The caterpillar sandal got its name from the unusual tracks it leaves as the students trek across the sandy desert floor. This style can be made in a matter of twenty or thirty minutes using the whole yucca leaf.

The earliest Basketmaker sandals were square-toed and square-heeled, made in either a plaited or wicker technique, in the basketry tradition. Plaited (over-one-under-one) sandals were often made from the whole yucca leaf, producing a large checkerwork, or with narrower leaves using a twill plaiting (over-two-under-two) resulting in zigzags or chevron designs. One interesting theory is that perhaps the larger-sized plaited or twilled sandal of wide yucca leaves was used in the winter as an overshoe to be worn over the finer, corded, fiber sandals.

Several different methods of securing sandals to the foot were used in ancient times: loops were attached to the sides through which heavy cords

Yucca "Caterpillar" Sandals

A fast, efficient sandal can be made from the leaves of yucca as well as other plants with long, fibrous leaves such as sedge, tule, and cattail. Sandals can even be made from the needles of various species of longleaf pine. But yucca is excellent material for this use because it is so durable and easily available in many parts of the country.

▲ Cut a bundle of leaves to about ten to twelve inches long and trim off the spines. Try the small Yucca glauca for these narrow pieces. Dry these leaves for several days, then dampen them before you begin making your sandals so they won't shrink afterward. Then, dampen them again when you are ready to begin making your sandals. You can use fresh yucca leaves, but the end result will shrink considerably after a day or two.

▲ Next, cut four long leaves to use for the warp strings. Once the spines are removed from these leaves, they should be about 14 inches long (the longer leaves of Yucca baccata are best for this use). These strings will ultimately be the deciding length factor, so if you have a large foot, you may want to cut the warp strings longer. If you have a really big foot, you may have to twine some three-ply cordage to use for the warp strings. Leave the strings long enough to tie on each end.

▲ Trim the four pieces down to a uniform width of about a quarter inch by shaving off the outer edges of the leaf, leaving the thick inner portion.

▲ Soften the warp strings by bending them over a branch, rock or running your fingers back and forth until they are flexible.

▲ Tie the ends of the warp strings together and place one end over a stake in the ground. Keep the warp string tight as you work.

▲ Fold one of the small leaves in half in one hand while holding the warp string tight with the other (this is when it pays to be ambidextrous).

▲ Weave the small leaves by looping one at a time over the warp string and criss-crossing the weft so opposite ends extend over the other warp string.

▲ Repeat this process, starting the loop on the opposite warp string. Pull each weft tight and hold them with the fingers as you weave.

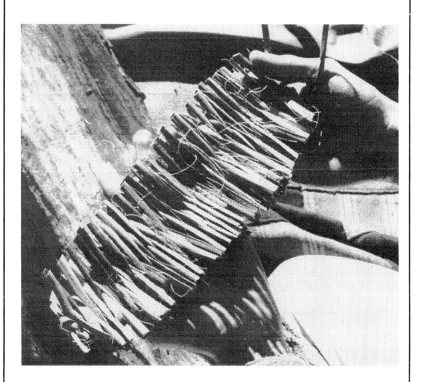

Measure your foot and trim the edges. (Photo by Richard Jamison).

▲   When you have filled the warp strings, or the sandal is as long as your foot with about an inch to spare to accommodate overhanging toes and heels, untie the loose end of the warp strings and retie them tightly to securely hold the weft in place.
▲   Measure the width of your foot, plus a little extra, and trim the outer edges. Be careful not to trim the outer edges too closely or the weft will come loose.

The sandal is tied to the foot by a piece of cordage which is threaded through and tied to the foot or around the ankle in any way that is comfortable.

These sandals generally don't last more than a few days, but the usefulness can be extended by adding a few more warp fillers if the weave gets loose.

passed to tie the sandal to the foot; toe loops were attached to some sandals with cords that went around the ankle; and an abundance of cords were threaded from several toe loops to cords encircling the heel.

Bags
It was common to use human hair or yucca cordage in non-loom looped bags. Usually the bag was made as a rectangle then folded over and sewed with running or overcast stitches down the side and across the bottom. It was a simple thing, then, to run strings of cordage through the top of a looped bag.

Another variety of bag, twined from finely processed yucca cordage, was straight-sided and almost flat-bottomed, like a deep container, or sometimes slightly narrowed at the opening and egg shaped. Other types of bags were also common; such as the coarse, larger ones made from whole yucca leaves and used as storage receptacles, and smaller bags made of a combination of human hair and yucca cordage.

Mats
For years, I spent many restless nights sleeping on uncomfortable lumps and holes in the ground before I took the time to devise a sleeping pad or mat. For my purpose, a bunch of long reeds or cattail leaves sufficed because we were constantly moving camp; but for the people who occupied the same area hundreds of years before, woven mats were definitely among their household furnishings.

Mats come in a wide range of sizes for different purposes and can be made of a variety of available materials, including whole or split yucca leaves, tules, grasses, willow, reeds, rushes or bark. Large mats are used for sitting, sleeping pads, floor coverings, partitions, and shelter construction. Smaller mats are used to set items on or to serve food. For decoration, the edges of mats can be fringed by leaving the yucca leaf unwoven at the edges and fraying the ends.

Fire starting material
Of all the materials I have used to start fires by friction, I like yucca the best. Once the flower matures, the outside leaves of the yucca die and the flower stock becomes very woody. At this stage, the small stalks of the Yucca glauca make great hand drills, or if they are too crooked, a five to ten inch piece can be cut out for a bow drill.

The larger plants, Yucca baccata and the Agave have stalks that grow as tall as eight to ten feet and three to four inches in diameter–just right to cut up for fireboards, which should be about six inches long (or even a little longer, considering that you hold them down with your foot).

I have also used yucca as fire plow material with success; this method takes a lot of hard work. Still, no pain, no flame!

Food

For the native Americans of the Southwest, the yucca plant was an important food source, providing sustenance throughout most of the year. Not only was it prolific, it was nourishing and provided some valuable nutrients to a sparse diet.

According to the *Cactus Cookbook* printed by the Cactus and Succulent Society, yucca blossoms have been found to contain 343-398 milligrams of ascorbic acid per 100 grams of flowers. The flowers and stalks are also rich in sugar.

Because the yucca is so prolific, easy to identify, and does not resemble any poisonous plant, it is an ideal species to experiment with, either in the field or at home. Here is an opportunity for the adventurous to experience textures and flavors that can't be found anywhere else. Just remember that a genuine interest in wild plants must also lead to conservation measures.

My only warning is for anyone not accustomed to a steady diet of wild plants to use moderation. According to one source, the fruits of yucca are reported to be cathartic to some degree. On the trail I once ate only one-quarter of a pod raw, and it caused severe swelling in the back of my mouth and throat. From that experience I learned that cooking the fruit is best for me.

I also prefer to remove the outer skin and seeds of the yucca fruit because the skin of some species has a slight bitter taste. We have tried steaming the fruit pods at home—with a touch of mayonnaise they tasted a little like artichoke hearts. On another occasion, we cooked yucca pods in a steam pit with squirrel and birds, stuffing them inside. It was great. There is nothing like sitting down to a big meal of skewered pack rats and all the yucca cakes you can eat.

The following parts of the yucca are edible, when available, in greater or lesser degrees depending on the species:

Central spike—when it first emerges in the spring it looks much like a large asparagus and can be peeled and sliced crosswise, then baked or fried.

Flower buds—should be collected just before they open. They should be parboiled, discarding the water, and rinsed thoroughly before serving.

Flowers in bloom—should be soaked overnight then boiled. The mature petals can be fried. (Be careful not to eat the yucca moth.) Flower petals are also good as an ingredient in soups or raw in salads. Some species can be somewhat bitter, however, but the flavor improves with parboiling.

Ripe fruits—should be peeled first and the seeds removed, then they can be boiled, roasted, baked or fried. The fruit pods can also be baked, then dried and mashed into meal and patted into cakes for storage. The boiled pulp can be simmered down to a stiff paste which is then rolled onto a sheet and dried in the sun for storage or eaten as a delicious sweetmeat. The fruit of the yucca can be picked before it fully ripens, then allowed to dry. This is a good idea because the pod is vulnerable to burrowing insects.

Ripe seeds—are collected from Yucca glauca when the pods open, or can be removed from the Yucca baccata before the fruits decay. They can be roasted and ground to use as a coffee substitute, or ground to make flour or meal.

Soap

I have often used the root fibers of yucca for cleaning my hands and the crown as a scouring brush to wash pots and pans.

An average yucca root is about seven to ten inches long and one to two inches in diameter and looks like a dried sweet potato (it may look like a sweet potato, but to be sure, it does not taste like one!).

In the 1800s a company in Illinois made soap from the plant and put it on the market. More recently, a company marketed a shampoo called "Yucca Dew." Whether it actually contained any part of the yucca plant, I do not know.

For soap or shampoo use one inch or larger yucca tap roots with green tops. Peel the bark from the roots and cut them into small pieces and pulverize them in a piece of cloth if you have one. Then place the roots in warm water and agitate them until the water has a milky appearance. The root may be used with some caution as a laxative.

Brushes

There is no archeological evidence that early people made scrub brushes from the yucca plant. But the women obviously cleaned their pottery by some means and, given the availability of yucca and the fact that it was employed for so many other uses, I can only speculate that they probably used it as I have, to clean cooking vessels.

A bristle scrub brush can be made from the crown of the yucca by trimming the leaves down to about one half-inch from the crown. If some of the root is left on the bottom the brush will produce its own soap (although not copious) when it is agitated in water.

Jim Riggs

Make Your Own
Hide Glue

● ●

I must confess that I consider hide glue, like sinew, to be
a nearly magical medium, sort of like a living organism
with a mind of its own! By most of our contemporary
concepts of logic and application, it should not be able to
accomplish what we know it can (by the laws of physics,
a bumblebee should not be able to fly either)....

Finding a natural glue evaded me for years. On my first two yew
bows—short, flat-limbed Northern California style, I used regular Elmer's
white glue with not-very-refined sinew. It worked fine, though no glue
would have held down those chunky sinew ends forever! But native
peoples did not use Elmer's to back their bows or haft points and blades.
I wanted something natural, something I could produce myself from raw
materials. The ever-present but low-key search was on.

Back in the '60s and early '70s there seemed to be neither large groups
of people into primitive skills, processses and technologies, nor much
awareness of, nor contact among, those of us who were. Nor was there a
lot of good, specifically written "how-to" information. The old Ben Hunt
books had their limitations!

In our isolated compartments, we ferreted out what information we
could and experimented, trial and error, having to solve needs and
problems mostly via our own ingenuity. In 1967, Larry Olsen's *Outdoor
Survival Skills* was published and, figuratively at least, initiated the more
recent and widespread revival of interest in aboriginal skills. Numerous
newer books, abo gatherings and networking have made a plethora of

The author demonstrates hide staking at the first annual Woodsmoke Rendezvous, back in the old days. (Photo by Richard Jamison)

knowledge and information readily available. Today one can learn in a single article or workshop methods and skills that have taken many of us twenty years or more to figure out on our own. This is the story of one such quest.

I was living in a little log cabin two miles up a trail in the Southern

Oregon Cascades immersed in a variety of primitive projects. Periodically, after running into enough dead-ends or accumulating enough questions, I'd make a trip out to do some library research. References to glue and binding agents were generally brief and ambiguous: pitch, pitch and charcoal, other plant juices, asphaltum, fish skin, sturgeon noses, bladders and something from along the backbone, bone joints, cartilage, sinew, antler, hooves and hide. At the time, I tended to amalgamate all of these into a somewhat ephemeral, surrealistic vision similar to the Macbeth witches' "Double double toil and trouble, fire burn, cauldron bubble." Gee, maybe eye of newt and toe of frog would make glue, too!

My early mentor, Buckskin Slim, used Elmer's for backing most of his bows, but had also used boiled-down salmon skin glue. I'd eaten hundreds of boiled trout on survival trips and knew how sticky the skins became, but at the time it made more dietary sense to eat the skins rather than experiment with glue making.

The category "hide glue" sounded simplest and stuck somewhat dormantly in my mind. I was not then aware that commercial rabbit skin glue existed. Finally, about fifteen years ago, the need for glue and the impetus for addressing that particular experiment coincided; I had finished a nice Serviceberry bow, wanted to sinew-back it and was determined not to use Elmer's!

The Original Experiment . . .
Since I'd been brain-tanning buckskin for several years, I always kept a stash of hides, and found some scrap pieces of deer and elk rawhide laying around. As whole hides, these had been fleshed while fresh, laced into frames to dry and the hair scraped off. The vast expanses had been used for quivers and other containers, knife sheaths, etc. With tin-snips I cut up a handful of dry scraps into one to two inch square pieces and plopped them into a #10 can of water boiling on the stove. An hour or so later, along with the interesting aroma that pervaded the house, I noticed the skin scraps were swelling and becoming somewhat gelatinous to the touch.

As the water boiled away, I added only enough to keep the skin from burning. A couple of times I'd quickly dip a finger into the soup, but noticed no discernable stickiness. A couple of hours later it had again boiled down, seemed a little thicker than plain water and was becoming a translucent brownish color. I again dipped in a forefinger, smeared it with my thumb to an evenly thin layer, blew on it a couple times to evaporate a bit more moisture then tightly squeezed thumb and index finger together for about thirty seconds.

The result surprised me, amazed me—and freaked me out—I honestly could not pull finger and thumb apart. Eureka, I'd finally discovered glue!

However, I still had the problem of my thumb and finger being stuck together. Fortunately, (and more rationally) I remembered the glue is water soluble, and a rinse in warm water returned my use of thumb and finger as separate appendages.

Since that enlightening day, I've made and used gallons of hide glue and can better describe my own "how-to" process in a sequential series of steps, tips, do's and don'ts, though I'm sure there is more to learn.

The Hides...
I suppose almost any skin will produce some glue, but larger, thicker hides such as deer or elk seem more energy-efficient. If a hide has been salted for storage, I think it advisable to thoroughly soak and repeatedly rinse it in water to dissolve as much salt as possible. You can use any pieces of skin, green or dried, but they should be fleshed clean of any meat or fat, and I prefer to have scraped off the hair prior to boiling them. Initially, the hair is not detrimental, it just adds extraneous bulk, but you don't want hair in your final glue.

Once I've boiled the mass to the point where the skin is well-cooked (swollen and gelatinous), and the glue has gone into the water, I pour all the liquid through a piece of window screen to strain out all skin pieces and hair. Cheesecloth or similar fabric is a bit slower but even more thorough in straining out hair.

For the past several years, I've refined my glue process even more by using hide shavings, a natural by-product of making buckskin. In the dry-scrape, buckskin tanning process I begin with a clean, fleshed, deer hide. It can be freshly peeled from the carcass, or one previously dried or salted for storage, then soaked in plain water twenty-four hours or so until it's thoroughly wet and pliable.

Either way, I cut inch-long slits parallel to the edge of the hide, a half inch from the edge, every three to four inches around the hide. Then I lace or tie it onto a rectangular pole frame fairly tightly and evenly stretched. As it dries over a day or two it shrinks and becomes even tighter, so some practice is required in not stretching so tightly at first that, as it dries, it rips out some of the ties. When dry, I begin scraping off the hair and epidermal layer of skin which lies beneath it. The scraper is a steel blade roughly four inches long with a rounded cutting edge sharpened on a single bevel. This blade is lashed or screwed onto an elbow-shaped handle of wood, antler or flat angle-iron.

If my goal is just getting the hide adequately scraped for the next step in making buckskin, I quickly shear off both hair and grain (epidermis) together with only one or two brisk strokes at any specific area as I work down and across the whole hide. When I want shavings for glue, however,

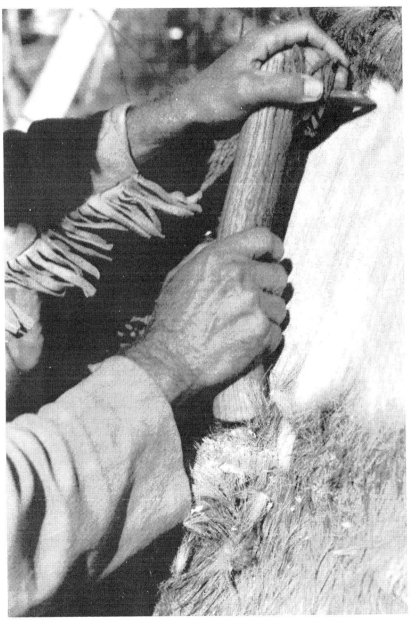

After a light once-over to remove most of the hair, go back over the whole hide again, shearing off the epidermis in thin curled shavings. (Photo: Richard Jamison)

I scrape lightly to remove only the hair. When done, I clear it away from the base of the frame. Then I go back over the whole hide again, shearing off the now mostly hairless epidermis.

With long, smooth strokes of the scraper blade, this comes off in thin curled shavings much like a plane removes shavings of wood. I collect all these shavings which, since dry, will not spoil and store them until I need a batch of glue. Some hair remains in the root follicles of the shavings, and other fluffs of hair unavoidably get mixed in, but are immaterial at this stage.

For additional information on obtaining and caring for hides, making and using hide scrapers and frames, etc., (as mentioned in this article), plus an in-depth "how-to" account of the complete buckskin process, aboriginal uses of the deer, making skin clothing and much more, all laced with both experience and humor, read *Blue Mountain Buckskin: A Working Manual To Dry-Scrape Brain Tan*, by Jim Riggs, 2nd Edition, 140 Pages. Profusely illustrated with photos and drawings. Order from: 72501 Hwy 82, Wallowa, OR 97885.

Making Glue . . .

My standard, all-purpose, old reliable camping pots, stew pots, tea pots and glue pots are #10 cans (a two- or three-pound coffee can size). I punch opposite holes just below the rims and attach wire bails for easy manipulation.

For glue, I jam a couple of big compressed handfuls of hide shavings into the pot, say, a well-packed two-thirds full, and fill the can with hot or cold water to about three-quarters full.

Since the shavings are so thin, they immediately soak-up a lot of water. I bring this to a rolling boil, uncovered to reduce boil-over potential, and maintain the boil for an hour or so, adding more water as needed. At this stage don't worry about too much water—more is better than less to prevent burning the skin.

I stir this glop frequently. After an hour, the shavings should be swollen and gelatinous. I pour all the liquid through a screen or strainer into a second pot, refill and reboil the first for another half hour, then strain that into the second pot. This time I also hand-squeeze the skin to get most of the liquid out and discard the skin as compost. By this time, most of the glue from the skin should be in the water.

Besides the fact that the skin shavings soak and boil up more quickly, I believe this mostly epidermal layer contains proportionately more glue than the rest of the hide, though this theory remains objectively untested. In my experience with shavings, one pot-full makes enough glue to back one bow, with a considerable amount of glue left over.

Again, for an expected ration of raw skin to finished glue, more experimentation could be done; I'm simply not into the real statistical end of it!

Whether you've boiled up fresh skin or dry skin, hairy skin or skin shavings, after straining the liquid you will have quite a pot of milky, to tan-colored soup, free of most hair and actual pieces of skin, but still too thin for glue. As you boil this down further and the water evaporates to a quarter pot or less, the incipient glue should become more viscous (thick and gluey) and somewhat darker.

I use different viscosities of glue for different jobs, but generally seek a consistency slightly thinner than the commercial LaPage's mucilage in the pear-shaped bottle with the pink rubber spreader on top (the stuff you probably used in grade school, if you're old enough, anyway!).

To check your glue for adequate adhesive qualities, try the previously described finger/thumb test. If it's not sticky enough, boil it down further. Make sure you cool it down before use though, or it'll cook and rubberize your sinew! For immediate use, that should do it, but, there is definitely more to know about your newly-made glue.

The Nature and Care of Hide Glue . . .

I must confess that I consider hide glue, like sinew, to be a nearly magical medium, sort of like a living organism with a mind of its own! By most of our contemporary concepts of logic and application, it should not be able to accomplish what we know it can (by the laws of physics, a bumblebee should not be able to fly either), but we must produce, manipulate and treat it within its own necessary parameters for it to serve us well. Ignore or forget it too long in the wrong condition (that can mean you, or the glue!) and it'll turn fickle quite rapidly, molding or rotting with the stench of death. Since I feel I've already done almost everything wrong with hide glue at least once, I feel qualified to offer some do's and don't's.

Let's say you've made a batch of glue but aren't going to use it right away, or have glue left over after a project and want to store it. The only way I know to store hide glue indefinitely is to completely dry it down, and this is an active process using a direct heat source. Without heat, a pot of glue, even perhaps only one to two inches deep, if left to sit, will soon glaze over and begin to harden on top, but under the glaze it will remain liquid and soon spoil. The glue does not have to be boiling to be drying, though with low heat the surface glaze should be broken through periodically to allow quicker evaporation from beneath.

Refrigeration or freezing may delay spoilage or mold for a few days, but I've had small cans of glue go bad within a week, whether frozen or just cold. The other two safe but temporary conditions are actively reconstituting dry pieces or crystals with water, and heating the glue to the consistency for use, or actively drying it back out after use.

My wood heater is perfect for either process as the heat source is continuous and the temperature adjustable by the amount and kind of wood and by moving a glue pot to different areas of the stove surface. I also keep a grate set on a couple of bricks a few inches above the stove top and have drying screens above and behind the stove. Thus, when I add water the glue is reconstituting and after use it is automatically drying back out. With a large pot of glue intended for storage, I usually just dry it down to a solid layer and leave it in the can. When thoroughly dry, this hard, flat, translucent disc of brownish glue has shrunk away from the sides and bottom of the pot and can be removed for travel or storage elsewhere if desired. Dry chunks can be pounded or ground into finer pieces or crystals like the commercial hide glue. The crystals, of course, reconstitute faster than chunks.

In actively drying down a pot of glue, it naturally becomes thicker and thicker until it congeals into the gelatine phase, then through the rubber and leather phases on its way to the inert rock phase. Once it is no longer liquid, care must be taken not to burn it. When congealed and dry enough to be rubbery and not sticky to the touch, the entire glob can usually be eased from the can with a butter knife and dried on a screen as is, or sliced like cheese into thinner slabs for quicker drying.

If you don't have time to carefully boil a whole batch all the way down, you can rapidly boil it until quite viscous but still liquid, then pour a thin layer into a flat pyrex or enamel casserole dish, onto a non-greasy cookie sheet or even foil, and sun dry it or place it in an oven set on "warm". A thin layer will usually dry quickly with little chance of spoilage.

Unless preparing to back a bow, I normally need only small amounts of glue, but quite regularly, for hafting, fletching, etc., so I always keep a tuna can with some dried down glue near the wood heater. This requires only a dash of water and a couple of minutes of heat to be useable, and quickly dries back out.

The Open-ended Finis...

There is a definite satisfaction in doing more with less and being directly familiar with and responsible for all phases and materials in any aboriginal project one undertakes. The ability to make your own glue is one such endeavor, one useful product of a process. As with any process repeated enough, you'll eventually learn what you must do to be successful, what you must not do and, yes, what you can get away with! Well-made hide glue, your very own hide glue, will forever bond you to its wondrous merits.

Pegg Mathewson

Traditional Basketry Materials

Gathering and Preparation with an Emphasis on the Western United States

●●●●●●●●●●●●●●●●●●●●●●●●●●●●●

Sometimes you can find "road kill" bark slabs that have

been run over by logging trucks so many times that they

have separated out into perfect fluffy shreds.

There is an old saying among native California basketmakers that goes: "When you start your basket, you're halfway done."

Anyone who has ever sat down to begin a basket knows there is a lot of preparation that goes on before that first twist or fold. Bark is peeled and stripped fine, shoots are split and thinned, roots are roasted and scraped, all in preparation for their use in weaving. At the very least, you have to go outside with your clippers.

Native peoples in North America used, and still use, basketry in a variety of ways. In the past, families had to rely on the strength and flexibility of their baskets for many subsistence needs such as carrying, gathering seeds, roasting, winnowing and boiling. As a result, they learned to understand the plants and how to prepare them to be long, flexible and durable when formed into a basket and dried.

Of course, today we do not rely on baskets as we once did, but many people wish to make a basket for the sheer enjoyment of forming a vessel from nature's greenery, or for less exacting purposes such as storing onions or for taking to the market. Perhaps you are out on a wilderness trip and you need to carry a load more efficiently. If so, a basket can help.

This chapter is an introduction to some of the many types of plant parts used in traditional basketry and ways in which native peoples have prepared them for use. I will not be discussing basketry techniques here, but I will mention the basics: twining, plaiting, wicker and coiling, and where a plant part particularly lends itself to that use. Some plants work well for basketmaking, others need special treatment and still others might as well be egg shells or iron bars for all the good they would be.

Since I have worked mostly in the western United States, I will focus on the plants in that area. The techniques described may be applied to similar plant parts anywhere you live, and a wide variety of city and ornamental plants work as well. If you're not sure, try it out and see if the plant is suitable for what you want to do with it. Be creative!

Shoots
Many plants, especially trees and woody shrubs, send out long, narrow, flexible shoots. These are called adventitious shoots or wythes. These may be used whole, or split into thin splints or skeins for finer and lighter baskets. Whole-shoot basketry is one of the simplest and best ways to start weaving if you are a beginner because there is little or no preparation (see chapter by Tamara Wilder and Steven Edholm on whole-shoot baskets). For the best shoots, prune the plant severely the previous winter to promote fast-growing, straight shoots for the following year. Many traditional groups burned their basketry plants regularly to promote new growth.

Try the shoots of the following plants: willow (Salix sp.), dogwood (Cornus sp.), hazel (Corylus sp.), sumac (Rhus sp.) except poison oak or ivy, redbud (Cercis sp.), maple (Acer sp.) as well as fruit tree suckers and fir (Pseudotsuga sp.), cedar (Thuja sp.), pine (Pinus sp.) and other conifers.

For whole-shoot twining and wicker basketry, use one year's growth harvested in the winter; that is, anytime between the dropping of the leaves and the appearance of new buds in the spring. Winter-picked shoots will have the bark adhering tightly to the wood. For white shoots, pick the shoots just after the first buds appear in spring, and the sap starts running. For smaller sticks, slip the bark off with your fingers by peeling it down about an inch, rolling the peels tightly around the stick, pinching this roll tightly between your thumb and forefinger, clamping the protruding peeled end in your back teeth and then pulling the roll down to the tip of the stick. This is a Yurok/Karok/Hupa method.

In the spring the bark slips right off. Some people use a strawberry top picker for smaller sticks or a split stick pounded into the ground. You may also buy or make a metal "willow break" for peeling large sticks.

For finer baskets and for coiling, you need a very thin weaver. Split the peeled sticks down into splints or skeins. To split a stick in half, start the cut with a knife and then set the knife aside. Gently pull each half simultaneously apart applying equal pressure on both sides. It helps to place your pinky fingers on the whole shoot down below the split for support as you go. Once you get good at that, try holding one half in your mouth and the other in one hand. Support and control the split with your other hand, pinching firmly where the wood is splitting, sliding down as you go. In both of these methods you need to watch out for one side getting larger than the other. If this starts to happen, pull more on the largest side to return the split to the center. This seems to be contradictory but it works.

The Paiute of the Great Basin and others in California split willows down into three splints at once, holding one in the mouth and one in either hand. In Europe, a wooden cleave helps split the weavers into three or four strips.

Now each part needs to be split again, flat-wise, to make it more flexible. This second split is done in exactly the same way and cleans out the pithy center of the shoot, leaving a thin ribbon of sapwood. You can do this in winter to keep the bark on your splints for color, or you can peel the sticks for white splints.

For very fine coiled basketry the splints may be split many times and need to be evened out in width and thickness. To do this, fold the splint over your thumb and pull it down the entire length to feel for any lumps or thin spots. Trim the lumps with your knife. If the splitting is done correctly, very little knife work is necessary.

To size for width, trim the edges with a knife. Many people size weavers today by running them through holes punched in the top of a tin can. The metal shears off tiny shavings of wood from the edges. You can tell the skill of a weaver by the garbage they leave behind; the best leave only long, even curls or centers and no tiny shavings.

Now you are ready to weave with your shoots. Most people store the splints in rolls with the splint side facing outward. These are wrapped around with bits of rag, strung together and hung up in a dry place to dry completely. Traditional weavers age their materials for at least a year before use to allow them to shrink completely. We once tried an experiment in which rolls were weighed every week until they stopped losing water weight. It took over six months. Materials must be soaked again before weaving, but if they are correctly seasoned they never loosen up when woven into the basket.

Roots

Roots provide some of the best material for basketry, but they tend to be overlooked by beginners because it seems like so much work to get them out of the ground. Don't be discouraged. Just don't bother digging in rocky or clay soils or in the dry time of the year. You usually don't even need to dig straight down anywhere if you look for the best places.

Look for roots growing along the sides of creeks, especially after the water has subsided from a heavy rainstorm. You can usually wade along and gather up the roots that have washed out of the bank. This is good for willow, cottonwood, alder and other river roots. Many plants, especially conifers such as cedar, like to grow in the looser soil and punky wood associated with stumps and fallen logs. These are called nurse logs in the Northwest, and are often full of long roots running along their length. You need only pull them apart and take what you want. All root gathering requires that you replace the soil and cover any roots you may have left. Don't leave a strip mine behind you, please!

Try the following roots: conifer including spruce (Picea sp.), pine, redwood (Sequoia sp.), cedar, juniper (Juniperus sp.); river roots including willow, cottonwood (Populus sp.) and alder (Alnus sp.); sedge (Carex sp.); maple (Acer sp.), oak (Quercus sp.); bracken fern (Pteris aquilinum); horse tail (Equisetum sp.); tule and bulrush (Scirpus sp.); briar root (Smilax californica); and yucca (Yucca sp.).

Small roots usually work just as they are, and modern weavers often like the fantastic twists and turns that a traditional weaver would shun. Roots peel in spring just like shoots do. For finer weavers, and those used to produce the watertight basketry of the western states, larger roots need to be split down into weavers with no outer surfaces. The split surfaces absorb water when the basket is in use and swell up to effectively seal the basket. Conifer roots are used most often in this way.

In traditional basketry, conifer roots are usually cooked. This softens the root slightly and allows the bark to slip easily at any time of the year. For split-root weavers, you may gather roots up to wrist-size and any length. But it is best to get roots that will fit easily curled in a canning kettle for cooking. I prefer finger-sized roots.

Very large roots were steam-baked in a sandy river bar in the old days. This is done by digging a long trench in damp sand. Next, build a fire in it for an hour or so, scrape out the fire, set the roots in and cover them with damp sand about a foot thick. Then build another fire on top and let it die down overnight. Uncover and split the roots in the morning.

Smaller roots can be boiled from ten minutes to an hour, but do not overcook them; this actually hardens the roots, especially if they are left standing in the water as it cools. Cook only as many as you can split while the water is still warm.   In the northwest, traditional weavers roast cedar roots over a coal fire until they crackle and the bark slips easily. Some California weavers use ovens and even microwaves. Be forewarned: If you use your oven, you may not want to cook food in it ever again. The sap gets into everything (experience of a Yurok weaver).

Split the roots in the same way you did the shoots, in half, and in half again, flatwise as many times as it takes to thin the ribbons down to about one-eighth of an inch in thickness. The width will be as wide as the root. These strips are then stored away and seasoned, as are shoots.

When you are ready to weave, soak them in warm water for one-half hour and then soften the root by working the ribbon over a blunt edge such as a mussel shell or butter knife. Rub the root over and over from the middle out to each edge and on both sides as if you were trying to scrape something off the surface. I like to pinch the root between my thumb and the tool in the same hand and pull the root away at about a ninety-degree angle. After about ten minutes the root will be fully softened and rubbery. It can be used as a flat ribbon or stripped into narrower weavers along the growth rings. Try not to trim roots with a knife as they will fray at the cut.

The other roots listed may be used whole or peeled and do not need to be either cooked or softened. Sedge roots, used in Pomo and other central California traditional weaving, are dug, split once, peeled and trimmed to size. They are light tan in color. Horsetail roots are pure black. Bracken fern roots have two flat, structural filaments inside the root that are encased in a white sticky matrix. These are cleaned off and soaked in a black dye to enhance their natural dark-brown color. Tule roots and briar roots are also a natural dark red-brown. Yucca roots have a beautiful magenta to dark-brown core. Gently crack off the outer root bark to expose this. The bark can also be used as a red dye.

Barks
Bark fibers may be divided into two categories: wet, or inner barks gathered from live trees, and dry, or exfoliating outer bark. I will deal with wet inner barks first, as these are the strongest and most commonly used. The best live bark includes the growing cambium layer directly in contact with the wood. This means if you strip all the bark off of the tree it will die. Which is alright if you cut the tree and intend to use the whole thing for firewood or building. If not, take only a small strip of bark running up the tree rather than around it. In the Northwest, you can still see ancient cedar trees showing long scars where people gathered bark for generations without killing the tree.

Try the following inner barks: cedar, birch, maple, willow, juniper, cottonwood, cherry (Prunus spp.), basswood (Tilia sp.) including tulip poplar, and hickory (Carya sp.).

Gather live bark in spring and summer when the sap is flowing. To gather a strip of bark from a standing tree, cut a slit horizontally no more than one-eighth of the width around the tree. The best bark is from small to medium-sized trees so that the thick outer bark is not so cumbersome and hard to cut through. Gently loosen the bottom of the strip and pull backward, stripping up. The strip will gradually feather out and pull free. For a slab of bark, cut a score on the tree the size you want and gently pry it off. If you cut the tree down, you can get an entire bark round, or you can score the bark with a knife and peel off exact-sized strips. These are especially suited for plaited basketry. In all these cases, try not to pull the bark off at an angle greater than about 45° or the bark will crack and bits may stick to the wood and feather off more quickly.

Bark strips may be split down flatwise into thinner pieces using the same splitting technique described earlier. It is easier to split bark because it naturally tends to separate into papery layers. Sizing the bark for width first makes it easier to split as well.

In the Northwest, weavers use a cedar bark sizing tool similar to those used to make rawhide thongs to measure width. You can make a primitive one by setting an obsidian blade into a notch in a flat piece of wood. The cutting edge should be perpendicular to both the notch and the flat plane

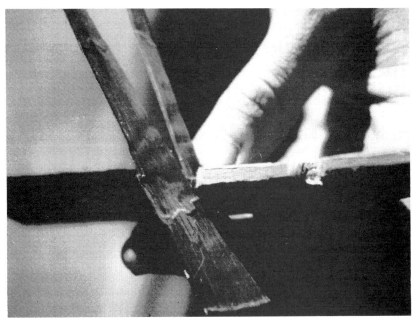

A sizing tool can be made by setting an obsidian blade into a notch in a flat piece of wood. The tool the slides down the bark, cutting uniform strips.

*The author uses a length of stripped willow bark to lace an external rim
reinforcement strip of juniper bark to her bark basket. (Photo: Jim Riggs)*

of the wood. Slide the tool down the edge of your bark. The sized strip will come through the notch.

Bark slabs and strips can be dried and stored at any stage. Heavy slabs may need soaking for more than a day to reconstitute them. Thin strips may need only a half-hour in warm water. Inner barks are sometimes pounded and stripped even finer for the weaving of cloth-like items such as the cedar bark blankets of the Northwest coast. Soak the large strips until the papery layers start to come apart by themselves. Then lay the strip on a flattened log and gently pound it with another piece of wood. Pounding with a rock tends to break the fibers instead of separating them.

Sometimes you can find "road kill" bark slabs that have been run over by logging trucks so many times that they have separated out into perfect fluffy shreds. Log yards are good places to find many kinds of bark, but ask first.

Another type of bark that is good for rough weaving, especially twining, is the soft, dry, shreddy outer bark which exfoliates, or hangs in festoons off of the branches. Try to gather not the outermost layers, but the layers between these and the live bark. These are the strongest. These dry barks need only to be rubbed or rolled between the palms to break up the clumps.

Try the following dry barks: sagebrush (Artemsia sp.), ninebark (Physocarpus capitatus), antelope brush (Purshia sp.), cliff rose (Cowania sp.), evening primrose (Oenothera hookerii), clematis (Clematis sp.) and reedgrass (Phragmites sp.).

Vines

Nature's twining and climbing plants are naturals for basketry, but they are not always as strong as you might think, they need support for their growth and often have weak wood themselves. Vines are seldom used in traditional basketry, but there are some exceptions. Experiment. They need no preparation at all, or you may want to split them once to get more mileage out of your material.

Try the following vines: grape vine (Vitis spp.), traditional in the west for rim finishes; honeysuckle (Lonicera sp.), traditional in Northern California and the Southeast; clematis, morning glory (Ipomoea sp.); blackberry (Rubus spp.), especially the native variety called devil's shoelaces; wisteria (Wisteria sp.); and kudzu (Pueraria lobata).

Seed Pods

This tiny section is added to include the useful and fascinating devil's claw pod (Proboscidea fragrans or Proboscidea parviflora) of the Southwest. It has been cultivated by the native peoples of Arizona for centuries, selected for its long black hooks on the pods. This is an easy annual to grow, but needs ample heat to produce good pods.

Collect the pods before the green sheath has completely fallen to prevent the sun from bleaching out the color. Split the claws in half, either directly on the pod or cut them off at the point where the claw joins the pod. Lay the claw on a board, stick an awl into the middle of it at the tip end, and pull the claw away to start the split. Continue the split as described above. Some weavers start the split from the fat end of the claw.

The fibers are very short in comparison to other weavers but they are incredibly strong. They are used mainly in coiled basketry for the black design, especially at the start of the basket where it receives the most wear. Some modern weavers incorporate the whole pods, like little alien heads, into fantastic art basketry.

Leaves and Grass
Leaves and grasses are widely used but usually in the more impermanent baskets or those destined to be used, like brown paper bags, until they fall apart. There are some notable exceptions, however, such as the yucca baskets of the Southwest and the tule baskets of the Plateau. Most leaves and grasses require a minimum of preparation. Those that are used for structural basketry are listed here. Those that are used for non-structural decoration are listed in the next section.

Tules, cattails, rushes, palm leaves and iris may be used in soft basketry where there is no strength requirement. These may be weavers or foundation.

In Klamath Lake and Modoc basketry, tules are carefully sized down into strips and tightly twined on a cordage foundation. Different parts—culms, basal leaves and roots—give different colors. These tule baskets were used for everything including hot rock boiling.

The grasses listed below can be used as bundle foundation in coiled basketry. They don't have the strength or flexibility to make the turns necessary for weaving. Wheat straw is an exception. Used for centuries in the Celtic nations, it is soaked and woven into "corn dollies" at harvest time. According to legend, the spirit of the grain lives in the weaving until the next planting season when it is buried in the new fields. New Zealand flax is an import used a lot in landscaping. It is used in traditional Maori weaving and is exceptionally strong, either whole or separated into cordage fibers.

Try the following leaves and grasses: yucca (Yucca sp.) and agave (Agave sp.), tule (Scirpus sp.), cattail (Typha sp.) including juncus rush (Juncus acutus), palm (Phoenix sp.), and iris (Iris spp.), New Zealand flax, bunch grasses including wild oats (Avena sp.), wild rye grass (Secale sp.), salt grass (Spartina spp.), wheat straw (Triticum spp.), sweet grass (Anthoxanthum sp.) and southern beargrass (Dasylirion sp.).

Yuccas, agaves and their kin are technically leaves but their structure requires some preparation. Only the narrow-leafed yuccas, such as Yucca elata and Nolina species have the flexibility to be used whole. To prepare yucca leaves for weaving, let fresh leaves wilt for about half a day. This relaxes them so they don't crack in splitting. Split the leaves flatwise as described above and trim them to the desired size. Leaves collected in early spring from the center of the plant are pure white like a cauliflower. The green leaves will eventually turn yellow.

Some yuccas and agaves can be retted and pounded to remove all but the inner fibers. These are suitable for cordage or bundle coiling particularly at the start of the basket. You can do this carefully and leave the thorn at the end of the leaf, especially on agaves. This is a natural sewing needle with the thread attached. Be careful of agaves. Some species, mainly the large century plants used in garden plantings, are toxic, producing a bad rash in most people. I have had no problem with the small native Agave desertii.

Wood Splints
In spring, when the sap begins to flow, a tree will produce a spurt of growth which is visible as a ring. In winter the tree grows more slowly. Trees produce a ring of growth each year. A healthy, fast-growing tree will have wide growth rings. These layers of wood can be separated into strips and used for weaving exceptionally strong plaited and wicker baskets.

Find a straight-grained, medium-sized tree in the growing season and cut it. You can use limbs if they are straight. Cut it into three-to-six-foot lengths and remove the bark. Make a score into the first ring of wood the length of the log, this gets a splint started. Begin pounding to one side of the score with a hard wooden mallet. Old, wooden bowling pins work well. A good log will begin breaking apart into flat strips along the spring growth rings. When you get a good section loosened, grab the end of the strip and pull it off of the log. Work the outside of the log first, and continue down into the lower growth rings. It is important to do this as soon as you can after you cut the log. The rough strips can be thinned by splitting flatwise as described above, or they can be planed down with metal shaves.

Try the following trees: ash (Fraxinus sp.), oak (Quercus sp), hickory (Carya sp.) and maple (Acer sp).

Decorative Overlay Materials
Though a strong, functional basket can be made with the materials described above, most people delight in the decoration of even the most

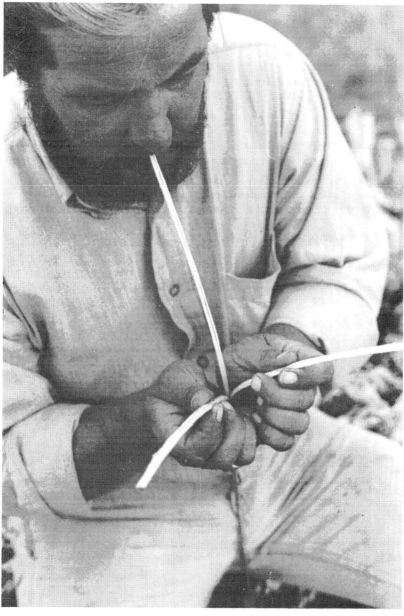

Richard Jamison demonstrates technique of splitting sumac splints into three thin weavers: Here he shows how to support and control the split using your hands or pinky fingers so that each weaver is the same thickness.

common household tools. The following materials have been used by native peoples in the west to give color and shine to their weaving, though they are weak and brittle by themselves. These materials are used by laying them over or wrapping them around a stronger weaving material during the basket making process. Overlay twining, wrapped twining, false embroidery and imbrication are all techniques done with these materials. Some of the shoot and root materials listed above are both strong and have a dark, contrasting color.

Northern beargrass is collected at high summer before the flower stalks begin to form. Reach into the center of the clump and pluck out the very center bunch of leaves. This includes the growing point. The plant won't flower in the year you collect leaves, so skip around and leave some to flower. The small central leaves are the most flexible and dry pure white if laid in the sun for a few days. Turn them frequently so they don't sunburn—they can become brittle and turn a dingy yellow. To reconstitute them for weaving, soak the leaves in warm water for 20 minutes and then wrap them in a damp towel while you work. Over-soaked beargrass turns grey and cracks. Some people remove the center vein of the leaf before using it to make it lie flatter. Be careful not to cut your hands on the sharp leaf edges.

Maidenhair or five-fingered fern has a beautiful shiny stem with a black side and a reddish side. The red side tends to be brittle and hard to work with, but some weavers save both sides. Pinch the fresh stem in your fingers or in a split stick and pull down the length of the stem to crack it along the line between the red and black sides. This can be tricky—the stems can spiral. Gently pull the sides apart and clean out the greenish center with your fingernail.

Wild cherry bark in the northwest is a beautiful shiny red, particularly up in the high branches where the wind rubs the boughs together. This natural polishing rubs off the dull grey outer film. Use a pruning saw to get at the high branches. Lower branches can be rubbed with a kitchen scrubber or horsetail rushes to polish up the red bark. Cut the branches at the leaf whorls. Make a small cut at the top to get a small tip of outer bark free. Then pull out and down at an angle to spiral off the outer bark in one piece. With some practice you can get a long strip about one-half-inch wide out of a single branch. The green inner bark can be treated as in the bark section. It is strong and beautiful but should not be used in any food processing baskets as it contains cyanide.

Chain ferns and some other ferns contain supportive filaments that run along inside the stems. These were described in the root section for the bracken fern. Filaments can be extracted by first removing the leaflets, then cracking the entire length of the stem by gently pounding it with a rock. Pull away the outer tissue and remove the two light green filaments. These are often dyed a rich orange brown with alder bark.

To make the dye, pound up some bark or grate the larger pieces to resemble grated carrots. Pour boiling water over about a cup of the bark in a bowl and allow it to steep and then cool for a few hours. Set your rolls of fern filaments or anything else you want to dye so that they are covered with liquid. You should see a change almost immediately. Some alders work better than others, but generally it is the exposure to air (oxidation) which brings out the rich color. After a few hours, wrap the filaments in a damp towel to fully oxidize. If you still don't get a dark enough color, add a pinch of baking soda to the dye and try it again. Alder acts as a natural litmus solution (a blue coloring matter that is turned red by acids and can be restored to blue by alkalis). Alkali will darken the color and acid will lighten it. If you get it too dark, add a little vinegar.

Porcupine quills are used in fine twined basketry in California and Oregon as an overlay. They are usually dyed yellow, red or pink. Many natural dyes will take on quills, but by far the best is wolf lichen (Evernia vulpina), the bright chartreuse moss that hangs on the trees at high elevations. It has a natural mordant and can be used to enhance other dyes. Wash your quills well with a grease-cutting mixture such as urine or pine cleaner (your choice!). Place the quills and moss in a pan in alternating layers about an inch thick ending with a moss layer. Pour boiling water over the whole thing and bring it to a boil again. Quills don't mind the heat. Set a plate in the pot to keep the quills under the liquid. Set the pot aside overnight and in the morning the quills will be bright yellow.

Try the following colors:

Shiny white or cream
northern beargrass (Xerophyllum tenax)
cane tops (Phragmites communis)
corn husk, rye grass (Elymus sp.)

Shiny black
maidenhair fern stems (Adiantum pedatum)
gold-back fern stem (Pityrogramma sp.)
deer fern stem (Blechnum spicant)
sea grass or eel grass

Orange brown
chain fern filaments (Woodwardia sp.)
dyed with alder bark (Alnus sp.)
cedar bark split very fine, spruce or cedar root skins

Shiny red
outer cherry bark, redbud skin (Cercis sp.)

Yellow
Porcupine quills or beargrass dyed with wolf lichen
dock root (Rumex sp.)
grape root
osage wood chips (Maclura pomifera)
rabbitbrush (Chrysothamnus nauseosus)
onion skins (Allium sp.)

You will notice I have listed some other dye materials. These are only the most commonly used dyes. Try getting books on dye plants and experimenting with the stronger outer fibers. Split willow, cedar and spruce roots, wood splints and yucca take natural dyes quite well.

Also try walnut (Juglans nigra) husks, iron shavings (or steel wool), marsh mud, or oak galls for dark brown or black. Bloodroot (Sanguinaria canadensis), willow bark and sand dock make other orange-reds. Spruce bark makes a nice lavender on rawhide. For greens and blues, try hawthorne berries, larkspur flowers (Consolida ambigua), pond scum algae, Queen Anne's lace center flowers or bear's hair lichen.

There are endless possibilities available for the modern basket maker. I have tried to summarize the traditional plant preparation methods I know about. There are many more plants out there to experiment on. Feel free to try these methods on any available plant parts you may find.

The author demonstrates and explains various basket weaving techniques indigenous to Native American cultures during a class at the Rabbit Stick Rendezvous. (Photo: Linda Jamison)

Ernest Wilkinson

Tracking Skills

• •

Having coordinated search and rescue teams for many years, I can verify that a good tracking team, on the scene before a large group of ground searchers arrives, can save many hours and often the life of the victim(s).

How often have you heard the phrase, "Tracks read like a book?" The premise is correct, but don't forget that you have to be able to read the book before you understand the story. Before you started school you couldn't read at all. It took a few years of tutoring and lots of practice to learn, and then gradually you became proficient. The same is true when it comes to tracking. Reading tracks is much like reading a good mystery novel—each chapter provides clues that add up to the final conclusion.

Animal tracking seems to be of interest to many folks, but since most animals are very clever and evasive of humans, it is sometimes difficult to become proficient at it. Hence, it is very important that you learn the habits, size and other details of the animals you intend to track so you will have more clues with which to put together the final picture.

Of course, it will depend on where you live—whether in a small, localized area with limited species, or in a larger regional area with a wide variety of animals. But regardless of whether you are an urban or rural dweller you can start practicing in a park, under bridges or on nearby roads. There may be squirrels and gophers in the parks, along with an occasional raccoon, or perhaps a muskrat in the waterways or canals. In fact, you might be surprised to learn the variety of animals that live in urban areas providing a chance to start forming your tracking skills. If you

Bear tracks in sand (Photo: Ernest Wilkinson).

live in an area with lots of snow you have ideal conditions to practice tracking in the early morning after a skiff of snow has fallen.

With a little practice you will soon be able to see that different animals have different sizes and shapes of feet. Animals with four toes include fox, coyote, bobcat and cougar. Animals with five toes include skunks, badgers, weasels, raccoons and bears. Then, to complicate matters, there are some mammals such as squirrels that have four toes showing on the front feet tracks and five toes on the hind feet.

Porcupines are similar except that the tracks are larger, with a very rough pad. The porcupine sort of waddles along with a pigeon-toed (toe inward) track, and leaves tail-drag marks. Badgers also leave pigeon-toed tracks.

Each animal also has a standard gait or step pattern to their track. The canine or dog family has different gaits such as walking, trotting and loping which you can learn to identify. Other animals have a hopping pattern. The rabbit track shows the back feet in front and to the side of the front feet tracks. The smaller, front feet land first with the back feet coming down in front and producing the spring for the next hop. Weasels and martins do not have a walking gait, but use sort of a bounding hop, with the front feet landing together at a slightly diagonal angle.

In addition to the size, shape, number of toes, gait patterns and other clues, it is important to learn the habitats of different animals to help you identify their tracks. For example, bobcats prefer rough, brushy and rocky areas, whereas coyotes prefer open slopes and meadows. This can vary and overlap somewhat depending on where you are.

Beaver would naturally be in wet areas with ponds or streams to provide a food supply, while the martin inhabits spruce forests which contain squirrels and rodents for food. You might find groundhog (marmot) tracks in the alpine country above timberline, but you would not find prairie dog (a close relative) tracks there. They would be at lower elevations in meadows and on the grassy slopes.

The location of various animal tracks will also vary according to the season of year. Groundhogs and prairie dogs hibernate during the winter which eliminates confusing their tracks with others during the winter months. Let me give you another example: you would not expect to find deer and elk tracks in the high altitudes of the western United States during the winter because deep snow buries their food in higher elevations. They are usually forced by deep snow to migrate long distances from their high summer feeding grounds to the lower valleys to feed during the winter months.

This brings to mind another family of tracks: even-toed ungulates such as deer, elk, antelope, big-horn sheep, peccary and other similar animals. Again, each species of ungulate has a generally distinctive track. For example, the deer's track is sort of heart-shaped, while the antelope is a bit concave on the outer edge, and the toes a bit farther apart than the deer. An elk track is larger and more rounded on the toes than a deer track.

If the animal is running, the hoof tips will be spaced farther apart than when it is walking. That provides a clue to the rate of speed the animal is traveling. Of course you must take into account that the size of tracks of the fawns and females of the species are smaller and more trim than the older males.

Which reminds me of an incident that happened many years ago while I was guiding Bob Lee, President of Wing Archery Company. He shot an elk at about seven o'clock in the morning; the arrow hit high between two ribs and the arrow didn't penetrate very deep. After the elk jumped a couple of times the arrow flipped out and fell to the ground. This meant there would be very little external bleeding, but we felt obligated to do our best to track the animal down even though we figured it was not a fatal wound.

After being hit, the elk ran off through the spruce trees. The impact of the hooves on the pine needles during the running gait made tracking very easy to start with. But the animal soon slowed to a walk as it continued across the slopes and grassy meadows. At one point it crossed through the tracks of another small group of elk, making it necessary for me to get on my hands and knees and search out one track at a time; but by this time I had the size and shape of the hoof print ingrained in my mind.

There was no blood in the tracks except for an occasional drop every fifty yards or so that might be spotted on a blade of grass or on a rock. This let me know I was still hot on the trail. Later, as the elk moved across the terrain, the external bleeding completely stopped and the only way I could verify that I was still on the correct track was to occasionally locate a bit of blood on an overhead leaf or tree branch that had brushed off as the animal passed by.

To make a long hunting story short, I finally found the elk dead in some willows. Apparently the arrow had just penetrated the lining of the chest cavity, which had gradually filled with blood. With very little visible blood on the trail, tracking had been slow, taking five hours. However, I was glad I persisted.

Now you can understand a little of how the art of tracking is similar to a detective game. You must gather all the possible clues before reaching a conclusion, since one track can sometimes create the wrong impression. Clues will include geographic locations, time of season, habitat, ground cover, tracks or partial tracks, scat (feces), hair, gnawed branches and any other information you can find that adds to your conclusion.

It is impossible to go into details on each individual species here, but if you're truly interested in becoming more proficient at animal tracking, I recommend *A Field Guide to Mammal Tracking in Western America*. Check your library for books that offer specific information on animals found in your area. I also recommend *Tracking, A Blueprint for Learning How*, by Jack Kearney, published by Pathway Press, 525 Jeffree Street, El Cajon, California 92020.

Man tracking
Man tracking is another art, used mostly by law enforcement officers to locate children and others who have lost their way. If you have ever been associated with a successful search for a lost child, you will appreciate the value of man tracking expertise. In some of the standard searches there are sometimes several hundred ground searchers involved with no success. On other searches, a good tracking team gets involved and greatly minimizes the potential search area, which in turn makes for the best possible use of helicopters and ground crews.

For example, let's suppose a person has been missing for five hours

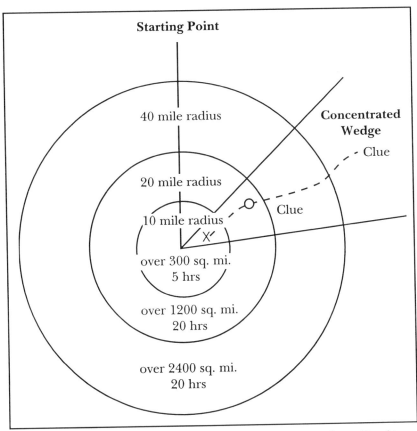

Mathematical theory of lost person traveling a two miles per hour. Tracking can establish direction of travel of victim to trim 360 degree search area to less than half or even as small as a 30 degree wedge. Terrain is also factored.

and it is estimated he or she is traveling at a rate of two miles per hour. That would put them approximately ten miles from the last point seen, but we have no idea which direction they are traveling. A 10-mile radius is mapped out that includes about 300 square miles. Assuming another five hours has passed before searchers arrive at the location, the potential search area can increase to a 20-mile radius and involve more than 1,250 square miles. This area can continue to increase until it is virtually impossible for a standard ground crew to cover it.

However, if an experienced tracking crew is called immediately, they can usually determine the direction taken by the victim. The terrain of the area is also a factor in determining the direction of travel. Even a track of several feet can often give a clue to the direction taken and eliminate searching the other half of the circle. And, when the track can be followed for a distance to determine the direction of travel, the shape of the search area can be reduced from a 360° circle to a pie-shaped wedge of perhaps 30°. This is a mathematical theory, but it seems to hold up quite well in most searches. The above-mentioned potential search area is larger than general, but illustrates how the size of the search area can get out of hand.

A tracking team generally consists of three people: a point man (or woman) and two flankers. The point man is in front of the others and to one side of the track, while the flankers are several feet behind on each side of the point man. They never step in front to avoid obliterating a clue. In this manner, each tracker is looking from a different angle, increasing the chance of spotting a clue. Such a clue might be a disturbed pebble or stick flattened into the ground, even a flattened blade of grass—any notable disturbance to the natural surroundings.

Early morning or late afternoon are the best times for tracking because the angle of light make clues easier to detect. The sun casts a longer shadow when low than when it is overhead, and every little pebble and stick becomes more apparent. Where small rocks or sticks have been stepped on by a flat human foot, the flattened area does not have the small shadows behind each upraised pebble as is evident in the area surrounding it.

Using a Tracking Stick

A tracking stick can also help in spotting small clues. It can be a ski pole without the basket, a straight willow limb or similar tool.

When you see a normal track, mark the stride (the distance from the toe of one track to the heel of the next) on the end of your tracking stick with a pencil mark or by carving or scratching it in with a knife. Remember that the length of stride will vary when the person is going uphill or downhill.

Your tracking stick should also have the length and width of the track marked on it. And you should make a sketch of the track showing any nail marks, grooves or other distinguishing marks which might be found in a clear footprint left in mud or dirt.

What if you locate a toe mark on the last track but cannot find the next step? By placing the tracking stick on the toe of the last track and measuring the stride you can make a slow arc with the stick and find the next step.

Your eye has been on the general area where that next track should be, whereas now it is focused on a small section at the point of your tracking stick as it moves in an arc. You are then better able to locate a bent blade of grass, disturbed pebble, discolored foliage or other clues because your focus is more concentrated.

While you are learning to track, do not take shortcuts. For example, perhaps you might not have located any clues on finding the victim's next step, but can see a track ahead. Do not jump ahead on that track. Stop and train your eye to locate the clues that lead to it before you proceed.

In the case of a lost child or in the event that darkness or a storm is threatening, experienced tracking teams can work together. As one team works out a located track, the other team makes a half-circle several hundred yards ahead of the first team on the chance of locating the extended track, being careful not to erase or obliterate any clues. This can sometimes save time, not having to work out the entire trail track-by-track. Once a clue is found, the first team can then leap-frog ahead of the other team and vice-versa.

Having coordinated search and rescue teams for many years, I can verify that a good tracking team, on the scene before a large group of ground searchers arrives can save many hours and often the life of the victim(s). Often the sheriff, who is in charge of any county emergency, calls for help and the general public responds by offering to assist in looking for lost children. But any time a group, or even one individual, traverses an area, many clues become completely erased. That is why, particularly in the case of accidentally lost children, I highly recommend that a skilled tracking team or two be put into the area before a general ground search crew is called and the clues are destroyed. Search and Rescue teams are becoming more alert to preserving tracking clues and training others to do the same.

Still, I have seen searches with more than 200 well-meaning, untrained people meandering through the area hoping to assist. Many of them will walk on the established trails and destroy most of the tracking clues. Then the direction is often difficult, or impossible, to determine by tracking or other methods. As a result, the search time lengthens and the search fails; the victim is found dead several months later within easy distance of the search area.

The clues are usually there if you know how and where to look for them, but don't expect the impossible. We often hear of someone who can accomplish super-human feats, like tracking an ant across pavement or a porcupine up a tree. Perhaps it can be done under extraordinary conditions, but those kinds of stunts are not commonplace.

Over my many tracking years, I have experienced some incidents involving what I call "darn fool's luck," but it was only because the luck was combined with fifty years of practice that it produced so-called "amazing" results. The moral: don't neglect the clues while praying for a miracle.

Another side of tracking is learning to mark a trail for your own future use. As a licensed guide, I conduct various five- and six-day backpacking excursions into remote mountain areas. Most of the time we hike on the standard Forest Service trails that are marked with long and short blazes cut into trees, posts along the routes or piles of rocks. But occasionally I like to provide my customers with a feel for the pioneering spirit by leaving the standard thoroughfare and striking off cross-country, hiking from ridge to ridge or canyon to canyon. As you can imagine, there are often cliffs, rock ledges, tangled timber or similar obstacles in these places that block the path of the backpackers.

Add to that the fact that when going through tall timber you cannot see distant landmarks that would normally guide you in flat terrain. So years ago, when initially blazing these short-cut routes, I left small markers along the way that were identifiable to me for future use.

Sometimes I would follow an elk trail around the side of a mountain to a certain spot and then leave that trail to hike through the timber and come out on a certain ridge, creek valley, camping and fishing area or other designated location. When checking out the route I picked up several small two- to three-inch rocks. One of these would be left on top of a large boulder along the trail, another on top of a rock, or I set two of the small stones up with one on top of the other within sight of the last one. I continued this across the mountain, around swampy areas, cliffs or other obstacles. It is not natural for a small rock to be perched on another, so to a trained eye the unnatural placement can be used as a guide.

My markers are so small and unobtrusive that they are not offensive to the view of hikers, and my subliminal trail is fairly permanent because winter snow and winds do not disturb the rocks. I marked some of those areas through timber and criss-crossing elk trails more than thirty years ago. Each summer, I guide groups through these same courses to come out at an exact location two or three miles away. The hikers often wonder how I manage to come out precisely on course, but those small rock markers still catch my trained eye. I immediately detect that small, out-of-place stone that is missed by everyone else.

I have witnessed bow hunters and others going into remote timbered areas marking their trail with bright, orange-colored plastic ribbon tied to trees or bushes every few yards. But they do not retrieve those ribbons as they return. I have seen others, one a nationally-known person, use a spray-can of bright paint to mark a trail to follow back. Those ribbons and paint are still there years later, an eyesore for anyone who might venture that way or be taking photos. If you insist on using ribbons to mark a temporary trail, and circumstances are such that you might not return by that route (if you are on a search and rescue mission, for example), use bright-colored crepe paper. It is biodegradable and soon dissipates in the sun, rain and snow.

Other methods of trail marking can also be used on the spur of the moment that leave no aesthetic imposition. Let's assume it is hunting season and you have killed a deer or elk on a timbered mountain. The sun is down by the time you get it dressed out and propped open to cool. You have no way to get it packed out so late in the day, and it looks like a snowstorm is moving in. You quickly move down the mountain in an effort to get close to camp before dark.

If it snows a foot during the night it will cover all tracks and the area will look completely different the next day. I have known hunters to take an animal under these same circumstances, then spend several days in an unsuccessful search for their kill beneath the snow. But such a loss can be prevented by using a simple marking system.

As you walk along, snap off some evergreen boughs or other brushy limbs and hang them upside-down on protruding limbs or snags in a sight line. Because upside-down branches are not natural, your eye automatically focuses on them, allowing you to follow your route back to the dressed carcass the next day. Even if the snow is exceptionally heavy, it usually falls off the outer branches after an hour or two and the next morning your markers will be visible. There is no end to the kinds of markers you can devise, since they can vary a great deal from terrain to terrain.

Speaking of being lost, I would like to suggest a few things that might be of help if you find yourself in that situation.

To begin with, if the sun is going down, a storm moving in or any other circumstances arise that prevent you from getting back to camp—admit you are lost. Then, look around to see what is available for emergency shelter. By staying occupied with a project, you can prevent a panic attack and stay in control. It has been estimated that a person uses seven times more energy when excited than when calm.

When you are preparing your emergency shelter, pace yourself so as not to perspire. If your underclothes become damp from perspiration your body will cool down considerably, and may not be able to regenerate the lost heat, causing hyperthermia. One of the basic survival rules is: "to stay dry is to stay warm."

Another warning—don't continue to travel (unless, of course, to stay where you are puts you in additional danger). Stay put and if you left word with a responsible person as to where you were going, when you would return and your route, they will know approximately where to begin searching when you don't show up.

If you must move your location, you can mark your trail with some of the above methods to make it easier for anyone attempting to rescue you by tracking. Teach youngsters to occasionally scratch their initials and direction of travel in the dirt on open spots along the route, or to leave rows of pebbles and other signs if they become lost. Children should also learn to construct simple emergency shelters and be taught to find shelter. That way, if they become lost they will devote some of their time and energy to building a shelter. Once built, they will be more inclined to feel some attachment to their shelter and new surroundings, and stay put instead of wandering. Also teach children to stay in one place if they are disoriented. On more than one occasion our rescue teams would find the spot where a child spent the night then left at daylight, so our search would start all over again.

But enough about survival techniques.

You can gain a lot of personal satisfaction and confidence from being able to read wildlife tracks like a book, or better yet, if you have occasion to use your tracking skills to save a life. Practice sessions will sharpen your awareness to the enjoyment of the outdoors, as well as obtaining some fresh air and exercise. As you learn to read the animal tracks, you also learn more about the life and habits of your wild neighbors. Give it a try and have fun!

Richard Jamison

The Primal Gourmet

• •

*I have cooked everything from small ground squirrels to
a hind quarter of beef in a pit with good success. And there
is nothing quite like coming back to camp, exhausted after
a day-long hike, uncovering the pit and enjoying a tender,
succulent hot meal without having to go through all the
preliminary hassles. Multiply your delight ten-fold if a
rain shower has dampened your spirits and your firewood.*

I don't mean to brag, but I am a better outdoor cook than Linda
is. Not that she objects to this encroachment on her territory—it's a nice
trade off, actually. She gathers the firewood and has more time to explore
while I cook. But it surprises me a little since I had no maternal training
in the kitchen. Maybe it came about because of the trips I conducted where
food was scarce and it was important to make the best of each precious
mouthful. Maybe it is a matter of routine, learning to regulate heat and
experiment with various techniques of cooking the same food over and
over. Or, perhaps, it's simply because I have a personal relationship with
fire through countless years of making it a valuable tool and companion.

In ancient times, though, the women probably cooked while the men
hunted. This was a boon to the females—what woman in her right mind
would prefer to face a prehistoric bison with only a sharpened stick?
Hmmm, was this a conspiracy?

No one really knows how or when early humans started cooking their
food. Maybe scavenged animals killed in sweeping fires tasted better, and
was more tender "scorched" than raw. Or a piece of meat may have

accidentally fallen into the fire as early people gathered around the hearth for warmth.

Regardless of how or when it was discovered, cooking caught on and spread to include a number of ingenious methods of preparing food—all without the pots, pans and utensils that were developed later. A few cooking methods that were undoubtedly used by our early ancestors include skewering; spit cooking; grilling; cooking in coals and ashes; stone ovens; clay containers; and steam pits. It is interesting to note, as with many early living skills, these time-tested methods are still practical today.

Cooking fires

Of course, the first step in any outdoor cooking is to locate your fire-building materials.

For a fast start up, you can use the various softwoods like pine, spruce, or fir; especially when split, they produce a quick blaze because they are resinous. But a fire built entirely of softwoods burns out fast and needs frequent attention, so once your initial fire is started, add some hard-woods. Hardwood coals last longer and they don't make your food taste like turpentine, as resinous woods often do. Oak, when you can find it, produces steady, glowing coals and hickory, ash or one of the sweet black-smoking birches are also great for cooking. I don't recommend spruce and juniper because they contain moisture pockets that explode when trapped gasses and water vapor build up, and cause considerable popping.

Certainly poison ivy, poison oak and poisonous sumac should never be used as firewood. In fact, be careful when you gather wood in areas where it grows, so that it isn't added to the wood pile by mistake. As for quantity, a good rule to follow is to collect twice as much as you think you will need.

Your fire "lay" is crucial to proficient outdoor cooking. There are several different kinds of cooking fires and much of your culinary success will depend on building the right one for the occasion.

A word of wisdom here: in the process of deciding where to build your fire, consider positioning it against a boulder or sandy bank whenever possible. The smoke is then pulled into the partial vacuum created by the nearby object, and it won't follow you around as you cook.

A single round fire is generally not convenient for cooking. It's better to arrange a number of small cooking areas in a long trench fire. These can be broken apart for broiling, or the coals raked into several beds, just as you use different burners on your modern range at home. A trench fire is particularly good for skewering or cooking small game on a spit, grilling, or shishkabob-style cooking, or when you want to build a good bed of coals for ash cooking that will keep its heat for a long time.

Begin by digging or scraping a trench about six inches wide, six inches deep, and about two or three feet long. If the length of the trench runs the same direction that the wind blows it will assure a good draft. Bank the trench with standing rocks on both sides, leaving the ends open to take advantage of the draft.

The most important consideration when cooking on, near, over or in rocks is that they must be "fire-proven" (thoroughly dried near the fire for a couple of days) or they may explode when the heat creates steam that expands. Exploding rocks can be extremely dangerous. I speak from experience. Once you have "proven" a few rocks, protect them from dampness and rain so you can use them over again.

Now for the fire. On a dry, flat spot lay a tinder bundle made from dry grass, the dry inner bark of cottonwood, sage, cedar, or birch. Then build a small tepee over it from dry twigs. Over this lean a few larger sticks in tepee fashion so that ample oxygen reaches all parts of the lay. Have your supply of hardwood handy to add when the fire gets going.

If you know how, preserve the ambience of the event by igniting your fire with the coal from a primitive firemaking technique. If not, use one match to light your fire—even if you have more. The skill it takes for one-match firemaking may someday mean the difference between a warmly comfortable camp and a chilly, miserable one.

You may have noticed the way a piece of charcoal turns gray on the outside as it burns. The charcoal is actually turning to ash, and that ash has a purpose—it helps the coal continue to burn by covering it with a screen that lets just enough air through to allow the coal to stay alive. When the ashes are knocked off the coal, it burns red hot, and quickly burns itself out. A fire banked with ashes holds glowing coals for many hours, making it easy to control the heat or rekindle the flame when you want to; ideal conditions for spit cooking.

By the way, you can preserve charcoal for future use by removing the blackened hardwood, dousing it with water, then drying it, or just covering the wood with sand until the fire is out. These charred pieces of wood can be added to your fire just as you would add commercial charcoal briquettes. It's nice to have a small stash of "wilderness charcoal" in a dry cache in the event you come back to camp in a rainstorm and find your firewood soaked.

Skewering

Assuming you have something to cook, nature has kindly provided the means to fix most foods.

The most obvious cooking method of early people was to simply skewer food on a stick over an open fire. You can cook anything this way, from a whole fish to a wild-game shishkabob to dough wound snake-like (or a snake wound dough-like) around a green stick.

When you cook chunks of meat on a skewer, first sear the skewer quickly over the flames, then plant it in the ground near the fire and leave it alone for about ten minutes.

To skewer a whole small fish on a stick, secure it with a small green spike so it won't fall off, then place the skewered fish, head down, into the center of the coals. By placing the head down you prevent the rest of the fish from burning as the heat rises. Cook it just until the eyes turn white since overcooked fish tends to be dry.

Naturally, you shouldn't use sticks from poisonous plants like poison ivy, poison oak, dogbane or poisonous hemlock.

Spit Cooking

It most likely became a chore for our ancestors to keep turning sticks near the fire for long periods, (although it probably kept the kids out of trouble), so they eventually built a spit that would accommodate whole birds, or a hind leg of mammoth, and could simply be turned from time to time while they went about doing other important business.

The simplest kind of spit is made of green wood, with two forked limbs at the top and several outcropping branches, planted securely in the ground, and a crosspiece on which the meat is impaled.

The problem with spit cooking is that as the food cooks it slides to the lowest balance point, so if you use this method, a couple of things are important to remember: first, skewer the meat through the center and secure it with additional green spikes; second, tie it with cordage so it won't rotate until you want it to.

Once at a Woodsmoke primitive skills conference we barbecued a whole goat on a spit. This required about six hours of slow cooking, so the spit was situated well above the ground to prevent the meat from burning. The height of the spit can easily be adjusted by raising or lowering the crosspiece as needed. The distance between the food and the fire dictates the length of time necessary to cook the meat.

You can also make a "gypsy" spit by constructing a four-pronged tripod over a small pit. Then build a fire in the pit and let it burn down to a good bed of coals. Tie a chunk of meat tightly with cordage and suspend it from the fork in the tripod about twenty-four inches above the fire. Double-twist the cordage so it winds and unwinds, slowly turning the meat over the coals. (A little wild sage rubbed into the meat adds a nice flavor.) If your fire is too hot, or flames threaten to burn your food, simply cover the burning wood with ashes.

It is important to cook meat slowly and evenly. More game meat is ruined by overcooking than by any other misadventure because the cook has the idea that, 1) an abundance of heat is the way to assure tenderness, and 2) high temperatures burn away wild flavor.

I suppose I can reasonably say that we have developed taste prejudices against wild meat over the centuries—there is nothing at McDonalds that even mildly resembles venison—yet wild meat is actually more healthy than meat bred for the table. The fact is, game species average only 4.3% fat, compared to 25-35% in supermarket meat. The fat of game meat also tends to be much less saturated, which translates to less harmful.

Fortunately, these prejudices work themselves out with time as foods begin to assume a familiar taste, but one way to eliminate most of the wild taste in game animals is to remove as much of the fat as possible, since fat carries much of the game's flavor.

Grilling

Grilling, with the heat directly below the food, is a common technique associated with outdoor cooking. Theoretically there is very little difference between grilling and broiling, though the latter is usually done indoors in an oven, the heat coming from above the food. Grilling is dry-heat cooking. Compared with a steam pit (cooking with moist heat, a method that will eventually tenderize tough cuts of meat), prolonged grilling will only toughen meat and dry it out—so precise timing is important if you expect to turn out a meal you can eat.

I generally devise a grill, or grate, by weaving a number of green willow stems to form a lattice that can be suspended over low heat coals. It takes a little more time, but you may want to add a second lattice of branches with leaves attached over the grate to prevent moisture from escaping as the food cooks. Again, the trench fire is best for this kind of cooking.

About one and a half inches is a good thickness for grilled meat. At that thickness you can grill close to the coals—turning once without a lot of fussing with height adjustments. Just be careful not to place the grate so close to the coals that it burns through the wood, and you loose your food in the fire.

It's hard to give any steadfast times for grilling meat. Much depends on the distance between the meat and the coals, as well as on the meat's thickness and your own preference: rare, medium or (horrors) well done. With a one-and-a-half inch piece of meat, 5-8 minutes per side is a good rule.

Since dark meat (legs and thighs) cooks slower than white meat, it makes sense to section any birds you intend to grill. Fowl needs to be

A willow grill can easily be devised for large fish and fowl that require slow simmering to prevent moisture loss. (Photo: Richard Jamison)

grilled very slowly, well above the coals, out of charring range. The ideal grilled fowl is succulent and delicately browned, unlike red meat, which can stand a thin char. As I mentioned before, the greatest tragedy to befall most grilled meat, and particularly fowl or small game like squirrel or rabbits, is overcooking because it results in dry, tough meat and a charred exterior.

To the contrary, ducks and beaver are quite fatty and create another problem. As they cook, melting fat causes flare ups that often catch fire and scorch your food—not to mention, ruin your grate. One way to prevent this is indirect cooking. When your coals have ashed over, push the center ones toward the perimeter of the fire pit, that way the food isn't cooked right over the coals. By the way, beaver tails are a succulent treat roasted directly in the coals.

Fish causes its own problems because it is naturally tender and loose-textured. It cooks quickly, and as it begins to cook the flesh flakes. That helps little in the turning department, and the problem is generally compounded by skin sticking to the grate. Be patient and kind to fish. Don't tug at it, and don't keep flopping it around and poking it with a stick. All that will get you is a messy dinner. Most fish, unless very large and thick, only needs to be turned once.

If I have only one large fish, like salmon or bass, it's easier to construct a basket from green willow as a cradle of sorts. That way I can turn the fish easily or move it around over the coals without disturbing it. And the leaves help protect the fish from burning, since it takes a little longer to cook than smaller varieties that are best cooked on a skewer. If we are lucky enough to catch several big fish, then it's less trouble to build a large willow grate and cook them all at once.

Again, it is impossible to give precise cooking times because a lot hinges on the size of the fish and the distance the fish is cooked from the coals. In general, the standard rule for fish cookery applies: ten minutes per measured inch of thickness. As with all of life's greater lessons, experience is the best teacher—with experience comes technique and refinement.

Stone Oven

The predecessor of baking was cooking animals in their skins. In Australia, when a wallaby or other animal is killed by the aborigines, they throw it whole on the fire in order to singe it. Once it is singed, it is opened and hot rocks put inside to cook it from the inside out.

Another good way to prepare meat or fish is to wrap them in leaves or grass and bake them in a stone oven. A stone oven is easy to build by forming a box of large flat rocks. You can even parch seeds or nuts on top of the flat roof of your oven at the same time you cook inside it. (I can't stress enough the importance of being absolutely certain the rocks you use are fire-proven.)

Anything can be cooked in a stone oven, just remember it is dry heat, so you should wrap your food in leaves or other greenery to keep it moist. You regulate the temperature in a stone oven very simply by piling coals around the outside next to the oven walls for more heat and scraping them away to reduce heat.

On one of our treks we experimented with bread leavened with wild yeast gathered from aspen trees and Oregon grape berries. The yeast was used to leaven our ground-seed dough, which we baked very successfully in a stone oven. To top it off, we made a passable jam from wild thimble berries and huckleberries that grew in the area and drizzled it over the bread. It was a notable trip.

Clay also makes a handy cooking container that seals in juices and provides a serving dish as well. Clay-sealed food can be cooked in your stone oven, or directly in the coals of your fire.

Low-firing red clay is best when it is available because it can be molded, but plain old mud packed around the food works in a pinch.

First, knead the clay a little until it can be shaped and flattened. Then, line your makeshift roasting dish with edible leaves, such as dock or dandelion, and lay your meat or fish on the leaves. When you cook fish in clay, the skin forms a protective layer that peels away when you break the clay off, but I like to use leaves as a liner anyway to keep the food from burning and to provide moisture.

Be sure to know the identity of the greens you include in your clay dish: some plants, like sage and wild mustard, can be used sparingly to season meat and fowl but impart a bitter, unpalatable flavor to your food when they are steamed, and the resin from pine needles makes food taste like turpentine. This warning goes double for wild vegetable side dishes since poisonous hemlock is almost identical to wild carrot at some stages of growth, and death camas looks a lot like wild onion in the early Spring.

Next, seal the edges of your clay container carefully and place it into the oven, or bury it in the hot coals of your fire. Turning is not necessary and may even cause the seal to break, spilling juices.

Ash Cooking

As the coals of your fire burn down they naturally create the final phase of your cooking fire—a bed of ashes. To many people, ash cooking may seem a doubtful suggestion. And not surprisingly, what is the first reaction you hear when ashes blow into someone's camp food? Loud protests, followed by a scramble to scoop the soot out before it contaminates the food, right? I have never understood how a student can wear the same underwear for fifteen days yet complain about a little dirt that gets into his or her food.

I suppose the reason most people act this way is that they don't understand what ashes really are. Ashes are not dirt. Ash is the light, fluffy residue from burned wood. You may even be surprised to learn that food cooked in ashes is indeed more sanitary than food cooked in pans, because the fire kills the bacteria. The ashes are actually purified by the heat of the fire.

And, despite the way it may look, cooking in ashes does not affect the taste of your food—once it is cooked you can easily blow the ashes away, leaving food clean and free from soot.

During our primitive living treks, in times when animal and plant life was scarce, the staple of our diet was ash cakes. Each student was given a small portion of wheat dough mixed with a pinch of brown sugar to make ash cakes until they adjusted to the new wild foods diet. Ash cakes were later made from ground, roasted seeds and roots mixed with water and shaped into a flat patty or tortilla. They were cooked directly in the ashes and eaten like crackers, or packed with us for trail food. Incidentally, excellent "wild" flour can be made from ground, roasted cattail roots mixed with ground sunflower seeds and pinon nuts for flavor. When we could find them, we added wild berries or currants to make ash cake turnovers that were a real delicacy. Kids love them.

You also need to make some tongs for putting the food in and taking it out of the hot coals and ashes. These can easily be made by heating a green willow stick in the ashes until it becomes pliable, then bending it in the center to make a usable tool.

As with most primitive skills, the key is patience. The secret to cooking in the ashes is not to get in a hurry—wait for your coals to turn to white ash, or you will burn your food. It is easy to cook food on flat rocks amidst the ashes, too. You've heard of frying eggs on hot pavement? This is the same principle, in fact, the predecessor of frying was parching on flat rocks. Before the Iron Age ushered in more durable devices with handles, a thin batter of acorn mush (like a tortilla) was baked in the ashes on soapstone griddles that had a little hole on one side to accommodate a hook to push it in or pull it out of the fire.

Steam Pit

The Cochise Culture (whom archaeologists believe lived on the North American Continent over 10,000 years ago) used the steaming pit as a method to prepare their foods, which consisted mainly of small game animals, nuts, berries and other seasonal plants. In Hawaii today, you can go to a luau where the main course is cooked in a pit. So the technique has obviously withstood the test of time.

Although it takes a little extra effort to prepare, the results are worth it because the steam in the pit both tenderizes and moisturizes. In my opinion, this is the most foolproof method of cooking for any kind of food, from greens to roots to meat. And it frees you for other tasks.

I have cooked everything from small ground squirrels to a hind quarter of beef in a pit with good success. And there is nothing quite like coming back to camp, exhausted after a day-long hike, uncovering the pit, and enjoying a tender, succulent hot meal without having to go through all the ordinary preliminary hassles. Multiply your delight ten-fold if a rain shower has dampened your spirits and your firewood.

To construct a pit, you will need a digging stick (and soil that can be dug up), some green plants, some large slabs of bark, if they are available, and a pile of fire-proven rocks.

A digging stick is more than just a stick used for digging, but that's another story. A digging stick is made by beveling a green stick on one end, then fire-hardening it in the ashes to give you a good hard digging edge that can be sharpened.

On the trail I use my digging stick to scoop out the pit. This is a lot of work in an age of efficient tools like shovels, and it is amazing to think that the early Hohokom Culture, who lived in the southwest over 2,000 years ago, dug their entire irrigation system (which was thousands of feet long) with digging sticks. Yet, in some aspects a digging stick is preferable to a shovel, particularly for prying rocks out of the ground.

The size of pit depends on the amount of food you plan to cook in it. It doesn't have to be extremely deep and it can be used again and again if you are in a stationary campsite, so the effort you expend is not in vain. The pit should be a minimum of two feet deep because you should reserve about one foot of space above and below your food, before the stones are added.

Select enough fire-proven rocks to tile the bottom and sides of the hole, preferably flat ones that don't take up too much space.

Using hardwoods, build a roaring hot fire inside the pit on top of the rocks to create a good bed of coals. You can also build another small fire close by and place a few stones in it to heat. These rocks will go on top of the fire pit after the food is in place and covered with grass.

Once the fire in the pit burns down and you are sure the rocks are well heated, scrape out the coals as thoroughly as possible to avoid giving your food that yummy, wet-ash flavor. It's important to work quickly at this stage so the pit doesn't cool off too much.

Because rocks hot enough to fry eggs will also burn food, line the pit with grass or other green vegetation. Green cattail or bulrush leaves work well, but be sure not to use pine, sumac or other scented plants for this purpose because they will flavor your food. The natural moisture content in the leaves and grasses help create steam (thus the name "steam pit") that both tenderizes and moistens your food just like a big pressure cooker.

Birds, rabbits and similar-sized game will cook more quickly when cut in pieces. But if you especially want to cook them whole, stuff a couple of smooth, hot rocks inside the body cavity.

Cooking vegetables is tricky business. Many early plant foods were tough and fibrous and were eaten raw, or sometimes roasted in the coals. Unlike the cultivated species, there are few wild plant foods that can go directly on a grill without some prior cooking to moisten them and relax the fibers, yet they are quite palatable when steamed in a pit. Cattail roots are particularly good when cooked in a pit, and when they are collected in the fall, the starch and protein content are about the same as potatoes.

After the food is arranged in the pit, cover it with more grass or leaves, making sure the covering is thick enough to prevent dirt from sifting

Ash cooking was probably the first method known to humans. The residue is easily blown off once the food is cooked. (Photo: Richard Jamison)

through to the food. This is a critical step unless there is water nearby to wash off the inevitable grit. Large bark slabs laid over the top layer will also help keep the dirt off the food.

Finally, sprinkle on a little water to increase the steam pit effect, then put the hot stones from your second fire on top so heat will radiate from all sides. Cover the entire pit with dirt, and seal any steam vents. Again, use care to prevent dirt from sifting through the covering to the food.

Now go about your business for a few hours; two hours for a small pit, up to four hours for a very large pit. You really can't cook it too long, but you can get impatient and dig it up too soon, so be sure to allow plenty of time, then add another half hour for good measure—you will be surprised at how long the ground will keep your meal warm.

The weather will affect the time; cold weather requires a little longer cooking time. In exceptionally cold or damp weather you can create more heat by building another fire on top of the covered pit.

Boiling

A cooking pot, more likely than not, was used by primitives along with any other reasonable method of boiling food. I'm not talking about making a molded clay vessel, but rather a container into which hot stones can be dropped to raise the temperature of the liquid enough to cook food. It can be clay, or rawhide, or even a tightly woven basket. But clay is most likely to be available in a pinch.

One way to accomplish this is to dig a hole in the earth, line it with clay and build a fire in it to harden the pot. Once the clay is fire-hardened and cool, you can pick it up and dump out the ashes. Or, you can wait until the clay is dry, carefully remove it from the hole and 'fire' it over a very hot fire. I have made several large cooking pots this way in a day or two, whereas molded pottery takes much longer to construct.

Raw skins can be used to boil food by digging a depression in the ground, staking the edge of the hide to the rim of the hole, filling it with water and using hot rocks to bring the liquid to a boil. Rawhide cooking bags can also be suspended over hot coals via a tripod in the traditional native American way.

As the stones cool, remove them with tongs or forked sticks and add new ones. It takes six or seven hot rocks to start the water boiling in approximately ten minutes, then a couple every five or ten minutes to keep it going. Don't put wet stones back into the fire, as they will explode.

The disadvantage to the clay pot cooking technique is that it is so time-consuming, more so than the pit when you consider the time it takes for the pots to dry before firing. The advantage—a hot stock pot. A ladle and spoon can easily be carved from wood, as can a bowl.

Whether you are in a survival situation or just out for enjoyment, cooking can be far more enjoyable when there are no pots and pans to scrub. And, regardless of the method you choose, I hope you find as much satisfaction in doing things the old way as I do.

If, for some reason, we decide to abandon the hectic, "good life" of our modern age and start living the real life, we will have to learn new ways to perform old tasks, like cooking. And the "new" ways would, ironically, really be the old ways of our ancient ancestors.

Tamara Wilder and Steven Edholm

Whole-Shoot
Willow Baskets

•••••••••••••••••••••••••••••••

Willows also contain salicin (which is essentially aspirin),

so if you get a headache trying to follow our directions, just

chew a "willer" twig.

Twining is one of several basic basketry techniques which is used worldwide. It is also thought to be one of the oldest. Whole shoots—shoots of plants that have not been modified, except by sometimes removing the bark—are often made into baskets using this technique.

There are a great many styles and shapes of baskets which fall under the classification of whole-shoot twining. Generally, use as well as local tradition dictate how they are constructed. In Europe, for example, whole-shoot baskets tend to be relatively large, heavy and of designs which lend themselves well to a sedentary agricultural lifestyle. By contrast, the less sedentary native peoples of Western North America traditionally tended towards whole-shoot baskets which used smaller shoots and were of more lightweight designs. These are the type of baskets which we will be discussing in this chapter.

Most of these native peoples had, and still have, highly advanced basketry traditions and wove very fine baskets for gathering, cooking, eating and storage. Many of these were woven tightly enough to hold liquids. While whole-shoot baskets are not always tight enough to fulfill these functions, they are much easier to construct. To make a refined basket requires many hours of preparation, splitting and trimming each element to size. On the other hand, there is very little time spent preparing a whole-shoot. Thus, for baskets that don't need to be so finely woven and which are to be used for such activities as portaging or as bird and fish traps, it makes a lot of sense to use whole-shoots instead; saving finer

Steven Edholm begins an "open weave" whole shoot basket. (Photo by Tamara Wilder)

baskets from excessive wear. This is not to say that finer baskets were never used or wouldn't work for these purposes. It is only that, due to their relative ease of construction, whole-shoot baskets can be preferable for these applications.

These types of whole-shoot baskets can be made either close twined, open twined or more often a combination of the two. Close twining (each row of twining sitting directly above the other) is a stronger and more durable weave (fig.1). However, a basket completely close twined can get fairly weighty.

Open twining (each row of twining spaced a short distance above the other) is a lot lighter but also less sturdy (fig. 2). In comparison, a basket with a closely twined bottom and rim, but an open twined body, is a good compromise. There are also many variations in splicing and adding techniques, starts and finishes. Traditionally, these change from region to region and from use to use, but here we will stick to one start, weave and splice.

Materials
While a variety of species provide good material for whole-shoot twining (see chapter by Pegg Mathewson on basketmaking materials), this text will be restricted to the use of willow.

True willows are trees and shrubs of the genus Salix. They occur throughout North America and have managed to adapt themselves to most, if not all, of its varied climates. Perhaps the most obvious and consistent characteristic of this genus is an affinity for water. Willows must have a source of moisture throughout the year and are often found in areas which are flooded in winter.

So when looking for willow, look for water (and vise-versa). Most

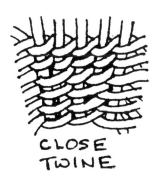

CLOSE
TWINE

OPEN
TWINE

Figure 1   *Figure 2*

rivers, creeks, seeps, springs, ditches and ponds have some species of willow growing on or near them. In fact, willows are so common that it's likely that a willow plant or patch exists within easy walking distance of wherever you are.

Unfortunately, however, not all willows are flexible enough to use for this type of tight twining. We normally use the types which have narrow, silvery leaves, reddish bark, and are found in the more arid areas of the West. Our test for pliability is to tie an overhand knot in a small shoot without it cracking. This test piece should be of one year's growth and without side branches, which brings us to the subject of management and what to collect.

Willows, under natural conditions, are often subject to fires and floods. They respond to these adversities with very rapid regrowth, producing clumps of long, evenly tapered shoots which have few or no side branches. These are the shoots that are desirable for basketry. As the tree grows from year to year, it branches out, the new growth becoming shorter, stubbier and more brittle. These are sometimes still usable, but the best shoots come from plants which were coppiced (cut back to ground level), burned, heavily pruned or damaged the previous winter and allowed to grow back through the summer. Harvesting every year, especially by coppicing, will produce the best results.

Harvesting
If you're lucky, you will find some adventitious (growing wild) shoots on plants which were cut back, burned or flooded out, in the past few years. (Be cautious, though, about harvesting shoots on road sides unless you are sure herbicides have not been sprayed.) If you can find no adventitious shoots, cut some plants back during winter or early spring to gather the following year. Don't clear-cut every willow patch you see; a few vigorous plants can yield quite a bit of weaving material.

If the shoots are gathered in the dormant season (from leaf drop to bud swell), the bark will adhere tenaciously. If they are harvested in early spring (just after bud break), the bark slips off easily. By mid spring, anything that was not cut will begin branching out and will become less desirable. We prefer to harvest during the dormant season and weave with the bark on. This way the shoots are less prone to cracking and have greater wear resistance.

You can harvest an array of shoot sizes, but you'll only use two basic sizes for each basket, one for twiners and one for spokes. The spokes, or ribs, of your basket are the larger of the two. We suggest that you start with spokes that are a half to two-thirds the size of a pencil at the butt ends. The twiners should be about half the size of the spokes. A good handful of each will go a long way.

After harvesting, the willow can be used fresh, or it can be dried out and then reconstituted later. If used fresh it will shrink as it dries, making for a somewhat looser basket. However, we use fresh shoots a lot and they work fine as long as everything is pulled tight. If the willow is dried and reconstituted, the finished basket will be somewhat tighter and more stiff.

To dry the willows, simply bundle them and put them in a dry place. To reconstitute them, completely submerge them in water for about forty-eight hours. Larger diameter sticks take more time. Don't soak them too long, though, or they will start to rot and the fibers will weaken.

To keep fresh shoots fresh, put them in a shady place sealed in a plastic bag or put the butt-ends in water. If these are left too long, they will begin to grow roots and then leaves. This can be used to advantage by planting them in a moist spot, thus starting your own willow patch.

Willow roots so easily that freshly cut, and even not-so-freshly cut, posts will often continue to grow. This is due to gibberellin, a substance in the willow, which in the form of willow tea or willow compost, can be used to help cuttings of other plants take root as well. In concentrated form, gibberellin is a potent herbicide. Willows also contain salicin (which is essentially aspirin), so if you get a headache trying to follow our directions, just chew a "willer" twig.

Hand Positions In Weaving
The fingers of the left hand reach through the spokes and pull them to the left so that the twiners may be laid snugly in place. The thumb remains free to hold down the twiners as they are brought to the front, and to assist in keeping things from unraveling.

The function of the right hand is to maneuver the twiners, pulling them tightly into place. Each twiner is pulled firmly down behind the spokes, around the back and then firmly down in the front.

Tools
The tools that you need are simple: a small, sharp knife and an awl. You can purchase a metal awl, or make your own out of bone or a modified nail. The awl need not be very sharp since it is for opening up spaces in the weaving and not for poking holes in the material. However, it must have a smooth, tapered tip.

Some Things to Remember
Keep everything pulled tight.

Make sure that everything stays moist. If anything dries out at all, soak it a little in plain water. It's a good idea to dip your whole basket periodically as well. You can also stop and let your basket dry out at anytime. Then when you're ready to work on it again, re-soak the whole thing.

Most baskets are constructed of many small pieces. For this reason, weaving (twining) is something you do between adding and splicing. Accepting this can save you a lot of frustration when your twining is constantly interrupted by the need to add new materials. However, once all of the movements become more natural, these interruptions will have a minimum impact on the weaving continuum.

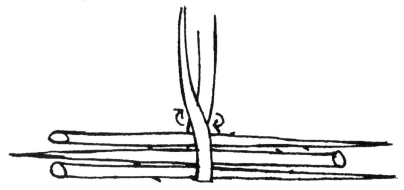

Figure 3

The Start

Select six spokes of similar length and thickness.

Choose a long twiner and fold it slightly off center, at a point a third of the length from the butt end. The butt and tip ends should alternate.

Insert three spokes into the fold, holding this together and flat with the left hand, grasp both twiner ends with the right hand, pull them hard and twist them a half twist away from you. This twist should pinch the spokes very tightly in place, but the spokes should lie side by side and not be allowed to bunch up (fig. 3). (Note: the length of the spokes and twiners in the diagrams have been greatly shortened in order to show tip and butt ends.)

Holding everything together tightly with the left hand, insert the other three spokes into the twist. Hold all of this tight and flat with the left hand, and repeat the a half twist away from you as before (fig. 4).

Rotate the second set of three spokes clockwise a quarter turn to form a criss-cross in front of the first set of three spokes (fig. 5).

Twine around the next two sets of three spokes. Bring Twiner 1, which is behind the spokes, forward and lay it in front of the last set of three spokes, now pull Twiner 2 around behind the last set of three spokes and then once again in front at point X where you started (fig.6).

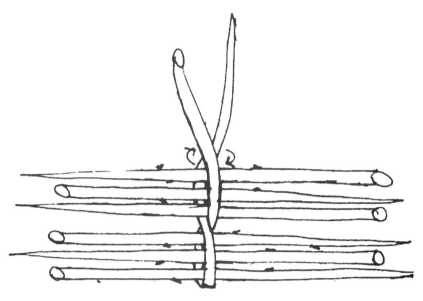

Figure 4

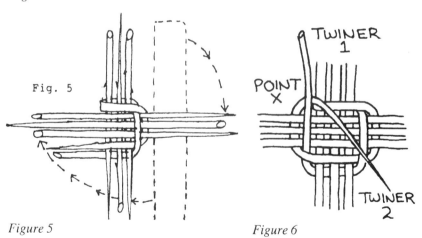

Fig. 5

Figure 5   *Figure 6*

Whether your start seems to have turned out well or not, we strongly suggest that you dismantle it and redo it a couple of times for three reasons: First, you will probably get everything a little tighter after several tries, secondly, you will be more likely to remember the start next time, and lastly, you may have done something backwards.

Twining

Having completed your start, you will now begin from point X twining around individual spokes instead of groups of three. Grasping the start with your left hand, hold Twiner 2 in place against the start with your left thumb. With your right hand, bring Twiner 1 back behind at Point X and then forward again between Spokes A and B (fig 7).

Pull it firmly into place and lay it flat against the front of the start. Transfer your left thumb to it, letting go of Twiner 2 which should now be pinched securely in place. With the right hand, bring Twiner 2 back between Spokes A and B, pull it back firmly and then forward between Spokes B and C. Pull it down to lay against the start. Releasing Twiner 1, hold it in place with your left thumb (fig.8). This is twining. Alternately each twiner passes in front of the following spoke, behind the next, and then forward again.

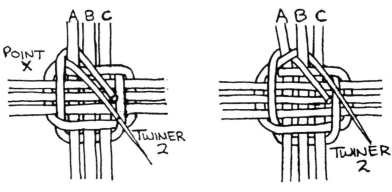

Figure 7   *Figure 8*

Splicing

All too soon you will notice that one of your twiners is getting short. Your first splice should be onto the butt-end of the first twiner (which was folded over). After this, you will be splicing onto the tip ends as they become thin. Always splice to the forward twiner, that is the one that you have just brought forward. Leave at least an inch of length on the old twiner to splice onto. Select a new twiner and insert it, butt end first, between the spokes and under the twiner being replaced (fig.9). The new twiner should stick out through the back of the start a half inch or so. Hold it there with the fingers of your left hand.

With your right hand, bring the end of the old twiner down to the left, under the new twiner, and up to lie parallel with the left spoke. Hold it in place with your left thumb. Again with the right hand, grasp the twiner that was not replaced and continue to weave with it, passing over the splice, behind the next spoke, and forward again (fig 10).

If everything was done properly and tightly, the splice should be pinched in place so that it cannot unravel (fig. 11). If not, unwrap and try it again. Continue twining until you reach Point X, splicing onto the other twiner each time it becomes too thin.

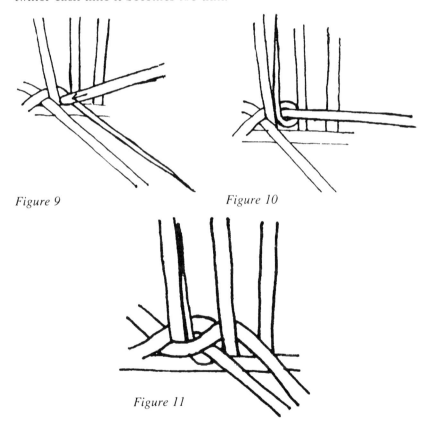

Figure 9

Figure 10

Figure 11

Adding Spokes

In order to make your basket expand you must add spokes. On the next row you will add a spoke to each of the four corners of the start. This will even things out and make it look more like the spokes of a wheel than a cross (fig.12).

Select four new spokes and bevel each butt end with a long sloping cut which is two or three times the diameter of the spoke in length.

Add the first spoke between Spokes C and D. Using an awl, gently open a space in the weaving alongside Spoke C. Remove the awl, and slide the new spoke deep into the start with the bevel facing Spoke C (fig.13).

Continue twining. Twine around the new spoke, as though it had always been there. Add a spoke to each corner in the same way (fig.14). On the next round, add a new spoke next to every other spoke. This will give your basket a good flat foundation.

Point X marks the beginning of each row. Try to keep track of it as it is the point where you begin anything new. If you like, twist a piece of colored thread around the spoke next to Point X to mark it clearly. When you change the rate at which you add spokes, do it at the beginning of the row and keep it up until the end. Doing this will keep your basket more uniform.

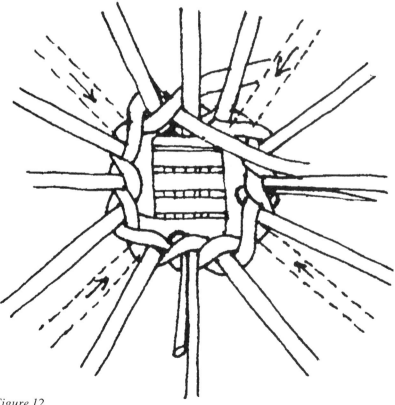

Figure 12

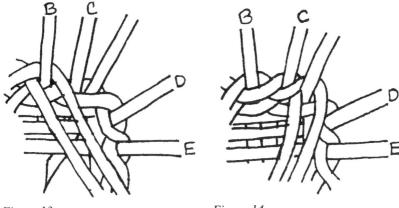

Figure 13   *Figure 14*

Shaping the Basket

The shape and size of your basket should be determined by the number and placement of the spokes. To make a flat tray, you need to add a lot of spokes consistently throughout the basket. If you add too many, however, the basket will become wavy like a warped record.

To make a cone-shaped basket, add fewer spokes but just as regularly. To make a bowl-shaped basket, add spokes for a while to form the base and then stop altogether, allowing the sides to turn up.

You can also shape your basket somewhat by bending the spokes into place. For a bowl-shaped basket, manipulate the spokes away from you as you progress. This way you will always be working from the outside of the basket and all of the splice ends will be on the inside. On a flat tray, however, the splice ends should stick out on the underside.

After you have twined three or four rows, you can decide whether you want to open or close twine. To close twine, continue just as you have, pulling each row down as close as possible to the previous row. Stop between rounds and pack each row of twining down with the side of your awl. To open twine, start sloping up at the beginning of a row. When you reach the distance you want to be from the previous row, continue parallel to it. It is even more important to use small twiners and keep everything tight when open twining.

Finishing

When you have achieved the size and shape of basket you want, you must do some kind of finish. The finish keeps the basket from unraveling and hides all the spokes protruding at the top. If you have been open twining, close twine a few rows to form a rim before you do the finish. Certain finishes also reinforce the rim, which is sometimes necessary.

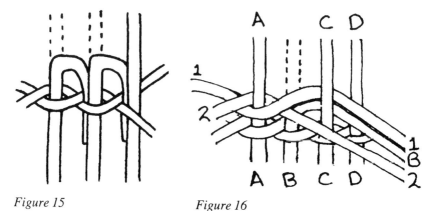

Figure 15   *Figure 16*

Before you begin the finish, you should soak the basket, especially the top where all the spokes are sticking out. You will be bending the spokes sharply and they will crack if they are too dry. Remember to start your finish at the beginning of a row. One simple finish is made by folding each spoke over and down next to the following spoke, and twining around both. The end of the spokes are left pointing down on the inside of the basket (fig.15).

A more complicated finish, one which also reinforces the rim somewhat, involves twining with the spokes. It is a little more intricate than the previous finish, but don't give up too easily!

Instead of twining around Spoke B, fold it over so that it pairs with Twiner 1 and bring both of them around the back of Spoke C and forward (fig.16).

Now fold Spoke A over so that it pairs with Twiner 2. Bring the pair A-2 in front of the following two upright spokes and then back between Spokes D and E (fig.17).

Now drop Twiner 2, holding it flat against the inside of the basket, and replace it with Spoke D, which pairs with A. This should pinch Twiner 2 in place. Bring the new pair D-A forward between Spokes E and F (fig.18).

Next bring pair 1-B back behind and to the right of Spoke F, drop them to the back and replace them with Spoke F. Fold Spoke C over so that it comes across the front and pairs with Spoke F. Continue around the back of Spoke G and forward with the new pair F-C (fig.19). Keep going the same way. Each left-hand pair of twiners passes in front of two upright spokes and then back. They are dropped to the inside of the basket and replaced by the spoke to the left which folds over to pinch them in place. The far left upright spoke then folds over to pair with this spoke/twiner and the two continue around the next spoke.

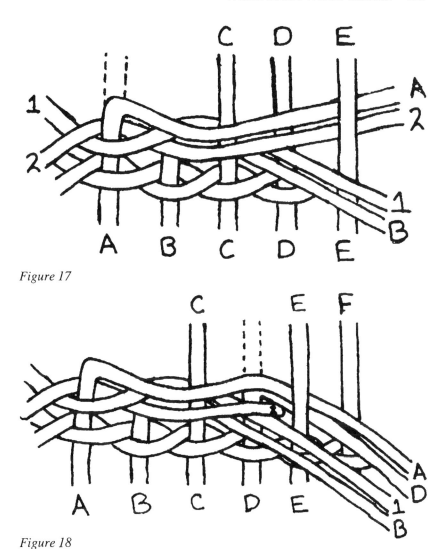

Figure 17

Figure 18

Final Touches

At the end of a finish, work the last twiners into the weaving so that they are held in place. You can either cut off all of the ends that you dropped down, or you can work them into the weave for a more finished look. If you cut them off, leave at least a half inch length until the basket dries.

Before the basket dries, you may want to add hoops or sticks to shape and strengthen it. This is especially important for larger baskets. Weights,

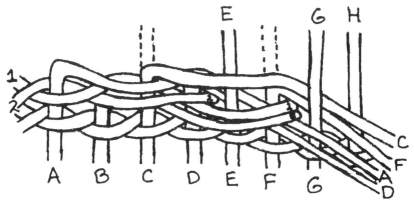

Figure 19

props, another basket or whatever you invent can be used to hold your basket in a desired shape until it dries.

Once the basket is completely dry, go back and trim the splice and finished ends closer on the inside of the basket.

You now have a completed basket. Congratulations. Now go use it!

Whole shoot willow baskets of various sizes and shapes serve many useful purposes and with practice are simple to construct. (Photo by Tamara Wilder)

Tamara uses a tump line for comfort and ease in carrying a conical burden basket, a common use among traditional peoples worldwide. (Photo: Steven Edholm)

Linda Jamison

A Paleo Prescription
The Hunter-Gatherer Diet

• •

The hunter-gatherer diet was eaten by all people on earth

before the coming of agriculture about 10,000 years ago.

It was refined over hundreds of thousands of years. So if

there is a diet natural to the human makeup, one to which

our genes are still best suited, this is it.

There was a specific diet we were designed to eat. The one we ate when we were evolving. It's harder to get, prepare, eat and digest than the foods we know and love, but it's low fat, low salt, low refined carbohydrates, high fiber, high complex carbos, and high protein. It's natural. And combined with the right exercise plan, which is natural too, people who follow it will start to shape up. It is the hunter-gatherer diet.

For Homo erectus to be able to adapt to the more temperate climate of Europe and Asia, it was necessary not only to tame fire, but to have both effective shelter and clothing to protect against heat loss, and to store dried meat and other foods for use in the lean months.[1]

These people were hunters and foragers who lived in tiny bands of a few families, perhaps only encountering a handful of strangers in their short lives. Among their many skills, they developed new techniques for meat preparation.

The limbs and carcass were first separated, then pounded so that the bones were broken into small pieces and the meat could be hung easily on nearby drying racks. Drying meat concentrates the protein, increasing the food value per pound. It also allowed the hunters to store meat, making them less reliant on seasonal movements of their prey.

But game meat was not their only source of food. Without question,

137

wild plant foods collected by the women were of paramount importance, perhaps eaten more frequently than animal flesh. By 130,000 years ago, plant grinders and pounders were in widespread use, so less palatable meat and vegetable foods could be processed, then cooked, before it was eaten. Everything points to a more efficient hunter-gatherer lifestyle, one based not only on game and plants, but sometimes on fish, shellfish, and some sea mammals as well.[2]

The first Homo sapiens who lived in the Savanna homeland enjoyed a virtual "Garden of Eden" that was even richer than it is today. South of Ethiopia and Somalia lies a vast region of plains, great mountains and plateaux that drain into the Indian Ocean on the eastern side, and into the lake basins of the far interior. It is a varied environment with subtle seasonal changes and great natural diversity. The rainy season brings lush grass amid a deep green woodland. Timid, small antelope and other woodland animals graze at the fringes of the forest. Vast herds of wildebeest and zebra range over open grassland plains, gathering near the ponds and seasonal water holes where lions and other predators lie in wait. A myriad of trees and plants yield edible fruit and nuts for humans and animals alike.[3]

In a sense, Africa was a giant nursery for modern humanity, a relatively undemanding environment where food was fairly plentiful, where Ice Age climatic changes were relatively benign.

According to physical anthropologist and ecologist Robert Foley of the University of Cambridge, early populations of Homo sapiens ranged over large territories, lived in groups with some kin-based social structure, and were highly selective in their eating habits, preferring meat and nutritious nuts and fruits. Plant foods were relatively predictable because they came into season at regular times of the year. Game animals, the major human prey on the savanna, are much less predictable, because they can redistribute at will. Even more important, they are far from easy to kill once located, especially if one has to kill them at close range. So how does the typical hunter-gatherer diet compare to what we eat now? The difference between our diet today and that of our hunter-gatherer forbears may hold keys to many of our current health problems. Particularly since the greatest single threat to the survival of our species is our diet.

Today's so-called balanced diet includes foods from four major groups: meat, fish, and poultry; breads and cereals; fruits, nuts and vegetables; and dairy products. Whereas, people living before the development of agriculture had no dairy foods at all, except for infants at mother's breast, and seeds and grains were available only in such small amounts as could be collected from seed-producing wild plants. So almost the entire diet was derived from wild game, uncultivated vegetables and fruits, and insects.

In fact, plant foods were the staples of diet even before the advent of agriculture. A great variety of plant foods were eaten, and the bulk of carbohydrates consumed in the past were complex, unlike the finely ground flours and refined sugars so abundant in our current diet. As a result, intake of non-nutrient dietary fiber was greater. Without knowing why, our forebears were on the right track. One of the greatest risks a human being can take is to allow the remnants of their food to remain in contact with the lining of the colon for three and four days at a time. Yet Americans and others who eat a modern diet are doing just that. Our grandparents had the right idea when they instinctively felt that there was something vaguely undesirable about becoming constipated. Analysis of 153 species of wild plant foods eaten by hunters and gatherers shows the average protein to be 4.13% and fiber content 12.6%–much higher than in our plant foods. Thousands of years of plant breeding and modern food processing have greatly increased simple, less desirable sugars, decreased many needed carbohydrates and increased calorie content. (*See table on the next page*)

As for meat, 43 game species relied on by various hunter and gatherer groups averaged only 4.3% fats, compared to 25-35% in supermarket meat. Overall, the average diet of hunters and gatherers consisted of 33% protein, compared to 12% in the modern American diet, an equal percentage (46%) of carbohydrates, and 21% fat with a high ration of polyunsaturates, compared to our 42%.[4]

The fat of game meat tends to be much less saturated, meaning less harmful, because the browse eaten by game animals is higher in polyunsaturated fat than the artificial stuff fed to cattle and pigs. And, the excess fat in today's meat animals is storage fat (found in layers under the skin, in the marbling of muscle tissue, and within the abdominal cavity) which is overwhelmingly saturated.

As for our fat-loaded dairy products–ice cream, butter, cheese, milk– early people had none at all. Nor did our ancestors garnish their roots with sour cream, add salad dressings to their greens or spread their wheat and seed cakes with a greasy layer of margerine.

Although early people did enjoy simple sugars from honey and fruit, studies of fossil teeth show that they ate far fewer sweets than we do. And, except for a deficiency of iodine in some geographical locations, our ancestors probably ate an abundance of vitamins and minerals (including calcium, even without any dairy foods). Their intake of potassium exceeded their intake of sodium. For most western people throughout the

Nutritional Composition of Wild Foods (per 100 grams)

Dashes denote lack of data for a constituent believed to be present in measurable amounts

Source: Composition of Foods, U.S. Dept. of Agriculture*

Plant	Calories	Protein (grams)	Fat (grams)	Calcium (mg)	Phosphorus (mg)	Iron (mg)	Sodium (mg)
Amaranth, leaf	36.0	3.5	0.5	267.0	67.0	3.9	-
Dandilion, leaf	45.0	2.7	0.7	187.0	66.0	3.1	76.0
Dock, leaf	28.0	2.1	0.3	66.0	41.0	1.6	5.0
Jerusalem Artichoke, root	75.0	2.3	0.1	14.0	78.0	3.4	-
Lamb's Quarter, leaf	43.0	4.2	0.8	309.0	72.0	1.2	-
Mallow, leaf	37.0	4.4	0.6	249.0	69.0	12.7	-
Mustard, leaf	31.0	3.0	0.5	183.0	50.0	3.0	32.0
Nettle, leaf	19.0	2.2	0.3	58.0	46.0	2.6	159.0
Onion, leaves	36.0	1.5	0.2	51.0	39.0	1.0	5.0
Poke, leaf	65.0	5.5	0.7	-	-	-	-
Poke, shoots (cooked)	20.0	2.3	0.4	53.0	33.0	1.2	-
Prickly Pears, fruit	42.0	0.5	0.1	20.0	28.0	0.3	2.0
Purslane	0.0	21.0	1.7	0.4	103.0	39.0	3.5
Rape, leaf	32.0	3.6	0.6	252.0	62.0	30.0	-
Salsify, root	13.0	2.9	0.6	47.0	66.0	1.5	-
Shepherd's purse, leaf	33.0	4.2	0.5	208.0	86.0	4.8	-
Sow thistle, leaf	20.0	2.4	0.3	93.0	35.0	3.1	-
Violet, leaf	-	-	-	-	-	-	-
Water Cress, leaf	19.0	2.2	0.3	151.0	54.0	1.7	52.0

Plant	Potassium (mg)	Vit. A (IU)	Thiamine (mg)	Riboflavin (mg)	Niacin (mg)	Vit. C (mg)
Amaranth, leaf	411.0	6,100.0	0.1	0.2	1.4	80.0
Dandilion, leaf	397.0	14,000.0	0.2	0.3	-	35.0
Dock, leaf	338.0	12,900.0	0.1	0.2	0.5	119.0
Jerusalem Artichoke, root	-	20.0	0.2	0.1	1.3	4.0
Lamb's Quarter, leaf	-	11,600.0	0.2	0.4	1.2	80.0
Mallow, leaf	-	2,190.0	0.1	0.2	1.0	35.0
Mustard, leaf	377.0	7,000.0	0.1	0.2	0.8	97.0
Nettle, leaf	795.0	4,300.0	0.0	0.2	0.6	30.0
Onion, leaves	231.0	2,000.0	0.1	0.1	0.4	32.0
Poke, leaf	-	6,500.0	-	-	-	76.0
Poke, shoots (cooked)	-	8,700.0	0.1	0.3	1.1	82.0
Prickly Pears, fruit	166.0	60.0	0.0	0.0	0.4	22.0
Purslane	-	-	0.0	0.0	0.1	0.5
Rape, leaf	-	1,355.0	0.3	0.3	1.1	118.0
Salsify, root	380.0	10.0	0.0	0.0	0.3	11.0
Shepherd's purse, leaf	394.0	1,554.0	0.1	0.2	0.4	36.0
Sow thistle, leaf	-	2,185.0	0.7	0.1	0.4	5.0
Violet, leaf	-	8,200.0	-	-	-	210.0
Water Cress, leaf	282.0	4,900.0	0.0	0.2	0.9	79.0

* Christopher Nyerges, Wild Greens and Salads, (Harrisburg: Stackpole, 1982) pp. 192-193.

world, the reverse is now true. In fact, hunter-gatherer sodium consumption is estimated at 690 milligrams daily, which came from wild game and plants and on rare occasions, natural salt licks, as compared to between 2,000 and 7,000 for present-day Americans. As for blood pressure, which has at least some relationship to salt intake, six contemporary hunting and gathering groups were below 120/80, normal for modern Americans and Western Europeans, and unlike us, showed no increase with age.

Our hunter-gatherer cousins were also physically fit throughout their lives. To get their game, the men had to walk until they were in throwing range, after which they may have had to cross thorn-ridden wilderness in a dead heat with, say, an antelope, then cart the beast home. Women had to carry 20-30 pounds of kids on their foraging treks, and on the way back home another several pounds of fruits, nuts and roots. To top it off, shortages were periodically imposed on early people, so they could not have become obese even if their unavoidable exercise were insufficient to prevent weight gain. And it's not surprising to learn from fossil remains that our remote ancestors possessed great muscular strength, considerably more than is typical of today's Westerners.

The hunter-gatherer diet was eaten by all people on earth before the coming of agriculture about 10,000 years ago. It was refined over hundreds of thousands of years. So if there is a diet natural to the human makeup, one to which our genes are still best suited, this is it.

Apart from the diet of early Stone Age people, we can evaluate other aspects of their life style. In isolated locations and in certain seasons, some pre-agricultural people probably chewed tobacco—as do modern-day hunters and gatherers like the Australian aborigines, for example. Tobacco was absent from most of the Old World, however, until the European discovery of America, and the New World was not populated until long after the appearance of anatomically modern humans about 40,000 years ago. Smoking almost certainly postdates the advent of agriculture 10,000 years ago and cigarettes were not even developed until after the Crimean War, in the mid-1850s.

As for alcoholic beverages, if pre-agricultural people had any local breweries they probably operated only seasonally and produced libations by natural fermentation, not distillation. This would have resulted in beer, for example, as opposed to whiskey. Furthermore, studies of recent hunter-gathering peoples show that among them drinking is subject to customs that limit the frequency and place of consumption, degree of allowable intoxication, and types of behavior that will be tolerated. In such circumstances, the solitary, addictive, pathological drinking found in Western and many European societies is almost nonexistent.

Overall, contemporary hunter-gatherers are healthier than we are, at least with regard to those diseases of civilization: heart attack, cancer, stroke, hypertension, obesity, and diabetes—that cause deaths in affluent Western nations. They do not suffer from atherosclerosis, which predisposes us toward heart disease. This is because they are not exposed to cigarettes, eat relatively little fat and generally maintain a high level of aerobic fitness. A diet low in sodium, but containing ample potassium and calcium, keeps their blood pressures constant over the years, while ours tends to rise with age, and they experience little or no hypertension.

Still, it is possible that our poor diet and resulting bad health is not altogether our fault. A taste for fat, like that for sugar, seems to be part of our human makeup. According to the theory of evolutionary surplus, our taste for fats, sweets and salt is a product of natural selection. Built into the taste centers of our brains is a little urge that says something like: "consume as much of those things as you can...stock up for a rainy day...a shortage will come along and overdraw your fat bank." Our brains go for what was once, under conditions of limited availability, the evolutionary surplus.[5]

Extensive mounting evidence, most recently in the form of two studies in the *New England Journal of Medicine*, points to a strong genetic component in obesity. Most of us have a genetic tendency, from the distant past, to load up on goodies under conditions of abundance.

Of course, some fat (polyunsaturated) is indispensable to our diets and to eliminate it completely would be harmful. But the kinds and amount of fat we eat hurts our health. For example, fast-food (or is it fat-food) chains have prospered on fried foods, which multiply the fat content of a base food item: fried shrimp have more than ten times the fat that boiled shrimp do, and French fries have more than eighty times as much fat as baked potatoes.

Fatty foods can even cause stress in your body and make you less alert; fatty foods take five to seven hours to digest. (Recent reports show foods that are high in carbohydrates release a calming chemical called serotonin, while proteins containing the amino acid tyrosine, increases alertness.)[6] Susan Shapiro, Ph.D., an L.A. psychotherapist who counsels patients on nutritional issues and eating disorders, explains that stress can trigger cravings. Most people snack because they think they are hungry when they are really reacting to stress, which prompts a physiological response very similar to hunger. Psychologically, we perceive eating the foods we like as a solution to problems.[7]

Frankly, if we "are what we eat" as the cliche goes, then as a modern western society, we are in serious trouble. Not only do we not eat the right

Nutritional Values of Wild Game and Fish

Nearly all fish and wild game are lower in fat and higher in protein than their domestic counterparts. Venison, for example, has only 6.4 grams of fat per 100 grams of edible meat, while beef has 25 grams of fat per 100 grams of meat. Furthermore, venison contains 33.5 grams of protein per 100 edible grams, while beef has only 17.4. Not to mention the fact that fish and wild game don't harbor growth hormones or antibiotics as most domesticated meats do. The main concern in eating wild game is possible pesticide poisoning of animals. For example, stay away from deer that range near the Rocky Mountain Arsenal!

Wild Game

Description	Calories	Protein	Fat
Bear	148	18.6	8.2
Dove	140	21.6	1.7
Duck - wild mallard	233	21.1	15.8
Duck - wild widgeon	154	22.6	2.2
Moose	123	25.1	2.5
Muskrat (roasted)	153	27.2	4.1
Opossum (roasted)	221	30.2	10.2
Pheasant	151	24.3	5.2
Quail	168	25.0	6.8
Rabbit	135	21.0	5.0
Squirrel	115	10.1	3.8
Venison	201	33.5	6.4

Domestic Animals

Description	Calories	Protein	Fat
Beef - trimmed, choice, raw	301	17.4	25.1
Chicken - fryer, raw	124	18.6	4.9
Duck - domestic, raw	326	16.0	28.1
Lamb - choice, raw	263	16.5	21.3
Pork - trimmed, lean-med fat, raw	308	15.6	26.1

Source: U.S. Department of Agriculture, Georgia, and Alaska Cooperative Extension Services. Based on 100 grams of edible meat.

Fish
Wild fish also are lower in fat and higher in protein content than farm-raised fish. Frog legs and turtles are also low in fat and high in protein. Obviously, care should be taken particularly with regard to fish taken from natural water sources to insure that the environment is not contaminated. This is critical in the Great Lakes area of Wisconsin and in New York; states that issue PCB contaminate advisories and, of course, definately don't eat any fish from Love Canal!

Description	Calories	Protein	Fat
Bass, largemouth	104	18.8	2.6
Bullhead	84	16.3	1.6
Carp	115	18.0	4.2
Catfish	103	17.6	3.1
Crappie	79	16.8	0.8
Perch	91	19.5	0.9
Pike, northern	88	19.5	1.1
Salmon, Atlantic	217	22.5	13.3
Salmon, chinook	222	19.1	15.6
Salmon, coho	136	21.5	5.7
Smelt	98	18.6	2.1
Trout, brook	101	19.2	2.1
Trout, lake	168	18.3	10.1
Trout, rainbow	195	21.5	11.4
Walleye	93	19.3	1.2

Source: published by the University of Wisconsin Sea Grant Institute. Based on a 3.5 ounce 100 gram portion of raw fish.

foods, but we don't eat them at the right times or in the proper amounts. Eating excessively diverts blood from the brain to the stomach, and the under-eater deprives the brain of essential nutrients.

Almost everyone has had sudden cravings for an orange, an apple, a piece of meat, a salad, a potato–something nutritious. That is why serious vitamin deficiencies are nearly impossible in healthy people consuming unprocessed food. Nutritional diseases only become manifest when the human diet is artificially manipulated. Until recently that was the result of wars, famines and plagues. Nowadays it is the result of a desire to consume white bread, nitrite-packed hot dogs, rainbow-colored low-fiber breakfast cereal, frozen pizza, chemical-laden Cool Whip, Tang (brought to us by Astronauts), Pringles' idea for potato chips and hundreds of other factory-made foods. Frankly, for the past fifty or more years, America's horses, pigs, cattle and sheep have been eating better than its human citizens.

Left alone, the human organism has the ability to select its own perfectly balanced diet. Food cravings triggered by physiological and psychological circumstances are nature's way of telling you what your body needs. The trick is to learn to read them. Since the body needs food fuel every four to five hours, people who skip meals or let too much time elapse between them may unintentionally set themselves up for cravings by allowing blood sugar levels to drop. Then we mistakenly go for a fat fix which is not the best choice.

So here we are, in an unprecedented evolutionary situation, surrounded by endless supplies of fat, sugar and salt undiluted by fiber and never exposed to the needed, corrective shortage unless we impose it on ourselves. And this progress, foolish as it is, continues to do us great damage.

But just changing our diet to bread, vegetables and fruit and lean meat won't completely overcome the problems associated with what we eat today. For example, the bread we buy in stores isn't really bread at all. Real bread is made from grains ground into flour, mixed with yeast and salt and sometimes a little milk. What is sold in stores disguised as bread is synthesized from what is left of the grain of wheat after everything worthwhile is removed—wheat germ, bran, and most of the vitamins and minerals. The starchy powder that remains is mixed with chemicals like calcium bromate, sodium stearyl fumarate, and tricalcium phosphate, to name a few. As a touching gesture, federal law requires bakers to add hard-to-absorb synthetic vitamins to replace the 24 or so nutrients removed in the milling process.[8] Is it surprising that the United States has the highest rate of colon cancer in the world?

There are several ways of restoring health to our daily diets. First, we could switch to the staple menu of rural Africans and Asians. That means ground corn, boiled bananas, freshly dug potatoes, rice and plenty of beans. Most Americans would be reluctant to make that kind of change. Or, we can adapt the modern diet so that it prolongs our lives—and the lives of our children—instead of shortening them. We can thread our way through the maze of potentially lethal, fresh-from-the-factory, simulated foods and eat the way human beings were designed to eat. We can nourish our bodies the way men and women nourished theirs for 50,000 years— before heart attacks, colon cancer, diabetes, and all the other degenerative diseases that we take for granted felled millions of innocent victims.

By picking and choosing the best from their life style along with the best from ours, we should be able to forestall, or even prevent, many currently prominent diseases and thus live longer, healthier lives.

Nor does our diet have to be boring. Dr. Leslie G. Freeman said of Cro-Magnon peoples at El Juyo Cave in Spain, "they lived well," as he and his colleagues dined on grilled oysters, salmon, mountain goat, and venison, along with wild greens and a fermented honey drink, a menu based on research at the cave. Among the finds were more than 1,000 identifiable seeds of 45 genera, brought from miles around. The plant remains (not fossilized, but protected by encapsulating clay for 14,000 years) also included grasses used for bedding or teas, wild pansy, rosemary, and raspberry.[9]

Evolution gave us a reasoning brain and if we can figure out why primitive people didn't get heart attacks, we should be able to modify our own hand-to-mouth existence. The struggle is our evolutionary legacy.

Wendy Schweitzer demonstrates convenient use position of bark basket resting on thigh while harvesting Golden Currents. (Photo by Jim Riggs)

Jim Riggs

Barking Up the Right Tree
Juniper-Bark Berry Baskets

● ●

...while picking currants one day, I suddenly realized that the curved basket bottom meshed perfectly with the opposite curvature of my upper thigh. This use-position, with the strap around neck and one shoulder, props the mouth of the basket upward and forward and frees both hands to rapidly and efficiently strip berries into it. How neat!

After attending the 1990 Rivercane Rendezvous in northern Georgia in mid April, I made a trip up into North Carolina to visit my old pal Doug Elliott. Having made dozens of one-piece folded and laced bark baskets using western juniper (Juniperus occidentalis) here in Eastern Oregon, one of my goals while in the Southeast was to gain experience making some tulip poplar baskets to note firsthand the similarities or differences in the materials and process. I figured I could find no better teacher than Doug—his house is bedecked with literally hundreds of tulip poplar baskets, more styles, sizes and forms than any one person could seemingly imagine, let alone produce!

During a marathon day-hike through his forest (alien to Western me— "What's this Doug? And this? What's this used for?"), we found a young tulip poplar freshly cut and left by loggers (it had been in their way). Later in the hike we fortuitously encountered a hickory sapling bruised, scarred and bent over by loggers. Doug's eyes lit up (Well, his eyes are really never un-lit!) and he showed me how to strip long narrow lengths of bark from the base to the top of the tree. We then split outer from inner bark, and coiled and kept the latter for our lacing material.

149

We also cut through several outer growth rings of the wood proper at the base of the tree and peeled away splints for the basket rim reinforcement hoops. It pleased us that all necessary materials for several baskets had been salvaged from others' waste. Back at Doug's place we began the actual basket construction.

Aboriginal Bark Containers
In the arid Northern Great Basin and semi-arid interior Columbia River Plateau regions of the Pacific Northwest, most of the native-produced folded bark baskets I've seen appear to be made of western juniper. While I've not experimented with them yet, the Common Juniper (Juniperus communis), the Rocky Mountain juniper (Juniperus scopulorum) and perhaps others should also work. In the moister forests of northern Idaho and western Montana westward to the Cascade Mountains and coasts of Oregon, Washington and British Columbia, natives used mainly bark of the western red cedar (Thuja plicata), occasionally Alaska yellow cedar (Chamaecyparis nootkatensis), and minimally a few others not identified in my available literature. (For an illustrated informative article, "Cedar Bark Baskets" by Mary D. Schlick, describing contemporary rejuvenation of the craft by a native Yakima man, see *American Indian Basketry Magazine*, Vol. IV. No. 3. Issue No. 15.)

To my knowledge, the actual antiquity of aboriginally produced bark containers in the Northwest is not known. Standing red cedars in the Southern Washington Cascades showing old bark removal scars—ostensibly peeled for one-piece, folded baskets—have been dated by growth ring counts to a little over 200 years ago. Most museum specimens with data seem to be of post-contact, ethnographic acquisition: although I've not undertaken thorough research, I know of no bark containers of this style that have been found in an archaeological context and subsequently dated. Exhaustive research into aboriginal, one-piece, folded bark containers is obviously a master's thesis begging to happen, but if you really want to just make your own bark baskets of juniper, read on!

Tools for the Task
As an aboriginal process, construction of a juniper bark basket from selection and procurement of the raw materials to the finishing touches, encompasses a number of well-defined sequential steps, each facilitated by the employment and application of appropriate knowledge, tools and action.

In my advanced aboriginal skills courses I've found it an excellent project involving multiple primitive technologies and skills using only

Aboriginal Examples

Two aboriginal examples of one-piece folded baskets of western juniper bark from the Harney County Museum in Burns, Oregon, illustrate considerable variation in construction and craftsmanship.

They are included here as examples from the past that may compliment contemporary construction and reinforce our ties with the past.

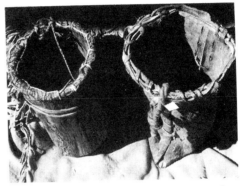

Burns is within the Northern Paiute culture area, but it is not known for certain if the two baskets were of local manufacture. The lacing and trim materials are not positively identified. Age is unknown, but portions of commercial cloth on each indicate use during post-contact times. Some measurements are included, but are not complete.

Left Basket Height: (corner to rim) 15"; (center of bottom to rim) 12-5/8"; diameter: (at mouth) 6-3/4"; circumference: (at middle) 19".

This is a finely crafted specimen showing external scoring at the base and tightly-laced rim. A cloth strip wrapped twice around the body with two-ply, hand-twisted, plant fiber cordage tied to the rim that appear to form part of the carrying strap. Another continuous length of two-ply cordage runs through periodic rim lacing holes and chain-links back under itself around the entire rim circumference. The specific function of this neatly affixed cordage is not known.

Right Basket Height: (corner to rim) 17"; Diameter: (at mouth) 7-1/8"; Circumference: (at middle) 19-3/4".

This is a more crudely made specimen of much thicker bark. The bottom has not been scored, but appears more to have been mashed and manipulated into shape as the sides were folded up. The top is not evenly trimmed and the rim binding is not continuously wrapped. A knotted length of twp-ply cloth rope affixed to one side of the rim appears to be part of a carrying strap.

natural materials and replicated aboriginal tools—no steel allowed! Therefore, you have to manufacture the tools. These include:

1. A percussion-flaked hand axe or "chopper" of obsidian, chert, basalt, etc., used to outline and groove through the bark panel on the tree and to initially pry up the bark edges for peeling. While some Acheulian hand axes were works of art, yours need not be, as long as it works. Sometimes you can just find a fortuitously shaped and sized rock that will suffice with minimal edge retouching. Hafted edge-ground axes and celts also work fine.

2. Spalled obsidian flake blades for trimming and scoring the bark, cutting lacing materials, etc. It's a good idea to back these (dull all but the intended cutting edge) so that bark and finger trimmings don't occur simultaneously!

3. A pressure-flaked stone drill, usually chert or basalt for strength, hafted with sinew, pitch, hide glue, etc., to a straight shaft for hand drilling side and rim lacing holes.

4. Occasionally, a spud for prying the bark panel from the tree. This could range from an appropriately shaped, unmodified antler tine to a stick found on the spot and modified to a chisel shape using a hand axe or flake knife, or by simply abrading it on a gritty rock. If you're not inclined to be a purist, just employ correspondingly appropriate modern tools. You'll learn less, but you'll still be making a bark basket.

Selecting a Suitable Tree

Unlike tulip poplars where most of the bark from a single tree can be utilized, juniper species in general are not noted for growing tall, straight, unbranched or clear-barked. You may have to scour dozens of trees before finding an unblemished and sizeable enough panel of bark suitable for making one basket. Denser stands of junipers will usually have proportionately more clean-barked, branchless portions of trunks than bushier trees growing in the open.

It is rare to find any single tree that will yield multiple suitable panels of bark. Trees about one foot in diameter are excellent. On much larger trees both the furrowed outer bark and the cambium are proportionately thicker, harder to cut through and peel from the trunk, and harder to accurately manipulate later in the process. However, huge-based junipers often branch into several parallel, smaller trunks; you may have to exercise the ape in you to climb up and survey them, but the sides of those facing each other, especially when shaded by dense outer foliage, are often quite free of twigs and knots. Clear sections of larger limbs will also work.

To replicate a typically proportioned aboriginal basket you are looking for a clear panel of bark approximately three times longer than it is wide. While aboriginal examples I've seen have ranged from quart-size and smaller up to baskets that could hold several gallons, the most common initial panel dimensions are nine to eleven inches wide by twenty-seven to thirty-three inches long. The surface should be as free as possible of any branch stubs, major scars or deep dives where the bark furrows down into the wood. These irregularities don't mean that cleanly removing the panel is impossible, just potentially more difficult. Since normally only a single vertically oriented rectangle of bark is removed from any one tree, the tree is not completely girdled and thus does not die.

Removing the Bark Panel from the Tree
When I've found what appears to be a suitable panel, I strip and peel off the roughest of the flaky, shaggy outer bark; it usually comes off in long strips. This sometimes reveals initially unnoticed flaws making the panel less desirable, but it also reduces unnecessary thickness of extraneous outer bark that you'd have to chop through with the hand axe. On most panels you can safely strip the brownish outer bark down to the depth of any furrows, but slow down when the newly exposed layers of bark begin to show a more reddish-purple color. The white cambium lies just beneath this. At this stage you needn't remove all extraneous bark; more can be cosmetically peeled later after the basket is bent to shape.

Depending on the style and sharpness of your hand axe, you might want to wear a glove. Using glancing, chopping, overlapping blows, outline the perimeter of your panel. If possible, make the panel an inch or so wider than necessary so a longitudinal strip can later be cut along one entire edge to be used for the rim reinforcement hoop.

Once you have the panel clearly delineated, use your hand axe as a grooving tool. Hold it with both hands, apply pressure and slide it back and forth in the cut to connect all the chop marks and deepen the groove all the way through the cambium to the wood proper. The cambium will be whitish and the wood more yellow-tan. It is especially important to make sure the cambium is cleanly grooved through to the wood in the top and bottom horizontal cuts; any still-connected spots there can cause splits in your panel if you're a bit careless in peeling it from the tree.

Begin at or near a corner in one side groove and, with fingers or the point of the hand axe, gently pry under and lift the edge. Work fingers or axe up and down, sliding under the bark, until an inch or so along the entire edge of the panel is free. If you're peeling during an optimal sap flow and the bark seems to be separating easily from the trunk, just continue shoving your fingers and hands further under the bark, then up or down toward each end.

On a large panel, if working under from only one side becomes awkward, repeat the initial edge-lifting along the opposite side and work back toward the freed area. If the bark is being a bit stubborn and finger and hand pressure are insufficient to cause separation, use your spud, but carefully! Prying too forcefully at any one spot may easily split the bark. Also be extra careful when freeing the panel at the top and bottom cuts (end grain of the bark) where splits are most likely to occur. Never try to just pull the slab off from one side or to back-bend it severely—it will split for sure.

Sometimes a few splits are inevitable. Short ones at the ends will be held in check later when the reinforcing rim is laced in place. Longer splits can be laced closed before the basket is bent to shape, but splits that extend more than half the length of the panel, even when laced closed, can make folding the bottom difficult without worsening them.

The main ingredient in successfully removing the bark panel reasonably undamaged is to begin slowly and carefully to get the feel of the material, then proceed accordingly. When the sap is extra juicy I've had panels literally pop free with very little coaxing. When more finesse is required, it is similar to carefully fisting the hide from a deer. Steel knives, axe heads, flat pry bars, etc., will work, but cause more unnecessary bruises, gouges, slices and splits in the bark than kinder and gentler methods.

In my experience in eastern Oregon I've found June through early August the optimal period for peeling bark without much difficulty. Years of drought or excessive moisture can vary those parameters. Typical western juniper habitat is a fairly arid environment though, and by late August many trees are too dry to peel. There are alternatives however, and one failed attempt need not mean another won't work. Moisture content can vary considerably between individual trees. Try trees growing more densely, higher elevation trees, trees growing closer to a direct water source or the north side of a tree instead of the sun-baked south side. Conversely, in early spring, the pre-warmed south sides of lower elevation trees may be ripe for easy bark removal.

Your freshly removed bark panel is best scored and bent to shape within a couple of hours of peeling or it may dry too much and become brittle. Sealing slabs in your standard, large-sized, aboriginal trash bag can keep them malleable for several days. Panels that have dried too much can be soaked in water until pliability returns, or even more quickly reconstituted by thoroughly wetting, sealing in a black plastic bag and placing in the direct sun for a few hours (the non-abo method).

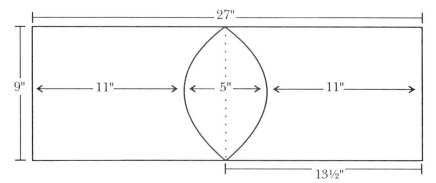

Template for an average sized and proportioned aboriginal western juniper-bark basket.

Scoring and Folding the Bark Panel

If you planned your rim reinforcement to come from your bark panel, lay the bark out, cambium side up, and cut an approximately one-inch-wide strip from along the entire length of one side of the slab (other rim options are discussed later).

Now measure and mark the midpoint of the panel's length with a straight line across its width (I use a piece of charcoal from the campfire). You don't need a tape measure; just stretch a piece of cordage to the length of the bark, then fold it in half to mark the midpoint. Now draw a symmetrical, bi-pointed ellipse (this is a contradiction of definitions that says exactly what I mean—eye-shape or football-shape) with its points and midline aligned along the midline of the bark.

The tips of the points should barely reach, or remain a hair short of, the bark margins. The width of the ellipse will be the width of the bottom of the basket. The width and shape of the ellipse, in relation to the width and length of the bark panel, will largely determine the shape or style of the finished basket. A narrow ellipse will dictate a flatter, more flask-shaped basket; a broader ellipse will produce a rounder, more cylindrical basket. Either way, the ellipse must come to a point at each side for the ensuing fold to bend and overlap properly. Most of the aboriginal juniper bark baskets I've seen were of the broader-bottomed, more cylindrical style.

The next step is to score or groove the entire circumference of the ellipse to a depth of approximately one-third to one-half the thickness of the cambium layer. Be careful not to cut all the way through! I use a sharp obsidian flake (large enough to hold securely) and cut a V-shaped trough, slicing out the cambium from inside the V. The V-cut, or kerf (a cutting slit), allows the sides to fold up with less binding.

Inside scoring appears to be the prevalent method on the aboriginal juniper bark baskets I've looked at, but the two examples illustrated here from the Harney County Museum in Burns, Oregon differ. One is neatly scored from the bark side (outside) as is most commonly done with poplar baskets. I personally believe the smoother, more uniform outer poplar bark lends itself to outside scoring more efficiently than the shaggier, uneven juniper or even red cedar bark, where it is easier to err in determining the appropriate cut depth. The other basket is much cruder overall, and appears to have not been scored, but rather mashed and manipulated into adequate shape as the sides were bent up.

An intermediate method on some abo bark baskets (that I've not tried yet) involves no actual cutting, but rather delineating the fold line along the ellipse by deeply compressing the cambium fibers with a wedge-ended stick used as a stylus. I imagine the spud, or similarly shaped antler, bone or stone, would work as well. These variations illustrate that no single method is prescribed, even within a single culture area, or considered the only right way to insure the bark will fold exactly where you want it to.

By whatever means, method or madness you've scored your panel, you are ready to form the basket by folding the sides up. Remember, the bottom is not going to be flat—as the sides are bent upward, the points of the ellipse must be free to bend downward. Thus, laying the bottom over a 'round' such as your leg or a small log gives you a solid surface to press against without inhibiting downward movement of the points.

To begin the fold, I like to spread one hand across the ellipse, thumb at one point and remaining fingers evenly spaced across to the other, and apply downward pressure, more concertedly at the points, as the other hand gently coaxes one side panel upward. Evenly distributed support and pressure from your hands, fingers, and arms contacting as much surface of the bark as possible gives you more control and lessens chances of lengthening existing splits or causing new ones.

Bend slowly, a little at a time, and make sure the fold is following the score line, especially at the points. If the panel really fights you and just does not want to bend, you may have to deepen or widen the score line and/or strip off additional outer bark that could be inhibiting flexibility.

Juniper bark does not often just flip into shape; it takes some manipulating and training. As you bend you may hear some cracking and popping. This may scare your ears, but normally it is just brittle sections of outer bark breaking and should not adversely affect the process or result. When you have won with one side let it relax but keep it at least slightly up-curved as you repeat the folding process with the other side. During this phase you may wish you had an extra arm and hand to help

Construction sequence for a single-fold style bark basket.

support, brace, hold and bend, and you may have to invent some interesting new holding positions to get both sides folded up evenly.

When you have trained both sides to fold up freely to a vertical position, you will want to bring them together to form the basket so the edges along each side overlap about an inch. Overlap will be less, of course, down at the corners, but if you drew and scored your ellipse well at the points, there shouldn't be any opening there before the overlap starts. If you are not quite satisfied, you can usually improve them with some specific pinching and manipulating.

At this stage, I tie a buckskin thong around the basket to hold it to shape, then strip off any remaining ragged outer bark that may have popped loose at the folds. I also check the evenness of the top circumference; if one side is taller than the other, or other irregularities exist, I mark with charcoal what to trim off. You can either open the basket back out flat to trim (easiest, I think), or wait 'til the sides are laced up and trim just prior to applying the rim reinforcement strip.

Drilling Holes and Lacing the Basket

The holes for lacing are drilled in two parallel rows up each side of the basket about an inch in from each edge, or just beyond where the overlap stops, and thus through only a single layer of bark. The lacing will run back and forth through the holes to encase the double layer overlap.

On the very first juniper bark basket I made, having neither instruction nor experience with the medium, I started punching lacing holes with an awl, but soon realized my error when all the holes started to connect by a long split. By switching to the stone-tipped hand drill, employing abrasion rather than punching, I eliminated the splitting problem. Holes can also be successfully burned in.

The number, placement, and spacing of holes depends on the size of your basket, your aesthetic whim, and the style of lacing you choose. The two most common are a single lace that spirals around and around

A chert-bitted hand drill is used to drill lacing holes through the side of a juniper bark basket. (Photo: Jim Riggs)

through the holes from bottom to top, and a double lace where each end crosses back and forth through the holes (which can be one long lace begun at its middle through the bottom two holes). This creates a pleasing X-pattern to the lacing. The sides can also be simply tied closed through corresponding pairs of holes rather than continuously laced. This could be advantageous in situations where long laces are not available.

Holes can be drilled while you have your basket temporarily tied to shape, although the edges tend to bend downward from the drill pressure unless you prop them in place with a couple of short sticks wedged inside. You can also shove your foot or a conveniently sized chunk of wood inside to serve as a back brace for drilling. Or you can just mark your desired hole placements with charcoal, then open the bark and lay it out flat on a more stable surface for drilling. If you already have your rim strip sized, you can measure its width in from the top edges of the basket panel and drill those holes too, though I normally wait until the sides are all laced up because some rim holes may have to be drilled through the double thickness overlap at each side.

Lacing material can be whatever you have on hand or can find in the immediate environment, including buckskin thongs, wet rawhide thongs, two-ply dogbane or other fiber cordage, sinew, long strips of willow bark, whole or split, thin willow withes, pliable roots or vines like honeysuckle or clematis, shreddy barks such as big sagebrush, strips of peeled juniper cambium, tule stems, cattail leaves, ad infinitum! While lacing material of high tensile strength is easier to use and to cinch tightly, super-strength is not imperative. The main function of the side lacing is to hold the overlapped edges in place while they're still pliable; as the whole basket dries, the bark becomes quite rigid and retains the shape it was trained to.

Forming and Lacing the Basket Rim Reinforcement Hoop
The main functions of the rim reinforcement pieces are to protect and prevent splitting or other damage to the top edge of the bark sides, to hold the basket mouth to desired shape while the rim and basket body dry and take on a set, and to increase overall durability of the basket. I prefer the convenient availability, flat configuration and neatness of the juniper bark strip for the rim, but I've also frequently used green lengths of willow or red osier dogwood shoots split in half. The flat side lays in contact with the basket.

Functional rims can be laced around either the outside or the inside of the basket mouth, or on both sides. Aboriginal baskets exhibit all three variations, and some have bundled rims that appear to be willow shoots, bark strips or other fibrous material laced on. The term rim "hoop" is slightly misleading in that I've never seen nor made a bark basket where the rim piece was first separately bound into a hoop shape before being laced onto the basket.

To prepare a juniper bark strip for the hoop, trim it to a uniform width (about an inch), then pre-bend it in your hands or over your leg to relax stiffness and train it to better conform to the curvature of the basket mouth. Lay it around the basket and cut it an inch or two longer than the actual circumference so that there will be some overlap of the two ends when it is laced into place.

Measure the rim strip's width down from the top of the basket, mark that, and drill your lacing holes roughly three-quarters to one inch apart all the way around. Begin lacing on the strip near one end (the distance in from the end that the other end will overlap) and continue lacing all the way around the basket mouth. Your final lacing stitches will bind down the overlapped area and end at your point of origin.

Leading ends, splices, and finishing ends of your lacing material are normally not tied off, but simply tucked under a previous or forthcoming stitch; once dry, they shouldn't come loose. Actual rim material, number of holes you drill, lacing material and technique can be whatever you choose to experiment with, as long as they work! The more baskets you make, the more interesting variations and refinements you'll come up with. For example, you can thin or feather out each end of the rim strip prior to lacing so that the over lap is hardly noticeable.

Finishing Touches and Variations
A freshly completed juniper bark basket should still be somewhat malleable and, if desired, you can do some cosmetic manipulating to adjust the shape of the mouth, flatten or round out the sides, etc. When I get one to the configuration I want, I place a short stick or two inside to prop and hold it in that position while it dries. Kept in the sun, sufficient drying should take only two or three days, depending on the thickness of the bark.

The final step is attaching a carrying strap long enough to loop over the neck and shoulder so the top of the basket hangs at about waist level. I usually affix a buckskin-thong loop to each side of the basket through a pair of lacing holes, then tie a longer shoulder strap to those.

When I first began making bark baskets I marvelled at the simplicity of the one-piece folded design, but the inevitable inverted U-shaped bottom (typically deeper on the standard aboriginal more cylindrical forms that were my only models) seemed impractical. Then, while picking currants one day I suddenly realized that the curved basket bottom meshed perfectly with the opposite curvature of my upper thigh. This position, with the strap around neck and one shoulder, props the mouth of the basket upward and forward and frees both hands to rapidly and efficiently strip berries into it. How neat! However, I've found no documentation that this handy position was either intended during aboriginal construction or practiced during use.

While the aboriginal use of juniper bark appears limited to constructing the basic berry basket type described here, I find it to be nearly as versatile as poplar bark, but much less efficient to harvest in quantity. Once you have made a basket or two, you learn to visualize exactly what size and shape of bark panel you need to construct specifically dimensioned baskets or containers intended for other uses.

For instance, juniper bark makes an excellent lightweight but sturdy quiver that provides more arrow protection than skin. But bark cylinders too narrow to reach one's hand into do offer a creative challenge for getting them laced up! Flat-bottomed, free-standing containers can be made from one or two panels laced up to form the sides, with a third circular or oval slab laced onto one end to form the bottom.

Various lids for containers can also be created. There is evidence that red cedar bark baskets were occasionally sealed with pitch along all seams and holes and used as water containers and/or for hot stone boiling, although I've not yet tried this with juniper (there's always more to do!).

A successful experiment I did recently try was substituting frame-stretched and dried elk rawhide for bark. The only significant construction difference I found was that the rawhide folded easier when scored on the outside.

A simpler style of folded basket I've seen pictured of cedar but not juniper bark eliminates the elliptical bottom and is simply scored in a straight line across the midpoint of the panel. Then, proceeding as normal, the sides are bent up, edge margins overlapped, drilled and laced and finally the rim piece affixed. Because this style has a V-shaped bottom produced by the straight-line fold, it holds less, but capacity can be increased by forming the mouth to a circular shape, gently spreading the panel sides apart to their limit and propping these both in place until dry.

Whether you are surrounded by tulip poplars in the East, live in the land of western junipers, or are somewhere in-between or beyond, where other trees may work just as well, one-piece folded and laced bark containers are fun to make and multi-functional for the modern abo. So, when spring rolls around, your blood's flowing, the sap's up, the weather turns hot and you experience uncontrollable urges to begin peeling things off, embark on a new kind of basket project—bet you can't make just one!

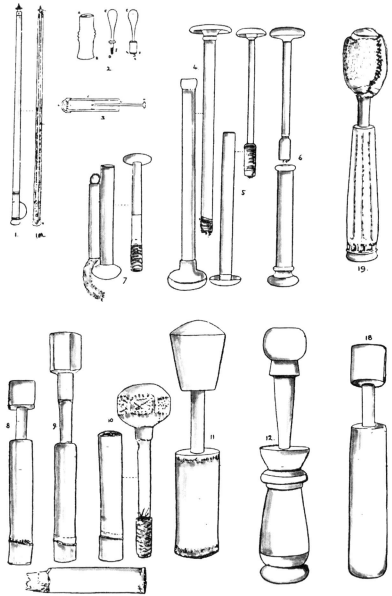

Examples of fire pistons from Europe (1-7) and farther India (8-12, 18-19). Illustrations reprinted from Henry Balfour, M.A., "The Fire Piston" Annual Smithsonian Report, *1907.*

Richard Jamison with Mel Deweese

The Remarkable
Fire Piston

● ●

Learning to operate the fire piston is the easy part. Ideally,

you would "practice" with a proven model, experiment

with different materials, then go on to make your own.

Unfortunately, there are so few working models available

it seems that we are destined to start from the other end of

the spectrum and first experiment, then practice.

I first read about the fire piston in *Bushcraft* by Peter Graves. Being a visual person, the reference didn't hold much significance for me until I saw one demonstrated at the Woodsmoke Rendezvous. But when I did see it, I immediately knew how the Australian aborigines must have felt when they saw a Bic lighter for the first time. I was seeing this incredible discovery, a primitive fire machine, and I was absolutely fascinated. That was in 1979. I thought about the fire piston quite a lot after that—I wanted one and tried to find out where I could get my own.

It was Mel Deweese, then a senior survival instructor for the U.S. Navy S.E.R.E. program, who first showed me the fire piston. His came from an isolated village in the Philippines. He and his group landed in the jungle in a helicopter and the local people came out to see what all the commotion was about. They were wearing loin cloths and carrying bows and arrows. Out of the corner of his eye, Mel saw one of the natives push something in and pop it out, and light his cigarette with it. He couldn't communicate because of the language barrier, but he managed to trade the fellow a Zippo lighter and two pieces of Hubba Bubba for the fire piston. They were both happy!

I doubt Mel understood the significance of his remarkable new "cigarette lighter" at the time, and after hearing his story, it was pretty unlikely that I was going to just go out and buy one–so I decided to make my own. I studied Mel's fire piston carefully and tried to duplicate it.

A fire piston is a remarkable device. It operates on the same principle as the diesel combustion engine. There are three absolute essentials necessary for producing heat in this manner: 1) A cylinder with accurate bore, usually closed at one end; 2) a piston accurately fitting the cylinder; 3) tinder which is very quickly flammable.

As air is forced into the shaft by a rod or "piston" the velocity condenses the air and creates heat. The intense heat ignites a small ball of tinder which is packed into a concave depression at the end of the piston. The piston is quickly withdrawn, and the glowing tinder (coal) is picked out of the depression and dropped into a tinder bundle, then blown into flame. It sounds very simple, but there are a number of elements that have to be "just right" to get it to work.

I started with ash (Fraxinus) as the material for both the cylinder and the piston and drilled the shaft with a power drill. It didn't work. I tried different types of tinder, thinking that would resolve the problem. I used juniper bark, dogbane fibers, cattail down, and cotton with no success. Next I tried maple with no more luck. I tried wrapping the piston with more string to form a tighter gasket, nothing. I used more, then less "grease" on the piston, but that didn't work either. (I should mention that there is no "degree" of success with the fire piston, either it works or it doesn't.)

At a loss, I turned to my knowledge of auto mechanics to follow the example of the diesel engine, and made some adjustments to my experimental model. Still no success.

My son Scott, who is an aeronautical engineer, says you can always tell an engineer because they tear a project apart and put it back together before they read the instructions. I'm not an engineer, but I am a mechanic of sorts, and I am persistent. So I resolved to "read the instruction manual," so to speak, and do my research.

I checked the local library. Nothing. There were no references to a fire piston at all. I checked other sources and asked people I thought should know. Still nothing. So I did the logical thing and shelved the project.

Then, as fate will have it, in 1980, I was doing research for the movie *Windwalker* and happened to run across a 1907 report on the subject of fire pistons. Not only were examples shown in the form of illustrations, but the history of it's discovery and evolution were cited. As a result of the references listed, I was able to research additional writings and reports. I was back on track.

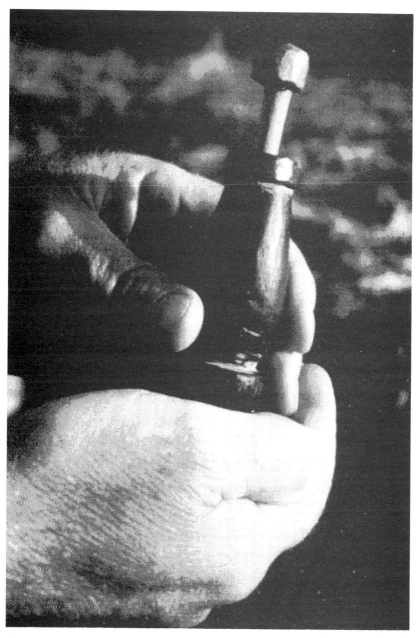

Fire piston cylinder made from buffalo horn with wooden piston. From Mel Deweese collection (Photo by Richard Jamison).

I will abbreviate some of the information contained in those reports for you here. I apologize for the lengthy reference to early accounts and descriptions, but I feel it is important to turn to a time when the fire piston was in practical use for examples. I think these references are valuable to anyone who intends to build a working model of the fire piston. The reports also present some interesting ethnological questions that illustrate academic thinking around the turn of the century and which, to some degree, still exists today.

Discovery
According to various reports, the fire piston appeared almost simultaneously in two very different parts of the world—Europe and Asia. We will begin by taking a look at the discovery of the fire piston in Europe.

France—On December 29, 1802, M. Mollet, professor of physics in the Central School at Lyons, announced to the Institute of France that he had noticed that tinder could be ignited by placing a small piece of it in a narrow channel into which air is condensed by means of a tight fitting "pump." On the strength of this announcement, Mollet was credited as the discoverer of the Tachypyrion (an instrument for producing fire by compression of air).

As often happens, the actual discovery was not made by Mollet at all, but rather by an unnamed workman in a small gun factory near Lyons when he observed a "luminous appearance" caused by the discharge from an air gun in the dark. He also found that tinder could be ignited from the great amount of heat generated by charging an air gun with an ordinary compression pump. The workman is said to have communicated this discovery to Mollet, who in turn reported it.

So the actual "discoverer" of the principle in France was a workman, and not a scientist. In fact, the details of the discovery were not understood by the French scientists, who were inclined to discredit them. Nevertheless, very soon after Mollet's report, the experiment with the air-compression pump was repeated by others and became a common one in laboratories where fire pistons were specially made for that purpose. They were usually made from brass cylinders, closed at the lower end and very accurately bored or gauged. Some were made of glass so the experiment could be easily seen. The glowing tinder was then used to light a sulphured match.

Not only was this principle adapted for scientific illustration, but it was also applied to domestic use not long after scientific interest had been aroused, although it is not known who developed the fire piston for practical purposes.

On January 1, 1803 the editors of the French *Bibliotheque Britannique* wrote to a Mr. Tilloch in England who was associated with the *Philosophical Magazine*, to announce Mollet's "discovery" and stating that the phenomenon had never been noticed before. But sources in the scientific community affirmed that the flash from an air gun had, in fact, been known for some time in England and was mentioned nearly a year and a half previously by a Mr. Fletcher at a meeting for philosophical experiments as a "curious phenomenon which deserved investigation." At the time no one could explain the cause of the phenomenon, which had been accidentally noticed and had not been arrived at by scientific experiment. Thus the first observation of the physical effect was credited to an Englishman sometime around the middle of 1801.

England—In England physicists knew that heat and cold could be produced by the mechanical condensation and rarefaction of gases because a paper on the subject was read by John Dalton in the year 1800, giving the results of experiments.

And in the year 1807, Richard Lorentz patented "an instrument for producing instantaneous fire" in England. His drawings and the specifications he listed are as follows:

> The illustration shows the construction of my machine or instrument for producing instantaneous fire. *A* represents the cap or head of a staff or stick, having therein a cavity or space for containing the prepared fungus known by the name of German tinder, or for containing common tinder of rags, or any other very combustible substance. *C* is the outer end of the rod of a syringe, which works by a piston in the upper part of the staff and by a stroke of about twelve inches forces the common air with great velocity and in an highly condensed state through a small aperture against the combustible matter included in the head *B,A*, which is well screwed on against a shoulder or face armed with a collar of leather. *B* is the hole for admitting common air when the piston is drawn quite back. The manner of working consists simply in pressing the end of the rod of the charged syringe strongly against the ground so as to drive the air suddenly on the tinder, and the cap *A* being without loss of time unscrewed, the tinder is found to be on fire.

Lorentz' patented fire piston is different from those used in laboratories in one important aspect. In the lab models, the air is merely compressed in the bottom of the cylinder, whereas in Lorentz's machine the air is not only compressed by the drive of the piston rod, but it is also forced under high pressure through a minute duct. Thus, the term fire "syringe" seems to be more suitable. It is possible that the air, already heated by compression, gains additional heat from the friction caused as it passes through the small duct.

However, "duct-less" fire pistons seemed to have been more popular during the early 1800s. In the *Mechanics Magazine*, (Vol. XVII, 1832, p. 328) the following passage submitted by E.J. Mitchell occurs: (fig. 2, pl. I.)

> The following is a sketch of a simple instrument for obtaining a light. *A,B* is a brass cylinder, similar in appearance to a small brass cannon, having the hole rather better than three-eights of an inch in diameter, drilled true. *C,D* is the form of a piston to work in the cylinder, but unpacked. *E,F* is the same ready packed with thick leather and fitted up for use. *H* is a circular brass nut, working against the screw to keep the packing tight. *K* is a small hook, fastened in a hole drilled through the nut *H*. *C* is the handle to the piston and is made of wood.
>
> The method of use is described as follows: "prepare some thin cotton rag (the older and thinner the better) by steeping it in a solution of saltpeter and drying it in a warm oven: tear a small piece off and place it on the hook *K* introduce the piston *ef* into the cylinder *A,B* a short distance only, then take the cylinder in the right hand. Place it perpendicular upon the floor or a table and strike the handle *E* with the ball of the right hand so that the piston may rapidly descent to the bottom of *ab* and being suddenly withdrawn, the tinder will be found on fire, and will light a common brimstone match or tinder which may be obtained at any of the principal druggists, but I prefer the rag steeped in saltpeter.—E.J.M.

The magazine's editor added that "the invention, though not new, is very well known on the Continent by the name of the 'instantaneous light-giving syringe'."

Although a number of simple fire pistons can be found in museums and private collections, according to Dr. Henry Balfour, curator of the Pitt-Rivers Museum in Oxford, none of the screw-type syringe models have been preserved.

In 1893, Rudolph Diesel used these same principles to develop the diesel engine.

Asian—Surmising that the oriental fire piston was invented independently by the relatively primitive peoples in some parts of Asia, we can only speculate as to how they might have discovered this highly specialized method of producing fire.

One theory is that the fire piston could have been derived from the pestle and mortar commonly used throughout Indo-China and the

Malayan areas for crushing the betel nut or chavica leaves. Apparently there is a very strong resemblance between the fire piston and some of the small mortar and pestle specimens. In fact, according to some sources, examples in the British Museum are so similar to some of the Bornean fire pistons that it is hard to tell the difference.

Two English explorers in Indonesia around 1900, W.W. Skeat and Nelson Annandale, saw a fire piston in regular use in the most northerly of what was then the Siamese-Malay states. They reported the Siamese name of the fire piston was "lek phai tok" while the Malayan name was "gobi api." The word "gobek" is usually applied to the piston (pestle and mortar) used for crushing betel leaves; "api" in Malayan means "fire." The tinder was called "rabok" which is usually obtained from the leaf bases of the tykas palm (Caryota griffithii), and was also known to come from rattan. According to Mr. Annandale "it (the fire piston) was mainly used for lighting cigarettes in the jungle, as the spark was not easily extinguished by high winds."

From a practical point of view, this theory does not seem likely because the features necessary for the success of a fire piston would have the opposite effect in the case of the mortal and pestle. For example, in the case of the mortar and pestle, it is essential for the pestle to work loosely in the mortar, while it is equally essential that in the fire piston the piston fits the bore. There is no room for alteration in either case without making the instruments useless.

A more likely theory seems to be the accidental discovery during the process of boring and gauging blow guns. Particularly if made of solid wood, there might have been some compression of air within the bore, which might have caused the ignition of some material that had adhered either to the hole or the rod. It is also interesting to learn that the oriental blowgun was used in many of the same regions where the fire piston is found.

Another Englishman, Henry Louis, told how he obtained a specimen which might fit this theory while camped "on a little stream known as Ayer Katiah, a tributary to the Teluban River." Mr. Louis related that a party of Malays came down from some neighboring villages, squatted down in camp and began to smoke. One of the party, a young man, "in the most matter-of-fact way," took out his fire piston and lit his cigarette.

"In this the cylinder is of wood, 6.4 cm long, neatly bound round with bands of plaited cane," he reported. "The lower end is rounded off, instead of terminating in the point so characteristic of other specimens from the peninsula. The piston, of hard wood, is very short and has a large, roughly carved head. The packing is of pale vegetable fiber. A large bean shell serves as a tinder box: it appears to be an 'entada' bean."

Further, if the blow guns were made of bamboo, it is conceivable that a rod was jammed down the stalk, breaking through the nodes with enough force to create compression and cause bamboo shavings inside the shaft to ignite. In support of this theory, some simple, primitive-looking fire pistons from the Cachins were made of natural bamboo cylinders.

Origin and Distribution
It was known that the principle of producing heat by compression of air was discovered in England and France by both accident and scientific experiment, and that this principle was to some extent adapted to domestic use there by the invention of the fire piston. So it is at least clear that the European form was not derived from the east. But did the eastern instrument come from Europe?

By 1900 there were very few examples of the fire piston left in Europe. Some specimens had been donated to various museums from private collections, but it had apparently been discarded as a viable instrument for firemaking in Europe by that time. This was evidently not the case in some of the less developed Asian cultures however, where Mel found one still in practical use as late as the 1970s.

It is significant to note that in 1900 the scientific world refused to recognize that early Asians, referred to as mere "savages," could possibly discover, much less develop for common use, such a highly scientific instrument. This assumption was based solely on the belief that undeveloped people were also unintelligent.

As I see it, the big question is whether or not a thorough, unbiased study was made of the true discovery and evolution of the fire piston, given the attitude of the scientific community at a time when fire pistons were available for study. Even as late as 1907, when Dr. Balfour published his rather lengthy study of the evolution of the fire piston, they were scarce and seldom used or found in Europe. Yet, at the time of his report many examples of fire pistons of Malaysian and Siamese origin were still observed in practical use.

Apparently the scientific community in the early 1900s had trouble explaining how native peoples, in a comparatively undeveloped culture, could possibly have arrived independently at the knowledge necessary for the invention of this method of fire production. After all, it had only been 100 years since the first English patent was taken out for a fire piston, and the scientific knowledge of obtaining a spark by this method dated from only a very few years earlier. Since this was beyond grasp for people who believed themselves to be in the "highest state of civilization and scientific advancement," they presumed that the fire piston must have been introduced by some more highly cultured race.

Although Dr. Balfour, from a purely practical standpoint, eventually talked himself out of his prejudice, he remained skeptical. "It seems almost incredible," he surmised, "that so delicate and far from obvious a method can have been discovered, whether by accident or by gradual development, by any of the eastern peoples amongst whom it has been found in use. At the same time, it must be admitted that this is the only serious difficulty which lies in the way of admitting the possibility of an independent origin in the two main regions of distribution."

To the contrary, from references preceding 1907, we learn that prior to 1865, the fire piston was already well known in the east over a very extensive geographical area, including Burma, the Malay Peninsula, Borneo, and the islands to the east of Java. It seems likely that considerable time would be required to account for this extensive distribution, even if the fire piston had been introduced by travelers from the west, which it clearly was not.

Although Dr. Balfour agrees that the French made some use of the fire piston, they did not have contact with the eastern regions where it was distributed. Nor was there any evidence that the Chinese (except on the Burmese and Siamese borders) might have discovered it, although they are commonly credited with the invention of many strange and wonderful things.

There is also some controversy as to whether the fire piston might have been discovered by the Siamese and not the Malays, but it seems that the Malays were, nonetheless, the main source of distribution over the islands of the East Indian Archipelago from Sumatra to the Philippines.

It is interesting to note that the Europeans "discovered" the fire piston in the same manner as Dr. Balfour explains the discovery in the east, by accident. Still, being cultures of "high intelligence" he finds no difficulty in crediting the French and English.

At this point I would like to note my own theory based on purely scientific principles of observation: According to three parallel reports; the Nelson Annandale report, the anecdote of Henry Louis, and the account by Mel Deweese, we can credit the smoking of cigarettes by Asian natives as the most common use of fire pistons in that part of the world during the mid 1800s through 1970.

Certainly, this unfounded assumption is no more ridiculous than the declaration that primitive Asian cultures could not possibly have invented a fire piston because they were considered to be of "low intelligence."

But I digress...

In summary, the distribution of the fire piston seems to have been a wide one in the Malay Peninsula where it was found to be used by both the Malaysians and what were known at that time as Siamese.

As for distribution in other parts of Asia, there are reports of the fire piston having been observed in use in Burma, French Indo-China, the Malay Peninsula, Sumatra, Borneo-Sarawak, British North Borneo, Java, Flores, and the Philippine Islands.

Materials

With the single exception of the peculiar type from British North Borneo, all the eastern forms of the fire piston are essentially the same in general structure. The details which can be modified or varied include the materials used in the manufacture of the cylinder and piston, which may be of bamboo, wood, horn, ivory, bone, brass, or lead (or lead and tin); the external form; and the accessories, such as the tinder container, which may be separate from the instrument, made of bamboo, nut shells, beans, palm bark, or woven materials. Prickers for adjusting the tinder, grease boxes and a spatula for applying the grease to the piston packing are optional accessories.

The Philippine fire piston Mel Deweese owns is a proven, working model. He has used and demonstrated it continually for over 15 years that I know of, so it has obviously proven durable under repeated use. As such, it seems like an ideal model to study and duplicate. I asked Mel about it's construction.

"This one is made out of water buffalo horn and a hard piece of wood," he explained. "The tinder is from the palm tree, which I think is the real secret, finding the right tinder. We're back to the triangle again, oxygen, friction and fuel and you have the oxygen and the fuel, but where do we get the friction. It's the friction of the molecules being compressed."

The material used to wrap the piston and act as a "gasket" can, apparently, be made from anything that works. In some of the early specimens leather was used. Mel uses thread.

"I've put thread around the end to form a tighter seal. So this makes it tight, otherwise this (the piston) would just slip up and down. And in the end of the piston, the cup is filled with tinder from the palm tree. And on this end I have grease from the pig, the wild pig in the jungle, which is used to lubricate the piston so it will slide better.

"The old man in the jungle says only the pig from this part of the jungle, but sometimes you have to evaluate it, because I know that particular pig was somewhere else yesterday."

The illustrations show many combinations of materials and variations of form. For example, in Burma the cylinders were mostly made of bamboo, wood, or horn and the pistons were either wood or horn or made of a combination of both. In the Malay Peninsula elegantly lathe-turned and slightly engraved cylinders were made of horn while other examples collected from the area were of bone and ivory. A specimen from Sumatra was made of buffalo horn.

In the writings of F. Boyle, *Adventures Among the Dyaks of Borneo* (1865, p.67), he described the fire piston and expressed much astonishment at the method of procuring fire used by some of the Dyak tribes. Although he admitted to never having seen it actually in use, he said the "officers of the Rajah seemed acquainted with it." He refers to lead being used as a material in making the instrument and added that "the natives say no metal but lead will produce the effect."

Apparently the use of lead as a material is peculiar to Borneo and may be a character developed in the island itself, unless the Malays used the metal themselves and introduced its use with the fire piston.

A report in the *Journal of Anthropology*, (XV, 1886, p. 426) quotes W.M. Crocker. "The fire piston is found among the Saribus Dyaks only. Here we have a small brass tube lined with lead; no other metal, the natives say, would produce the same result. A small wooden plunger is made to fit the tube, the end of which is hollowed out in the shape of a small cup, in which is placed the tinder."

Dr. Balfour reports that there were two specimens from the same district presented to the Pitt-Rivers Museum in 1894, both of which have cylinders of lead-lined brass and pistons of hard wood. One specimen has a bamboo box attached to it for tinder, the other has a tinder holder of nut shell and also a small cleaning rod of cane and a metal spatula for grease.

A specimen from British North Borneo is wood and the concave end capped with lead. A sunken groove near the end of the piston seemed to be designed for holding packing. According to Mr. Beaufort, "fire pistons were becoming very difficult to obtain in British North Borneo, where they are confined to the west coast." He added that "the better ones are made of wood."

Fire pistons once ranged over a wide area of the island of Java. They were always made from buffalo horn. Dr. Balfour describes a specimen in his possession which came from Buitenzorg in the west of Java as being "made from black horn and carefully polished, with a cigar-shaped cylinder with two bands of ornamental engraving. The piston terminates in a large rounded head, which is fixed to it with a horn rivet. The knob or piston head is hollowed out, and serves as a receptacle for tinder, which consists of a brown palm scurf."

In *Gems of the East* (1904, II. p. 334) Savage Landor reports that the fire piston was restricted to the wild non-Negrito tribes of north central Luzon in the Philippine Islands, where it was used by natives of the so-called Indonesian group. "This instrument, called "bantin" was generally made of caribou horn."

In 1901, Mr. Bailey is reported to have sent a specimen to the Pitt-Rivers Museum whereby the cylinder was cast evidently in a two-piece mold of bamboo, and is composed of a mixture of lead and tin. The piston is of wood. Attached to the cylinder are a tinder box of catada bean full of palm-scurf tinder and also a brass-wire pricker.

A fire piston was given to the Pitt-Rivers Museum in 1889 by Mr. S.B.J. Skertchley which included half of a bamboo casting mold. According to Mr. Skertchley the "total of the cylinder is composed of two parts lead to one of tin. It is cast in a bamboo mould. The mould is a thick piece of bamboo, split lengthwise, on the interior of which the ornamental bands are incised. A piece of flat wood, plank by preference, has a hole made in it the size of the bore. Through this hole a rotan is pushed, which also passes through a lump of clay, tempered with sand, stuck on the upper surface of the plank. The rotan projects beyond the clay to a distance somewhat greater than the length of the cylinder. The mould, bound together with split rotan is placed centrally and vertically over the projecting rotan, thus forming a box closed below with clay, open at the top, and having a rotan in the center. Into this the molten metal is poured. When cool, the rotan is withdrawn, the mould open and the cylinder is complete. A good mould will make three or four castings, but as a rule, the first destroys it. The measurements of the cylinder are: Length, 3-1/4 inches; width 1/2 inch, bore 3/8 inch. this is the average size; larger ones do not work well; smaller ones are of no use.

Technique

Learning to operate the fire piston is the easy part. Ideally, you would "practice" with a proven model, experiment with different materials, then go on to make your own. Unfortunately, there are so few working models available it seems that we are destined to start from the other end of the spectrum and first experiment, then practice. Alas, the question will be whether a model does not work due to improper materials or technique.

I asked Mel Deweese, who is the only fire piston "expert" I know personally, to explain the technique he uses to make his fire.

"The Negritos in the Philippines call it sol pop, sol 'pop' because of the noise it makes," he explained. "It has to be one action, it has to be in and out. In and out, 'pop'."

"And then we will pick the coal out with a sharp piece of stick and then put it into our nest."

I asked if withdrawing the piston has anything to do with the overall success. "I don't think so," he responded, "but sometimes you can lose the coal down inside. Or it'll fall onto the ground."

Although many early travelers and scientists reported seeing the fire piston work, with the exception of Dr. Henry Balfour, few actually mention trying it themselves.

Charles Brook in *Ten Years in Sarawak* (1866, p. 50) writes, "There is a method used by the Saribus and Sakarang Dyaks for obtaining fire, which is peculiarly artistic, and from what direction such a practice could have been inherited is beyond my ken. The instrument is a small metal tube, about 3 inches long, closed at one end with a separate piston, the bottom of which fits closely into the tube and when some dried stuff answering the purpose of tinder is introduced, and the piston slapped suddenly down, the head of it being held in the palm of the hand in order to withdraw it as quickly as possible with a jerk, fire is by this means communicated to the tinder in the tube. The Dyaks call the instrument 'besi api.'"

A. Gantier (*Etude sur les Mois*, Bull, de la Societe de Geographic Commerciale du Havre, 1902, pp. 95 and 177.) reports that "the native moistens the end of the piston in his mouth, so as to lubricate it and also to make the small piece of tinder adhere to the cupped hollow."

According to John Cameron, when used, the cylinder is held firmly in the fist of the left hand: a small piece of tinder, generally dried fungus, is placed in a cavity on the point of the piston, which is then just entered into the mouth of the bore; with a sudden stroke of the right hand the piston is forced up the bore, from which it rebounds slightly back with the elasticity of the compressed air, and on being plucked out, which it must be instantly, the tinder is found to be lighted." It is obvious from Mr. Cameron's report, that he did not understand what made the device work, and that the "technology" was completely new to him.

D.C. Worchester (*The Philippine Islands* 1898, p. 297) mentions examples made of buffalo horn from the wild tribes of North Luzon. He adds, "To perform this operation successfully requires long practice. I have yet to see a white man who professes to be able to do it..how the savages first came to think of getting fire in such a way is, to me, a mystery."

In many ways the fire piston is still a mystery. It is a mystery how it was discovered, and how to make a successful model. But it is also a challenge, and in a world of "absolutes" the challenge presented by the centuries-old Tachypyron could be refreshing.

The author (foreground) competes against other modern-day "abos" in the accuracy competition held annually at the Rabbit Stick Rendevous (photo by Linda Jamison).

David Wescott

An Introduction
to the Atatl

●●●●●●●●●●●●●●●●●●●●●●●●●●●●●

...if a major league pitcher can hurl a fast ball at 100

miles per hour, just think what you would have if you

could fit a gorilla with 20% longer arms into that same

uniform (although you may have trouble getting it to wear

that little cap).

T he atlatl (pronounced similar to rat-rattle by some and rattle-rattle by others), dating back over 40,000 years, is perhaps the world's oldest compound tool (compound–a combination of two or more elements or parts) and perhaps the world's oldest machine (machine–any contrivance or apparatus designed to produce or utilize power or energy), and is indeed the first of the great developments in hunting implements. The word atlatl, as it applies to this specific style of weaponry, comes to us from the ancient language of the Toltec, meaning spear thrower (Tate 1987).

Atlatl technology, used for both defense and offense, is certainly one of the most widely adopted and longest used technologies on earth. Artifacts have been found on every continent in the world except Africa and Antarctica, and predate the development of the bow and arrow by over 10,000 years. Many civilizations continued use of the atlatl until well after contact with the modern world. In fact, there is evidence to show that some, such as the Australian Aborigines, preferred their woomerahs over the bow and arrow even though their closest neighbors, the Asmats of New Guinea had switched to bows and arrows centuries before. Mexican Indians have used the throwing boards well into the twentieth century, yet they posses artifacts that have dated to thirteen thousand years ago. The northern tribes of the Eskimo used both the throwing board and bow and arrow as contemporaries.

It is believed that the reason for the continuous use of the atlatl in only certain areas was due to (1) the simplicity and adaptability of the technology; and (2) the specific survival needs of the people.

Simplicity and Adaptability

The Australian primitive simply removed a slab of wood from a tree, shaped it with simple pebble tools or used it as is. As the technology was refined and expanded, its adaptability became more evident through the variety of designs, materials and modifications employed in the many geographic areas that it is found. As man evolved from the close-range interaction of megafauna and thrusting spears, to a need for longer range weapons to be used against faster and smaller game, the atlatl was a natural solution. As game became even smaller and faster, the bow and arrow took over.

Survival Needs

The natural shape of the aboriginal woomerah allowed them to adapt its use to a variety of daily chores, thus reducing their need for a lot of specialized gadgetry. It was used as a music maker, digging stick, scythe, two-man fire saw and much more. A flint chip was also imbedded into the handle with spinifex gum so it could be used as an adze or chisel. As the use of the technology continued, the knowledge of animal life and the stealth and body control needed to master it as a hunting tool continued. Once the need for stealth or dexterity dwindled as a result of modern weaponry, so did the basic survival skills of the people.

In most literature, the technology of the atlatl has been lumped into one category–that of a projectile propelled by a solid hand-held extension. Very little has been written about atlatls that helps to distinguish the broad variety of styles separated by design, construction and use. Without looking at the various types of atlatl as distinctly unique from one another, we fall into the trap of comparing throwing boards to casting sticks because they are both atlatls, but dissimilar in other ways.

This lack of distinction has caused some confusion when trying to decipher why the atlatl works, as well as interpret the many items found in association with different atlatl-using cultures (ie. weights, bannerstones).

Atlatl Systems

The following categories have been enlisted to provide a simple classification for deciding what type of system (the atlatl and projectile must be made as a set) you may wish to produce based upon local tradition, materials available and what you want to do with the set you make. The categories do not establish a hierarchy or distinguish one class as any more valuable than another. They are only divisions that may help you to determine what it takes to make the set you desire, the level of skill and technology you may have to employ, and the principles involved that make it work.

Throwing Board

A throwing board was employed primarily in the northern regions to propel a harpoon into fish or mammals. A similar style of rigid board was used in Mexico to catch fish. The board was very rigid with the grip and finger loops either carved into it (integral) or provided by pegs that are added. The harpoon was a relatively heavy projectile that carries a detachable toggle point. Once the point entered the prey, the shaft fell away and the hunter retrieved his catch by means of a line attached to the toggle. The atlatl allowed the heavy shaft to be propelled with power from a sitting position and added thrust to the shaft when it was thrown into the water. Since wood was at a premium in the north, the shafts were relatively short and were detachable so that they were easily retrieved. In the south, the fishing spears were very long and may or may not have employed a detachable point. Both shafts were heavy so as to carry the force delivered by the atlatl. The atlatl's main function was to increase leverage.

Spear Thrower

The spear thrower system was used by mankind through most of our hunting tradition. Some flex may have been built into the system by either the atlatl, spear or both, but it was not a highly tuned device. Its main purpose was to deliver a long, heavy spear a fair distance into prey that was either too fast or too lethal to get close to, or increase the accuracy of the placement of the spear. The extra power from the thrower and the mass of the spear delivered incredible kinetic energy (knock-down power) to the prey.

Ivory throwers from the times of the Neanderthal to the modern woomeras of contemporary Australian Aborigines fall into this class of atlatl. The spears were a solid shaft with either a fire-hardened tip, hafted point or detachable foreshaft. The detachable foreshaft allowed the hunter to retrieve the spear and reload with a new foreshaft, ready to fire again. Thus the weight of additional spear shafts was exchanged for numerous foreshafts–not to mention the extra labor needed to produce a full-length spear.

Flexible System

The addition of component parts, bannerstones, counterweights and a notable preference for very light, springy darts with detachable foreshafts gave this system the ability to be engineered specifically to the needs of the hunter.

The stored energy of the flexible atlatl and dart propeled the light projectile with amazing speed, force and distance. The adaptability of the system allowed it to be used under a broad range of conditions and constructed from numerous serviceable materials. Most evidence of this system has been found in the arid caves of the southwest United States.

Oak atlatls of less than a quarter inch thick and fragile darts made from the papery canary reedgrass were common. Weighted systems from the Great Basin display broad varieties of size and design that may suggest that quivers of atlatls and darts may have been carried to compensate for varying size and distance of game. The main distinction between this system and the spear thrower is that an obvious mental shift took place to harness and maximize the use of flex and stored energy.

Casting Stick

Was the "Baton de Commandment" a shaft straightener, badge of office or casting stick? It has been suggested that a thong attached to the baton made it a perfect handle for casting arrows over incredible distances (Comstock/Baker/Ratzat). An interest in this activity was nurtured at the turn of the century, but has enjoyed a new resurgence with efforts to establish modern flight records for hand-thrown darts and arrows.

The thong-thrown arrow employs the simple idea of a very flexible atlatl shaft. Today we see a variety of systems that employ sophisticated understanding of flex and counterweights. With distance being the goal, very light sets can be built that reduce air drag and maximize the benefits of flex and recoil in both the atlatl and dart (Brian). Distances of over 300 yards suggest an apparatus that was used to throw a projectile from a high-arcing flight into a crowd or a herd, literally taking pot-luck.

Atlatl Basics

The basic principle behind the use of the atlatl is that when you increase the arc of the throwing pattern, you also increase the length of time that force is applied to the projectile (the velocity of a point on a radius is higher the further it is from the axis point). In other words, if a major league pitcher can hurl a fast ball at 100 miles per hour, just think what you would have if you could fit a gorilla, with 20% longer arms, into that same uniform (although you may have trouble getting it to wear that little cap).

With this mechanical advantage, a 6- to 10-foot spear can be thrown over 100 yards, as opposed to only about 100 feet with the unaided arm. When used to propel a heavy harpoon with a rigid throwing board, the harpoon will travel farther and at a much faster rate than if thrown by hand.

For increased potential, add to this principle the idea that if both the dart and/or atlatl are made of flexible materials and allowed to act as springs, their flex and associated recoil actually make the dart a self-projecting missile that snaps off of the atlatl at a greater velocity than can ever be generated by hand (Perkins and Leininger).

A large spear with some flex, thrown by a long atlatl with some flex, will be propelled farther, faster and with more energy than by hand. If this idea is magnified and controlled by an increase in flex, and the addition of counterweights that time the flex and de-flex of the system's components, all of the above factors, as well as accuracy, are enhanced.

If long-distance goals are your target, refine these same principles even farther, and you have projectiles that can be thrown well over 300 yards. The speed and force with which the projectiles travel will also be markedly improved.

When using an atlatl system, there are typically two methods for gripping the atlatl: split finger and power grip, and two distinct styles of throwing: accuracy and long distance.

Split finger grip—The index and middle fingers are placed into the finger loops or holes from the back of the atlatl, with the spur extending away from the body. The third and little fingers wrap over the handle of the atlatl and are gripped by the thumb coming from the other side. The dart is held in place against the spur between the tips of the thumb and third finger, and lies along the shaft of the atlatl between the index and middle fingers. Some increase in short-distance accuracy may be achieved by this grip, but it may feel awkward.

Power grip—The thumb and index finger are placed into the finger loops or holes from the back of the atlatl, with the spur extending away from the body. The remaining fingers grip the handle. The dart is held in place against the spur between the tips of the thumb and middle finger, and lies along the shaft of the atlatl on top of the grip fingers. This is a more natural-feeling grip, and may provide some increase in distance.

Split-finger grip. (Photo: Wescott)

Throwing for accuracy—The motion is somewhat like a cross between pitching a baseball and throwing darts at a dart board—you try to employ a somewhat flat delivery while maintaining control and speed.

1. The atlatl is held flat at shoulder height.
2. As the throw begins, you draw the dart back for a wind-up and step forward.
3. As you begin to propel the dart forward, the body begins to lower slightly, allowing you to begin the power arc with the handle, yet maintain a flatter trajectory with the spur end. The dart is released toward the point of aim at this point.
4. Follow through as if you were pitching a fast ball.
5. The final portion of the throw is a slight wrist snap and follow-through.

Throwing for distance—This motion is identical to throwing a rock or baseball. You can wind up by running and then throwing as you would a javelin.

1. The atlatl is held flat at shoulder height.
2. As you begin to propel the dart forward, the shoulder and elbow rotate forward to increase power. The dart is released at a trajectory of about 41° at this point.
3. The entire upper body rotates forward to increase the force applied.
4. The arm and wrist follow through and the dart snaps out of the spur.

*Split-finger grip. The dart is held in place against the spur between the tips
of the thumb and third finger and lies along the shaft of the atlatl between the
index and middle fingers. (Photo: Wescott)*

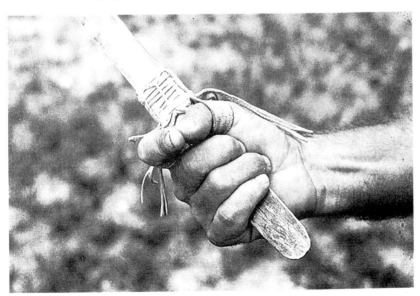

Power Grip. (Photo: Wescott)

A Suggested Comparison Of Atlatl And Projectile Types

Table A

Projectile characteristics and related throwing mechanism.

Projectile	Flex	Length	Mass	Mechanism
Harpoon	Rigid	Short	Heavy	Throwing Board
Spear	Some	Variable	Heavy to Light	Spear Thrower
Dart	High	Pi X Atlatl*	Light	Flexible System
Flight Dart	Extreme	Variable	Very light	Casting Stick

* Research suggests that for optimal performance in flexible systems there is a predictable relationship between the length of the dart and the atlatl. This may account for the variety of lengths and styles of atlatls found in areas that offer a variety of available materials—the atlatl and projectile must be constructed so that they compliment each other. Since few complete prehistoric darts have been found, we can't do a comparative study, but mathematics suggests that the length of the dart should be Pi X the length of the atlatl (Perkins and Leininger).

Table B

Atlatl characteristics and related projectile type.

Style	Flex	Length	Parts	Projectile
Throwing Board	Rigid	Short	Integral	Rigid/Short
Spear Thrower	None/Some	Variable	Added Tools *	Slight Flex/Long
Flexible System	Variable	Variable **	High	Flex/Light
Casting Stick	Extreme	Variable	Variable **	Extreme Flex

* In Australia the spear thrower is a multiple-use tool. More than a half-dozen uses are regularly identified with aboriginal artifacts. A flint chip imbedded into the handle is used as a chisel, the sharp edge serves as a fire saw, and the curved profile provides a natural bowl (Stokes). ** Both the flexible system and casting sticks may have finger and wrist loops, spurs, and movable weights added to the atlatl shaft, allowing them to be tuned with precision. The main distinction between the spear thrower and the flexible system seems to be a more complete understanding and control of flex and the component parts needed to employ its power. The difference between the flexible system and casting stick may simply be the degree of application of this understanding.

Making Darts

Most people spend far too much time on the aesthetics of their atlatl rather than on the mechanics of the system. But the dart is the most important component of the system (Perkins), and has to be custom-made to the thrower (Frison).

A spear is a hand-thrust or board-thrown weapon and has little flexibility. A dart is very flexible and is used with a flexible-shaft atlatl system. Regardless of what style of atlatl you make, the darts must match the style of atlatl you intend to use. A light dart used on a rigid atlatl shaft will overpower the dart and cause it to bend too far and snap. A harpoon used on a flexible shaft atlatl will probably force the shaft to bend too far and break as well.

A dart is surprisingly light and flexible, but the weight of the dart is much greater than any arrow and imparts more knock-down power (kinetic energy) than even the most sophisticated primitive bows. Most primitive darts vary widely in design, material and craftsmanship. But modern research shows that the laws of wave motions and aerodynamics can be applied to design extreme-precision components with primitive materials (Perkins & Leininger).

Darts must be a consistent length (specimens range from 4 to 10 feet) that fits your throwing style. They must be flexible yet made of a durable material (willow, lodgepole pine, canary reedgrass, giant river cane, elderberry, red osier dogwood, cedar, hickory, etc.).

After cutting the material, remove the bark and slowly heat the shaft over a fire until it becomes pliable (do not char it). Heating and straightening may take parts of three days for the wood to gain a memory of its new form. Even after seasoning and greasing, you may have to slightly re-bend the darts by hand before each use. As you heat and bend the shaft, scrape (don't whittle) it with a knife or glass to evenly reduce its size to match the set (at least three darts).

Proper flex may be checked by loosely holding one end in your hand near your shoulder and letting the other end rest on the ground. With your free hand, pluck the shaft like you would the string on a bass fiddle. The shaft should bend towards you and then fly into the air with a quivering rebound. As it comes down and hits the ground, it should bounce two or three times and still feel springy, but dampen quickly. Don't take off too much wood or your dart will snap in two from lack of strength.

Fletching on the butt end can be left off or comprised of two to four feathers. If you want the dart to rotate rather than plane, you can put a slight spiral in the fletch. Some people do not split the feather vane as on an arrow, but simply lay a full feather on either side of the dart and lash them in place with sinew.

The spear point may be a simple fire-hardened tip, or a foreshaft may be inserted into a small hole in the tip of the dart. A foreshaft adds strength to the tip, carries a replaceable point or blunt and adds weight (about 6 grams) to the front of the dart. This is important as it slows the motion of

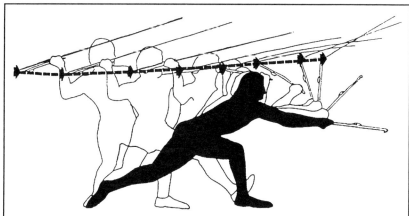

The Finer Art of Throwing

1. Grasp the dart with the grip hand, between the loop/hole finger tips as far forward as possible (the fingers used to hold the dart are determined by the type of grip used on the atlatl). This grip will cause the butt of the dart to press securely against the spur and reduce the chance of misfires.
2. The throw should be smooth, with a gentle increase in force until the last snap of the wrist. The motion is most like the wind-up and release of a baseball pitcher. The wrist snap at the end of the throw lends a controlling motion to the dart's flight.
3. For long distance, the wind-up and approach is like that of a javelin thrower. The release is at a much higher angle (41°) for maximum distance.
4. For accuracy, a subtle lunge seems to give you better follow-through. Some believe this is due to the fact that the lowering of the body keeps the pivot point at the spur on an even plane with the original starting point (see illustration).
5. The release of the dart becomes almost imperceptible, as is the aim. If you can throw a ball well, you can refine your ability with the atlatl.

the front of the dart in the throwing sequence, thus requiring the dart to store more energy in the shaft until the flex in the dart and atlatl meet, cancel one another and propel the dart away from the thrower at a greater velocity (Perkins and Leininger). It also works as a shock absorber in the front of the dart to reduce the stress on the shaft from impact (Harwood).

Modern substitutes can be used for faster results until you refine your work with native materials. This substitute may fly in the face of aesthetics, but until one first knows what to do, how to do it, and can do it habitually (Callahan), you save a lot of time, and waste of good native materials. Simply join two XX 2317 Easton Arrow shafts together by cutting and gluing a short piece of 2117 shaft into the junction. If you glue only one end, you have a breakdown shaft. Fletch and add a field tip just as you would any arrow. (Never throw this near people. To add safety, substitute a rubber blunt for the field tip.)

Glue a regular tip insert into the butt end, and ream it out with a counter-sink bit. This gives you a solid and well-shaped cup that will rest securely against the spur. You can make a dozen of these practice darts in one evening for about $35.

Making the Atlatl
The atlatl and dart must be tuned to match each other. The ancient Basketmaker atlatls described below provide a good model to start with, and work well with the darts from the Easton "tribe". Rigid models work well with heavy harpoons and long abo-spears, but the atlatl and dart must be designed with some flex to it if you expect distances to increase. Just about any wood will do (mahogany, oak, ash, birch, cedar, cottonwood, alder, etc.), and the design and size are as limitless as the number of people making them, although most share the same common components.

Handles—The handle allows you to control the atlatl during the throw without casting it down-range with the dart. It must be long enough to extend across the palm of the hand and allow full leverage on the wrist snap.

Finger loop or holes—These may or may not be used. The size of the loop is determined by the type of grip you choose to use. Many atlatls provide notches, finger holes or a narrowed waist that improves grip.

Shaft—The length of the shaft may range from 6 inches to 3 feet. An average length of 60.2 centimeters (24 inches) found on ten Basketmaker atlatls is a good size.

Flute—Many atlatls have no center groove (male). The groove in the atlatl may be a short one or run the entire length of the shaft. Its function is to hold the dart in line with the atlatl (long flute and flush spur–female) or to simply allow the butt cup to line up with a raised spur when the spur is part of a short flute (mixed).

Spur—The spur is a blunt nipple that allows the butt cup to pivot as the atlatl completes the throwing arc. It should be blunt so that it doesn't hook the dart upon release. It may be inlaid into the flute, carved into the flute (integral) or added to the flat surface of the shaft (attached). It may be made of bone, antler, wood, metal, etc.

Weight—Artifact weights average about 40-60 grams. Their function is to slow the bend of the atlatl, concentrate force and time its recoil to that of the dart. It should be placed at the point of flex on the atlatl shaft, and can

Trouble Shooting Your Technique

1. **Dart goes into the ground at your feet:** You are holding the dart too tightly and releasing too late. Relax. Release the dart at the same point you feel you would release a baseball.
2. **Dart sky-rockets away with no control:** Either you released too early or your darts are too stiff. If you try to control your throw with no results, then it is your dart. The flex in the dart allows it to bend and recoil into a proper flight path. Shave down the dart to give it more flex or tune the atlatl to match the flex of the dart.
3. **The butt of the dart drops too much as it is released:** Add fletching to the butt to control its flight. If the problem persists, the spur on the atlatl is probably too long and is hooking the butt of the dart just prior to separation.
4. **Dart hits the target sideways:** This could be a combination of problems. As the dart flexes, it takes a certain distance for the quiver in the shaft to dampen and straighten out the flight of the dart. You may be too close to the target for the size of the dart and atlatl system you are using. Your dart may be too stiff, or you may need fletching to control the flight. You may also need to re-tune the dart and the atlatl.
5. **Dart keeps falling off the atlatl as you throw:** Don't do this. You can ruin both the dart and the atlatl. You are not seating and holding the dart against the spur tightly enough or long enough.

be moved up and down the shaft until it is properly tuned to the dart. Multiple weights can be added.

Why did the bow and arrow take over in some cultures?

Velocity—A dart travels at about two-thirds the speed of a primitive arrow, one-half the speed of a 50-pound long bow, and one-third the speed of a modern compound bow.

Stealth—It is easier to launch an arrow with less movement at close proximity.

Release—The motion and effort needed to release a dart may spook the quarry. Compare this to an arrow which takes about two-thirds of a second for release.

Mastery—The body control, dexterity, and release are much easier to master with a bow and arrow than an atlatl and dart.

Accuracy—Success with a bow and arrow depends on good aim and gear. Success with an atlatl and dart depends on the complex coordination of many body movements, stealth and technology.

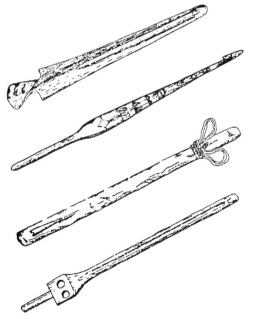

(top to bottom) An Eskimo throwing board, Australian woomerah, Basket-maker flexible atlatl, and a Northern Mexico fishing atlatl.

Why did the atlatl and dart survive in some cultures?

Momentum–A dart carries twice the momentum of a primitive arrow, and still greater force than an English long bow.

Kinetic Energy–A dart carries more energy than any other primitive weapon. The Spaniards feared this Aztec weapon as it penetrated their armor even when thrown from great distance.

Function–A bow takes two hands to operate. While duck or seal hunting, an atlatl can be used with one hand while the other handles the boat.

Stealth–Skill and knowledge let the hunter get so close there was no need to change to a new and unfamiliar technology.

Cultural Context/Tradition–The atlatl held a solid place in many cultures as a multi-functional tool. Fire making, woodworking, mixing pigments and tobacco, water dipping, chipping, chiseling, making music, clearing ground, and carving maps to water holes were all part of the functional atlatl.

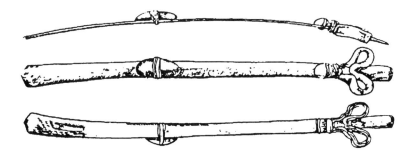

Finger loops or holes may or may not be used according to preference. The size of the loop is determined by the type of grip you choose to use. Many atlatls provide notches, finger holes, or a narrowed waist that improves grip.

Larry Dean Olsen

Badgerstone

• •

Miss Romain wanted my eyes on the blackboard. But out

the window and westward across the desert lay the cave,

and my eyes saw only the treasure in its deep floor. That

day I formed in my mind an expedition to reach the cave.

It was spring, and I was aching for a plunge into the Stone Age. I was already making excursions into desert places to hunt and to find arrowheads, and I was learning many great things about hides, rocks and mouse digging. But I felt ready for the long trek, the quest for my "Wyakin," for the feel of total Stone Age living–or something.

Then one day I saw it. I was staring out the window of Miss Romain's class, and there it was, in my mind's eye. A cave. Deep and hidden in a narrow twist of a lava gash that cut through the great Snake River plains. Below the cliff's base the talus dropped steeply to a creek I named "No Name."

In my inventiveness I saw that the cave was large enough to sleep twenty people on its flat floor. Its amphitheater shape caught the winter's sun clear to its back wall. The west wind was deflected around the living area by a narrow column of rock projecting neatly from the canyon wall.

Beneath the dusty cave floor I imagined buried ancient treasures of Anasazi living. It was a treasure of the greatest value to me. It was the proof of more than Paiute. It was Anasazi, unknown in these parts as declared in writing by the experts. It was something they believed but didn't know for sure–but I knew I couldn't have been born in a valley where Anasazi had not hunted!

Miss Romain couldn't understand me, but she was hopeful for me. Spring vacation was almost upon us and my chances for an academic rather than a social promotion looked good. Ever since the day I learned to read, Miss Romain had tried to coax me into interesting grade-school-level novels. That was until one day she caught me engrossed in Julian Steward's book, Basin-Plateau Aboriginal Sociopolitical Groups, an anthropological study of Paiutes. I had discovered the book in the Idaho State College library while on a trip to Pocatello.

In the basement of the local library was hidden a reclusive group of archaeologists and their artifacts. They ventured forth each summer to dig sites and get their names in the paper. They returned each fall with their treasures to spread on big tables in the basement. Then, during the winter months, they arranged, pondered and speculated on these tidbits of pre-history. This usually resulted in great pontification on the archaeology of certain sites, very technically written in ugly-looking journals read by a few devotees and then lost in the library stacks.

But I found the writings and I tracked down the lair of the archaeologists in the library basement and I boldly entered their domain. I was not welcome—but for two hours they tolerated my youthful questions and probing. I laid low over each long table and noted the minute details of each tiny flake and tool. The archaeologists and their student fellows kept their eyes carefully upon me and said many times, "Don't touch anything!"

Then there entered into the lab another person who commanded the entire attention of the experts. It was as if he was their medicine man, or the Great One who gave meaning to their work.

I melted into the huddle around him and listened. He was Sven Lilliablad and he knew things like I knew them. It was instinctive knowledge supported by some pre-existent memory as if the ancient peoples he studied were somehow personal friends. This little white-haired man was intense but spoke softly, and ideas flowed from his experiences like a vision. He gently touched artifacts on the table and explained their intent and function as if he had made them himself.

When I left the lab and walked to where my Dad was waiting for me, I carried, tucked under my coat, Julian Steward's book and a paper manuscript that Sven, my friend, had given me.

I had learned the difference between those who were academic professionals and those who also knew about the breezes. I knew then that I was not the only dreamer of Anasazi dreams who walked in the 20th century. It helped a lot to know this, and after that, when kids at school called me "Chief Oogie," I only smiled and let them compliment me to their hearts content.

Miss Romain wanted my eyes on the blackboard. But out the window and westward across the desert lay the cave, and my eyes saw only the treasure in its deep floor. That day I formed in my mind an expedition to reach the cave. My two best friends were invited along, but they didn't want to miss the Saturday matinee. I determined to go it alone.

On Tuesday I started making a new pair of high-top moccasins from an old pair of field boots. I cut off the soles, turned the boots inside out and started sewing on soles of cowhide leather.

On Wednesday I rolled up a blanket pack, sharpened my pocket knife and a small hunting knife and made a long "possibles" bag from the leg of an old pair of Levis. I filled it with survival supplies: fishhooks and line, bandages, matches, a notebook, pencils, two muskrat traps, a roll of waxed linen string, three apples, one large onion, three potatoes, three carrots, a poke of salt, a small canteen of water, three dry biscuits and one Hershey bar (in case of emergency).

By midnight I had the soles stitched on my moccasins and a long piece of clothesline rope tied onto my blanket roll. I was ready.

My mother had watched my preparations carefully and had suggested enough additional gear to fill a covered wagon. I told her I wasn't going clear to Oregon. "Besides," I said confidently, "you're lucky I'm taking even this stuff. If I really went whole-hog Paiute, I'd have to go naked, 'cept for my moccasins, cause they're the only things I have that're real Indian."   Actually, the field boot moccasins were only part Indian; the part where I did the stitching myself.

Momma sort of nodded a vague understanding of my plans. She understood my need to go, and skipping school for important projects like this wasn't totally against her personal plans for my success in life. Daddy wasn't too concerned about my schooling either, but he had plenty to say about me going into the desert alone. After two days of stern warning on everything from mosquitos to rattle snakes, he ran out of advice. On Thursday morning he drove me to the west desert and left me there. I later learned that he followed me for the first mile just to see if I was really serious.

My trail led down a steep gully for the first two miles. From that point I climbed up a long side wash to the bluff above. The desert stretched flat to the horizon. In the distance there appeared a thin dark line which I took to be No Name Creek canyon. I headed for it, with a sure expectation of a powerful adventure.

This was my first solo expedition. I had absorbed a great deal of interesting facts about Paiutes, Anasazi and the flora and fauna of the Great Plateau deserts of Idaho. As yet, this potfull of facts had been tested only in my mind, aided by the breezes. I was counting on my instincts to bring me success. My father truly did not know just how far I planned to hike. Actually, I hadn't realized it myself, and I wondered right off if I could get there and back to the drop point by Saturday evening.

I had previously spent parts of days alone working on my Uncle Bill's farm, and had spent several, one-night campouts in the desert by myself. As I hiked along the flat, three days seemed like quite a big chunk of time in this unknown, roadless place. But the land felt good under my new moccasin soles, and each step brought me more and more in touch with the breezes. I walked and tossed between a tiny grip of fear and a peaceful blending with the desert.

Sagebrush grew skimpy and short. Scattered on the flats were countless red ant mounds, each surrounded by circles of bare earth where the ants had stripped the land around their little pyramids. As I walked along observing each ant mound, a general pattern began to emerge.

The ants had constructed their rounded mounds with one side a bit steeper than the others. This steep slope was almost always facing south-southeast. At the base of the steep side was found their entrance holes. I noted in my journal that the few exceptions were always due to some natural obstruction on the south side of a mound, like a tall brush or rock that shaded the mound. From this observation I concluded that the ants depended on the sun to warm their lives each day, especially in the winter when the sun swung low along the southern horizon and the ants were deep below the frost line.

The steep exposure sucked up heat which reduced the grip of winter cold on the mound. I knew that ants remained active all winter. They stored food all summer in anticipation of the cold times; now I had discovered that they also built heat-efficient housing. I wondered what else these little tribes of desert dwellers could teach me. I thought about the story of the Ant and the Grasshopper, and I thought about my parents and our grocery store and the Prophet who taught Mormons to store food and fuel for two years ahead.

Somehow, I couldn't relate the ants to Miss Romain's class at school. I wondered whether ants found it necessary to hold classes of instruction for all upcoming "antlets" in order to maintain their organized and busy mound building society. Red ants seemed ever-ready for a fierce fight though, so maybe they did have a school of sorts after all.

Finally it struck me: the ants could serve me, as well as teach me. No longer were those little creatures mere teachers of philosophy, social organization and architecture. They could also be my professional guides as I hiked. It was so very simple. At any time of the year, whether cloudy or in blizzards, the little mounds, averaged together, faced south. I knew then that I would never lose my way in the land of red ants.

Red ants were also troublesome. The flat stretched on and on, and despite my many new thoughts and discoveries, the desert heat began to press down upon me. I had to move faster toward the still thin rim of No Name Canyon.

The stitching of my moccasin broke slowly at first. Then, stubbing against a rock, the whole toe end tore loose and started flopping. My once-pleasant walking on the new soles of my moccasins suddenly became agony as my right foot scooped up sand and stickers. Worst of all were the red ants. I hobbled on each step. Then the big toe on my let foot poked through and I tripped along in double plop in the middle of nowhere.

My feet were fairly tough, and the sand didn't bother me too much, but the stickers and red ants soon found the tender spots between my toes. finally I stopped, sat on my blanket roll and pondered my dirty feet with little red pricks and bites all over them. They looked wholly unsuited for this terrain. In only four miles or so of hiking, my Paiute stitching had failed me.

Now I was totally un-Paiute and wondered if I had been walking backwards or something. I drank some of my water and slumped in the dirt on the big flat in the miserable west desert.

Going back seemed the only sensible way for me. The treasure was far away and the vision was fading. I dozed in the pungent shade of a sage brush for a few minutes and as I lay there, all my thoughts disappeared. The vision was gone. The sky was white in the heat and alkali dirt purged my lips and tongue. Quiet settled in all around me. I could feel the thump of my heart as it performed its duty without any effort or desire on my part.

Slowly, thumpings came through the ground under me, in time with my heartbeat. They filtered a rhythmic pounding in the soil. I felt it in the ground around me but could hear nothing. In the stillness there came a sense that I wasn't alone out there after all. Was it someone walking? Legends say that Indians could hear the cavalry coming every time they put their ear to the ground. I just lay there, straining.

In a few minutes I could hear a muffled growl and spitting noise. It was really close. I sat up and turned toward the sound. The hairs on the back of my neck prickled. There was a small mound of sand, just behind my shade bush. The brush was blocking my view, so I carefully crawled about three feet and peered over. Less than five feet away was a large hole dug in the ground. It was almost big enough for a boy my size to crawl into. Sloping upwards away from the hole was a ramp of dirt tailings that peaked sharply at its top, clearly testifying of the enormous amount of earth moving that had taken place there.

The muffled growls and hissing were coming from the hole. Then a furry rump emerged. It was a badger, a big one, coming out of the den backwards!

My curiosity faded as fear swept over me. I was too close. Every boy in southern Idaho knew that badgers didn't back down from a fight. They chased worse than cactus. I was barefoot; no chance to outrun this monster. Right then I wanted someone to appear and rescue me. I almost cried out, "Momma!" The badger was growling fiercely and hissing. I could hear my heart right between my ears.

Old Badger came out of the earth and backed up the long dirt ramp. He held in his front claws a fist sized stone, and he was dragging and rolling it along up the ramp. His flat body topped the ramp and pitched awkwardly down the other side. This brought the stone to the top of the mound, but it slipped from his grip and went rolling back down the ramp and into the hole. Old Badger seemed to realize the failure of his attempt to remove the pesky stone. He let out a low growl and thrashed a bush near his nose, I lay low.

Old Badger finally lumbered back into the ground grumbling and hissing with typical badger temperament. I had my chance to slip on my broken moccasins and get out of that place, but I didn't. Old Badger hadn't seen or smelled me on his first trip out of the hole. Maybe I could watch for awhile. I could hear him deep underground almost beneath me, spitting and struggling.

Presently Old Badger's rump emerged and once again he backed up the dirt ramp, pulling the stone along. Once again he backed his flat body over the crest and lost his grip on the stone. It rolled back down the hole. Old Badger spat out a whole string of unique sounds and followed the path of the stone back into the ground.

The badger and the stone repeated the same dance over and over again until I became weary of watching. His situation seemed hopeless with the ready-made ramp and track for that stone to roll back on. His only hope was to keep a hold on the stone. This he seemed unable to do once his body tipped over the crest of the dirt mound. I wanted to crawl over and give him a hand.

Then, on about the fourteenth attempt, Old Badger held on to the stone and pulled it over the crest. It tumbled down the back side away from the hole. Old Badger just sat there and rested for awhile. The growling and hissing stopped. He seemed really pleased with himself for a moment.

Then I got nervous. So taken was I by the drama of the badger and the stone that I forgot how dangerous badgers were and how close my nose was to his. The sudden tension I felt must have caused a movement or a scent that reached the awareness of Old Badger. He rose up and our eyes met. His nose sniffed me out, but he didn't bristle. I almost fainted. If he chased me, he would catch me. I knew it. We stared at each other for a long moment.

Old Badger made the first move. Without any show of anger or bluff he gave me a nod, and slipped smoothly down the ramp into his den. I could feel him digging new ground below me. Then, I realized that my heart had stopped pounding and I felt warm, at ease and somehow very privileged.

I put on my torn moccasins, picked up my gear and started to leave. I glanced back at the hole and noticed the stone Old Badger had struggled with for so long. It was cleaner and smoother than the rough native lava of the area. I stepped quickly over to the dirt mound, picked up the stone and walked quickly away from the Badger's den. To my surprise it turned out to be a broken half of a well-crafted Indian mano, or handstone. I could smell Old Badger on it. I held it in my hand for a long time before slipping it reverently into my possibles bag.

From Old Badger's den I had scoop-plopped along for almost a mile before realizing that my despair and give-upitis was completely gone. My feet still suffered from the loose stitchings on my moccasins, but not unbearably as before. What had happened? What had Old Badger done to make such a change in the way I felt in this harsh and endless desert?

Had I been taught by an animal messenger? Truly this had happened, and a surge of genuine toughness flowed through my whole body. I was and would ever be, Badger Clan. Then I spit right into the breeze and pointed my tattered toes westward toward the ever-thickening black line of No Name Canyon.

Some examples of sizes and shapes of baskets you can weave. Top left-clockwise: A water basket in progress, shallow bowl, large tray with filigree work on top, small feather-decorated basket, flat tray decorated with corn husk design. Center front: hot pad sewn with a wheat stitch, the basket I purchased from the BOSS instructor and center a basket start (Photo by Richard Jamison).

Margaret Wilkinson

Pine Needle Basketry

● ● ● ● ● ● ● ◦ ● ● ● ● ● ● ● ● ● ● ● ● ● ● ● ● ● ● ●

When you begin, don't be concerned with making a perfect

basket, just start. Enjoy learning to work the needles and

see what you come up with. And regardless of how you

think your first attempt looks–KEEP IT.

I have always considered basketry a beautiful art and have especially enjoyed seeing the ancient Indian baskets displayed in museums. So when I had a chance to watch a basket actually being constructed, I sat spellbound, my attention focused on the hands of the weaver as he worked. This man was using a technique that I had never seen, and he was weaving long pine needles that were in a wide-mouth jar of water to keep them pliable. I asked him where he got the pine needles he was using, since we were in cottonwood and cedar country, and he told me he had picked them up from under the ponderosa pine trees on the campus of Brigham Young University.

At the time I was in Diamond Fork Canyon, Utah at the Woodsmoke Rendezvous, and the weaver was one of the instructors from the Boulder Outdoor Survival School (B.O.S.S.), a private organization that conducts primitive living expeditions in Southern Utah for B.Y.U. students and others.

I continued to watch as the basket developed. He wrapped raffia around the coil of pine needles and then took a stitch down over the bottom coil to tie it together. It was absolutely fascinating, and I bought that little basket during the Rendezvous trading session.

Traveling over Wolf Creek Pass on our way home to Monte Vista, Colorado we drove past some ponderosa pine trees, and I encouraged my husband, Ernie, to stop so we could gather needles for me to try my hand at this newly-learned craft.

Once home, I pulled out my craft catalogs and found where to order raffia. Ernie was going to Denver to get taxidermy supplies, and I decided to go along and look for basket weaving instruction books. From the many books displayed at Western Trading Post, I chose three basketry books that provided enough information to get me started. After determining what materials I needed, I did just that.

Since watching that first pine needle basket being made, I have had occasion to spend many precious hours creating what I consider to be my own masterpieces. I know they probably don't compare with the baskets made by many of the talented Native American basketmakers, but it has been a thrill for me to develop my talent and to teach others this craft as well–including some native Americans. It is very humbling for me to see their joy in re-creating something in the tradition of the Old Ones.

I'd like to share the experience of making a pine needle basket with you, too. Here are the things you'll need to get started:

▲ Pine needles
▲ Raffia, yarn or whatever material you choose to use to sew the coils together (Long grasses work well, too, but they should be dried first, then dampened before they are used.)
▲ Blunt-end sewing needles (tapestry #18, 20 or 21 are my choice)
▲ Scissors
▲ A gauge–this can be made from a piece of bone with a hole in it the size of the basket coil, a three-quarter-inch plastic tube like those used for aquariums or even a plastic drinking straw
▲ A pair of small needle-nosed pliers
▲ A plastic bag
▲ A thimble
▲ A pan or jar for soaking the needles

Making a pine needle basket can be an adventure, and the first step is to gather plenty of needles–whether from your own back yard or by taking a day trip to the mountains. Either way, you should begin by appreciating that Mother Nature has provided this wonderful material for you.

If you live in a warm climate, you may find longleaf pines like (P. australis) with their long nubby needles or (Pinus palustris), whose needles are often 12 to 18 inches long and ideal to work with. Pine needles can be gathered at any time of year, but in high elevation areas you will have to gather early enough to beat the snowfall. Choose from the top layer of brown needles that have just fallen from the trees. If you dig down too deep, the needles will have started to deteriorate and they will have dark mottled or mildewed spots, which make them weak and unsuitable for weaving.

I seldom collect green pine needles from the trees unless there has been a wind storm that has broken off branches, in which case I collect the needles and lay them in the shade to dry. Once dry they will stay pale green. If you use fresh pine needles without first drying them, they will shrink and your basket will be too loose.

Wash the needles by swishing them in water with a little natural soap to remove dirt or insects, then rinse them several times to remove all remaining residue. Next, spread the needles out over a blanket in the shade or on some other flat surface to dry.

If you don't plan to use all the pine needles right away, you can store them. If you've used a blanket or towel to dry them, just pick up the corners, shake them into a pile and put the whole thing in a box until you are ready to make a basket.

If you don't have much space for storage and you have plenty of time, you can bundle the needles. Group them according to size with all the sheaths in one direction, and wrap them with a piece of raffia or bind them with a rubber band. These bundles can then be stacked in a cupboard or put in a drawer. This works great when I am teaching a class because the bundles can be distributed quickly. But it is also very time-consuming, so I generally sort as I work the needles into coils, using short and long needles alternately. I usually use the same species for each basket.

The instructor from BOSS kept his needles in water as he worked, but when I tried this I found that my baskets became wobbly as they dried. So I experimented and found a way to make a nice firm basket that stays that way. Granted, the center, or start, of the basket does require dampened pine needles; but, how long do you need to soak them? It depends on what needles you use. The Canary Island (P. canariensis), digger (P. sabiniana), loblolly (P. tacda) and longleaf pines all have soft needles and take 10 to 15 minutes in warm water to soften them enough for the start (1-2 inch center). While coulter (P. coulteri), jeffery (P.jeffreyi), ponderosa (P. ponderosa), torrey (P. torreyana) and slash (P. elliottii) pines have rigid, thicker needles that require 2 to 4 hours of soaking in cold water, or 45 minutes in warm water. If you use hot, boiling water, they will be ready in 15 to 20 minutes, but boiling water darkens the needle color.

A good way to judge the flexibility is to bend the needles around your finger or tie them in a knot. If you can do this without the needles splitting or breaking, they are suitable to work with. Once the needles are pliable,

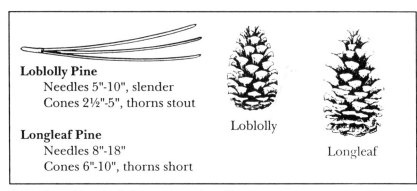

Loblolly Pine
  Needles 5"-10", slender
  Cones 2½"-5", thorns stout

Longleaf Pine
  Needles 8"-18"
  Cones 6"-10", thorns short

Loblolly

Longleaf

Loblolly and longleaf pine cones and needles.

remove them from the water and put them in an airtight container (a zip-lock bag works well). If you don't plan to use them right away, dry them out or they will mildew. Or, circumstances permitting, put the baggies of wet needles in the freezer until you are ready to use them.

I use raffia as my weaver. Raffia comes from the raffia palm that grows in Madagascar, an island off the east coast of Africa. The young palm leaves are cut green and the outer, transparent skin is pulled off and hung to air-dry in the sun. It is then stripped and graded into different categories and exported. I particularly like the raffia that has a waxy feel because it seems to work unusually well with the pine needles. I avoid dyed raffia because it is too dry. Sometimes, I prepare the raffia by letting it stand overnight in a plastic bag with a little water and some glycerin. This seems to make it more pliable and easier to work with, but it can be used either wet or dry.

Sometimes the edges of the long strands will be rolled; just dip the strands into a pan of water and manipulate them a bit until you can unroll the curl and have a nice wide piece. You should also remove the side hairs from the raffia, and if it is extra wide, you can split it to the size you prefer to work with. Threading the raffia through the needle the right way is very important. The fiber starts to grow at the palm leaf stem and continues out to the width of the leaf, and the short, less mature fibers are shorter than some of the others. So if you examine it closely, you will see that one end is thick where it was cut from the stem of the palm leaf and the other end has a slight taper. If you thread the thickest end through the needle, the fibers will lay flat and flow through the eye smoothly. Otherwise, the edges will fray and cause extra splitting and ultimately the strand will be too narrow to work properly. You can reduce the possibility of fraying if you keep the raffia a little damp as you work with it.

Threading the needle isn't too difficult if you make certain that the eye of the needle is the right size. Tapestry needles have nice large eyes and work well for this purpose. If you smooth the end of the raffia it will slip easily through the opening. If it tends to split when you try to thread it through, simply bend it over the needle to crease it, then force the creased end through the eye of the needle. Sometimes, if the raffia strand is too wide, you will have to split it into a smaller piece.

Coiled weaving is one of the oldest and most universally used methods of basket making. By adding one coil to another and then stitching them together you can make many different sizes and shapes of containers and mats.

To begin your basket, first pull or break off the sheaf at the top of the pine needles. Then, pointed end first, fill the gauge with as many needles as possible. This bundle of needles is called the core. Once the gauge is full, stagger the pointed end of the needles so they taper down to a small tip. Next, lay the narrow end of the raffia (threaded through the sewing needle) along the core that is sticking through the gauge and wrap about 2 inches over the raffia end so it is held in place by the wrap (fig 1). This ties the raffia and needles together. Now, flex the core of pine needles around your finger until it bends into a very small doughnut. Then thread the sewing needle through the center of the doughnut, and pull it as tight as possible (fig 2). Next sew around the doughnut, going down through the center, up and over the top, then down through the center again until you have circled the doughnut completely. If you mark your starting point with a small colored thread, it will be easy to know where to stop. To secure this wrap, take a stitch into the core.

At this point you should know approximately what type of basket you plan to make. It's a good idea to begin with a small basket so you can see your progress quickly and don't become discouraged.

Now you are ready to begin building the coil around the start. Be sure to keep your gauge filled and work from the back to the front (this works best for pine needle basketry). Hold the doughnut between your thumb and middle finger and wrap the raffia around the needles in your gauge

Figure 1: To start, wrap the core of needles with raffia about 2 inches.

Figure 2: Thread the sewing needle through the center of the donut, and pull it tight as possible.

of the needle is the right size. Tapestry needles have nice large eyes and work well for this purpose. If you smooth the end of the raffia it will slip easily through the opening. If it tends to split when you try to thread it through, simply bend it over the needle to crease it, then force the creased end through the eye of the needle. Sometimes, if the raffia strand is too wide, you will have to split it into a smaller piece.

Coiled weaving is one of the oldest and most universally used methods of basket making. By adding one coil to another and then stitching them together you can make many different sizes and shapes of containers and mats.

To begin your basket, first pull or break off the sheaf at the top of the pine needles. Then, pointed end first, fill the gauge with as many needles as possible. This bundle of needles is called the core. Once the gauge is full, stagger the pointed end of the needles so they taper down to a small tip. Next, lay the narrow end of the raffia (threaded through the sewing needle) along the core that is sticking through the gauge and wrap about 2 inches over the raffia end so it is held in place by the wrap (fig 1). This ties the raffia and needles together. Now, flex the core of pine needles around your finger until it bends into a very small doughnut. Then thread the sewing needle through the center of the doughnut, and pull it as tight as possible (fig 2). Next sew around the doughnut, going down through the center, up and over the top, then down through the center again until you have circled the doughnut completely. If you mark your starting point with a small colored thread, it will be easy to know where to stop. To secure this wrap, take a stitch into the core.

At this point you should know approximately what type of basket you plan to make. It's a good idea to begin with a small basket so you can see your progress quickly and don't become discouraged.

Now you are ready to begin building the coil around the start. Be sure to keep your gauge filled and work from the back to the front (this works best for pine needle basketry). Hold the doughnut between your thumb and middle finger and wrap the raffia around the needles in your gauge

Figure 1: To start, wrapt the core of needles with raffia about 2 inches.

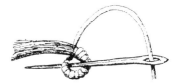

Figure 2: Thread the sewing needle through the center of the donut, and pull it tight as possible.

once, then start around once more and insert the needle into the middle of the doughnut, pull the raffia through. This makes a wrap and a long stitch. Continue doing this until you have completely circled the doughnut. Each time you take a stitch, use your forefinger to push the needles down and forward to make the stitches tight, this is called the lazy squaw stitch or the short and long stitch (fig 3).

Sometimes more than one wrap is taken around the top coil before wrapping around the two coils–and sometimes more than one wrap is taken around both coils. Every few stitches, be sure to feed your gauge with more pine needles.

Other types of stitches are easily adapted to pine needle basketry, such as the split stitch, where you work two rows in the plain stitch and on the third row, pierce through the center of the stitching material, taking with it a portion of the core (fig 4).

An open wheat stitch or double split stitch can be made by taking a second stitch through the split stitch, into the same hole. This results in a slanted stitch and a straight stitch coming from the same place. It adds firmness to the basket and can be used either throughout the basket or just on the rim (fig 5).

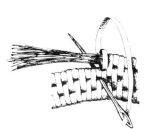

Figure 3: Squaw Stitch

Figure 4: Split Stitch

Figure 5: Double Split Stitch

As you pull the needle through the basket, pull the raffia to tighten your stitch and reduce the chance of breaking the weaver. Another trick to keep the raffia from breaking is to change the position of the strand on the needle occasionally.

When adding a new piece of raffia, try to select one about the same width as the one you end with, this will make the overall appearance more uniform.

If you make a basket with steep sides, you will have to work each coil on top of the next, but in order for it to hold you need to stitch through the center of the bottom coil using a plain stitch (fig 6). Do one complete round with your needle in a horizontal position; your coil will be locked into the correct alignment, and from there you can go back to the one wrap and then the long stitch. This makes a beautiful, solid basket.

If you decide on a basket with a gentle slope, just build the sides gradually, manipulating the coils as you work. If you want a small neck on your masterpiece, there are ways to accomplish that task, too. Your imagination is your only limit. If you want a lid for your basket, make it the same way you made the bottom of your basket and add a lip that fits down inside the opening or, if you prefer, over the outside of the basket. The lip can be made from a slender willow (Salix) or red osier dogwood (Cornus sericea) stem attached to the lid with raffia wrap.

There are several ways to splice your stitching material, but the easiest way is to lay the new end along the core and wrap the new end with the old

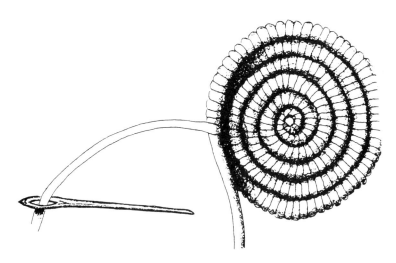

Figure 6: To form the sides, work each coil on top of the next.

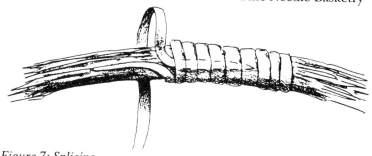

Figure 7: Splicing

Figure 8: Weaver's Knot

for several wraps (fig 7). Then lay the old end along the core, bring up the new strand and continue wrapping it over the old end and core, or you can simply tie a knot and keep weaving (fig 8). Personally, I don't like to tie knots except when I do fancy filigree work, so as I come to the end of a strip, I thread the needle back through the pine needle coil to conceal the end. Then, when I start again I thread the needle through another coil to the place where I left off. If you want a simple quickie basket, this is the way to do it.

Finishing the basket is sometimes a problem. To avoid a chopped-off appearance, gradually taper the pine needles for a few inches as you continue wrapping, make a lock stitch then thread your needle under several wraps and cut it off (fig 9). Your basket is officially finished. Or, you can add another decorative round, perhaps a different color wrap, working right over the already-wrapped top coil.

You can decorate your basket with different colors of raffia or corn husks, small bird feathers or other diversities. Or you can leave the sheafs on the pine needles and thread them through the gauge, sheaf first, to give

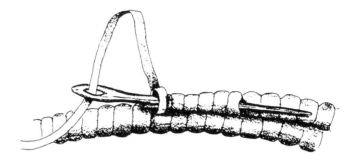

Figure 9: Ending

an unusual look to the basket. The sheafs can then be alternated to form a spiral design or be woven into row patterns. Beading or overlay can also be added by laying a flat strip over a coil, and wrapping alternately over the flat strip for a few wraps, then under the strip for a few wraps. Use your own ideas to come up with some wonderful designs.

You may want to pitch your basket to make it watertight, like the native Americans did before they had pottery to carry and hold liquids. Gather globs of pine pitch off the trees (once it falls to the ground it collects dirt and leaves) and melt it over low heat. Then strain the liquid to remove impurities and mix in some white wood ash to make the pitch harden when it dries and to prevent it from melting in the sun. Paint the basket with pitch mixture, inside and out, sealing all holes quickly before it hardens.

When you begin, don't be concerned with making a perfect basket, just start. Enjoy learning to work the needles and see what you come up with. And regardless of how you think your first attempt looks—KEEP IT. It is very special to look back on years later; you will love your basket and appreciate every bit of effort that went into it.

Jim Riggs

"Rocking On" with the Paiute Deadfall

●●●●●●●●●●●●●●●●●●●●●●●●●●●●●

For simplicity's sake, I choose to label the specific trigger

components described and illustrated in this article as <u>the</u>

Paiute deadfall, state of the aboriginal art, if you will!

Although a bit more complex than the simpler "two-stick"

deadfalls and occasionally trickier to set, the bottom line

is—<u>It works</u>.

T he major geographical and cultural focus of my studies and experience in archaeology and primitive technology has been the Northern Great Basin, those contiguous, high-desert portions of southeastern Oregon, central and northern Nevada and western Utah. Physiographically, this region of hot, dry summers and cold, dry winters is characterized by hundreds of parallel-oriented, 4,000- to 6,000-foot, flat-to-rolling valley floors, separated by predominantly north-south running fault-block mountain ranges occasionally reaching 12,000 feet in elevation.

In this vast region of internal drainages, run-off water from adjacent higher country is sufficient and constant enough in a few widely scattered valleys to create large, resource-rich, freshwater lakes, marshes and meadows. But most valleys, plains and intermediate uplands are considerably drier—sinks, playas, dunes, low escarpments—seemingly endless expanses of xerophytic shrubs and grasses with infrequent, intermittent stream courses and springs. Long ago, I figured if I could sufficiently internalize the natural history, ecology, aboriginal survival strategies, material culture and skills necessary to comfortably exist in this marginal environment, I could probably get by primitively almost anywhere.

While the overall human carrying capacity of the Great Basin environment is considerably lower than most of North America, the appearance of barrenness is deceptive. For more than 10,000 years in this setting, the Northern Paiute, Western Shoshone and earlier peoples became masters, through necessity, at seasonally and successfully exploiting nearly all food resources—grass seeds to grasshoppers, roots to coots—from all habitats within their territories.

Vital to this success was knowing "when to be where," especially with regard to variables in weather patterns, spatial fluctuations in floral productivity and more predictable faunal population cycles. Lacking a plethora of easily obtainable large game, predominantly elusive pronghorn and bighorn were advantageously hunted when appropriate, while the more prolific and regularly available rabbits and rodents provided the bulk of animal protein over the annual cycle.

Concerning the evolution of aboriginal human subsistence and adaptation in the Great Basin, Cressman states:

> "Long before the bow and arrow came into use the archaeological record shows that hunters were using other devices for taking small game. Various kinds of traps—the snare, the deadfall, and others—were in use, together with nets which may have been used in a variety of ways. Using traps in the food quest represents a sharp psychological break with the method of killing the quarry with a weapon in that there is no longer direct involvement between the hunter and the hunted. The man with a trapline thus had a device for supplementing his food supply beyond that which his skill and luck as a hunter could possibly provide. The traps set along the game trails, whether those of rodents or large mammals, would work for him while he is engaged in some other activity or doing nothing at all (Cressman 1977)."

Contemporary Considerations
In any primitive living situation where one is depending on the natural environment for sustenance, employing one or more forms of traps or snares is prudent and often quite lucrative. With minimal initial effort (and some practice), one can assess the available small game in the area and set up a number of appropriate traps.

Once the trapline is established, it need be checked only once or twice a day for harvesting, re-baiting and resetting. In effect, it becomes a passive potential provider of meat, as Cressman indicated, freeing you to actively pursue hunting, fishing, collecting or processing plant foods, manufacturing tools or even sleeping!

You'll also experience a definite anticipatory thrill, mentally and gastronomically, as you check your traps...Wow, Food! Sounds idyllic, but what traps do you choose to try, especially if you are just learning and have no backlog of experience? I'm convinced that in the history of humankind there have probably been more traps, snares, trigger mechanisms and various combinations thereof conceived than any one person could ever catalogue, let alone try. On a global scale, many of these were ingeniously designed for catching some very specific creature indigenous to an equally specific climate and habitat and may not be seriously applicable elsewhere (no need to continue brainstorming your surefire traps for wooly mammoths or California condors!). But others, no matter where their origins, are quite adaptable to a variety of creatures and environments.

Pertinent considerations in selecting and setting any particular trap include:
1. What animals are available and, of these, which seem most lucrative to try for?
2. Does some sort of trap seem the best means for success, say in contrast to direct hunting?
3. What tools and/or raw materials are necessary and available?
4. What projected energy and time are required to construct and set any trap?
5. What seems to be the most efficient investment for the best return?

The more elaborate or complicated—the more parts and materials requiring collecting and modifying—the more time you'll spend on any one set for one animal. If you're seeking larger game, especially with a group of people working collectively while "living out" for an extended period, this might be time well spent. But for smaller critters—some birds, occasional lagomorphs and especially rodents such as mice, chipmunks, woodrats, marmots and multifarious squirrels—I've concluded the simpler a proven-effective trap is, the better.

While I've experimented with dozens of primitive-style traps over the past twenty-five years, the two I emphasize most in teaching, and actually use most frequently to regularly put animal protein into my stomach, are (1) the simple snare (many variations and sets) and (2) the Paiute deadfall. This chapter will be limited to the construction and use of the latter.

The Paiute Deadfall
Several older archaeological and ethnographic reports concerning Great Basin cultures briefly mention, describe and/or illustrate (often incompletely and inaccurately) a variety of deadfalls involving a main rock and one or more sticks, pebbles, lengths of cordage, etc., that could be

inclusively labeled "Paiute deadfalls." For contemporary descriptions and illustrations of some of these variations, see writings by Olsen. While I believe these to be viable and advantageous to learn and practice as part of one's "deadfall repertory," I personally have found them less effective.

For simplicity's sake, I choose to label the specific trigger components described and illustrated in this article as *The* Paiute deadfall, state of the aboriginal art, if you will! Although a bit more complex than the simpler "two-stick" deadfalls and occasionally trickier to set, the bottom line is—*it works*.

Although it was born in the Great Basin, the Paiute deadfall has successfully served me in a wide variety of habitats in the American West. I'd consider it viable in any region that harbors small-to-medium sized, mostly ground-dwelling rodents or other creatures susceptible to a baited trap.

I don't pretend to wholly understand the physics involved, but I believe the deadfall's effectiveness is attributable to two main factors:

Primarily, the weight of the rock is efficiently and successively diffused and/or distributed via eight or more contact points amongst the stick and cord components. In setting, when the bait stick is lastly positioned, baited end in friction contact with the underside of the rock and butt end against the trigger pin, only minimal pressure from the initial weight of the rock remains to hold it in place. This in effect creates a hair trigger (with luck, a hare trigger!) in that the tip of the bait stick contacting the rock surface which is the most easily dislodgeable (weakest) part of the whole apparatus.

Secondarily, when the bait stick is tripped, the falling rock neatly flips the lever assembly and post out of its path, leaving only the thinner, unobstructive bait stick under the rock with the quarry.

The subtleties of the perfect Paiute deadfall are many, but only a few basics are truly critical to a potentially successful set. Once you've practiced enough to understand how the components must work together, you'll be surprised how quickly and sloppily (visually, at least) you can make and set a line of deadfalls—they don't have to look pretty, they just have to work! Many times I've set lucrative deadfalls employing no tools (steel or stone) and no pre-made or specifically modified parts other than simply breaking dry sticks to appropriate lengths, quickly twisting an adequate length of cordage from even marginally strong or long plant fibers (sagebrush bark, moistened dry grass, etc.) and baiting with a fortuitously found rose hip, wild onion or grasshopper. In some situations or environments I suppose unavailable natural fibers for cordage could seem a problem; remember, you are almost always wearing something that already is, or could be twisted into, an 8- to 10-inch length of string.

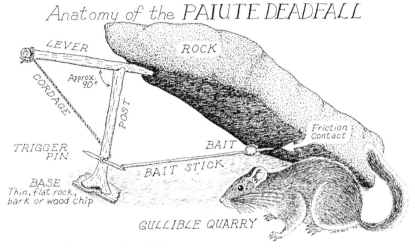

Anatomy of the Paiute Deadfall.

I suggest studying the accompanying illustrations to familiarize your-self with the anatomy, relative proportions, positionings, and possible variations of the deadfall components. The configuration and angles of lever and post to each other and to the rock that I have come to prefer are closest to those illustrated in Wheat (1967), and differ considerably from Olsen.   Among the criteria for my preferences here are overall deadfall stability and ease of setting, lower angle of rock to the ground, and increased likelihood the rock will flip lever and post out of the way when it falls. The terminology I use here for deadfall components has been adapted from a handout from the School of Urban and Wilderness Survival (SUWS), Hagerman, Idaho. The following descriptions of dead-fall components should become increasingly meaningful as you gain some hands-on experience with the deadfall and subsequently discover and incorporate whatever best suits your needs and options in any specific situation.

Deadfall Components

The Rock—Fortuitously, many of the best places to set deadfalls—rimrock outcroppings, bouldered hillsides, bases of talus slides, along streams—also harbor adequate deadfall rocks. I suggest gearing the size of the rock you select to the size of the largest potentially catchable quarry you believe to live in that habitat. If mice or chipmunks are the only critters you assess to be in your trapping area, smaller, flat rocks will suffice, but ideally a rock size large enough to kill a cottontail or marmot, set with a trigger mechanism delicate enough to be tripped by a mouse, will provide you with the most meat. Wily woodrats, for example, seem to delight in gleefully running through lightweight deadfalls!

The configuration of my ideal, generic, deadfall rock for up to cottontail size would be rectangular in shape, roughly 15 inches long, 3 to 5 inches thick with a flat bottom, gritty surface texture and weigh 30-plus pounds. The back end should be squarish so that when the front is lifted there is no wobble, rocking, or sliding, as if it were hinged to the ground. Any side-to side instability can make setting trigger components extremely frustrating.

Often you can square-up irregular spots by percussing them off with another rock used as a hammerstone. If reshaping isn't feasible, you can sometimes shim the back to stability with smaller rocks. If the deadfall rock wants to slide backwards, slightly gouge the back end into the ground or butt it against another rock. I cannot emphasize enough taking a few minutes to carefully select or modify the most appropriate rock available.

The underside of the deadfall rock should be as regularly flat as possible to mesh closely with the ground surface to insure a quick, clean kill. This is most important toward the back where the bait is and the animal's head should be. An extremely irregular or deeply concave rock surface may only maim the quarry or temporarily confine it until it digs its way out, unscathed. Toward the rear area of the underside of the rock, where the tip of the bait stick must hold itself in place by friction contact, a grittiness or some other flaw or irregularity of rock surface is necessary. If that surface is too smooth to grip the bait stick, peck it with a hammerstone to roughen it or even create a small concavity.

Frequently, I've set deadfalls in areas where tabular rocks were perfectly sized and shaped, but too thin and lightweight to be effective. Here the solution is to stack additional rocks on top of the deadfall rock until it's heavy enough to work. Rock on!

Also, be aware that sandy, dusty, wet, or other soft ground can ineffectualize a deadfall. Some compensations include placing a base piece, a thin flat rock, wood or bark chip, under the post to stabilize it and prevent it from sinking into the ground. You can also pave the ground beneath the deadfall rock, especially where the quarry's head and chest should be, by slightly imbedding smaller flattish rocks or a few hard, straight sticks laid paralleled to each other to create a more unyielding surface. Or you can set the whole deadfall on bedrock or on top of another flat rock or bark slab that you can move to where you want the set to be.

Trigger Parts—Always use dead (not rotten), dry wood if possible for all components. For lever and post, I prefer barkless, somewhat weathered,

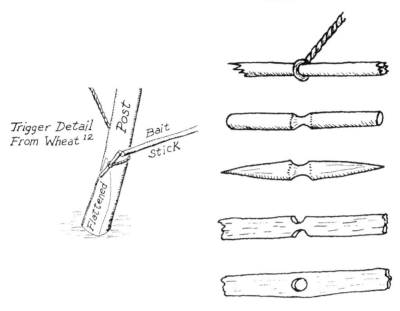

At left: Trigger detail (from Wheat[12]). At Right: Trigger pin variations from top; unmodified broken twig, cut and grooved, bi-pointed, notched flat splinter, and flat splinter with hole for knotted end of cordage.

straight shoots up to about finger thickness of willow, currant, red osier dogwood, etc. Anything rigid, straight, and preferably not smooth-surfaced will work. Green shoots or really wet wood can be too pliable, tend to slowly bend or buckle from the weight of a large rock, and can prematurely trip the deadfall.

Actual lengths and thicknesses will vary with your rock size and intended quarry, but a handy relativity for sizing trigger components is to make the lever, the post, and the working section of cordage all the same length. For my standard woodrat or squirrel sets this is 6 to 7 inches long and approximately a half inch in diameter. Remember, the initial piece of cordage must be a few inches longer so it can be affixed to the trigger pin and lever. The above proportions are not gospel—you may encounter sets where more dissimilar lengths of components work better—but I've found it efficient to make up a bunch of matched trigger pieces ahead of time, then choose rocks that suit them.

As previously mentioned, completely functional deadfalls can be spontaneously made and set with little or no modification of materials, but given the choice, I prefer to make some refinements. For example: I normally groove the back end of the lever so the wrapped and tied cordage won't slip, and I slightly flatten the top side of the other end to increase its surface contact and stability where the leading edge of the rock will rest. This second modification can wait until you are matching individual levers to specific rocks. It is also advantageous to shape the top of the post and/ or the underside of the lever to prevent sliding or rolling where those two contact each other.

With sincere thanks to John McPherson for the tip (why didn't I ever think of this?!?), I'm now a devout convert to selecting posts that have a natural fork or at least a broadened diameter at the base; this configuration retards the post from twisting, greatly increases stability and can make setting infinitely easier.[1]

The trigger pin, stiff, straight, approximately 1 to 3 inches long, can be round, partly or wholly flattish, bi-pointed like a gorge hook for fishing or a completely unmodified twig, but I prefer to point at least one end and groove its center. It can usually be slipped through the initial twist loop of your cordage and will hold itself in place in the groove, eliminating the need for a bulkier knot.

Since the bait stick remains under the rock when it's tripped, you want something as straight and thin as possible, but having a strong enough spine (rigidity) to span the distance between the trigger pin and the rock without undue bending or finally buckling from the pressure the trigger pin will exert against its butt (non-baited) end. A flimsy, rubbery bait stick just won't work.

In the Great Basin, I generally use dead willow or rabbitbrush shoots or basal stem sections of giant wild rye grass. Always, cut bait sticks a few inches longer than you believe necessary. Unless you've found one of those perfect rocks, uniformly gritty enough to grab the tip of the bait stick anywhere you position it, you can't predetermine its final working length until you locate a solid friction contact point. I do this by feel with the tip of the bait stick probing for a spot as far under the rock as possible. When a spot is found, I note where the back end of the bait stick should be cut or snapped to abut with the trigger pin.

If you happen to have such goodies as nuts, raisins, candy, cheese, peanut butter, carrots, doughballs, etc., your success is almost predestined. Of course, with all that on hand, why would you want or need to kill small furry animals?

I normally try to rely on finding adequate bait within the natural environment–wild rose hips, berries in season, seeds extracted from pine or fir cones, a succulent bulb, root, or mushroom—anything your quarry might eat that it finds more easily obtainable on the end of a bait stick than by working for it (by digging, climbing, traveling, etc.). Normally, herbivorous critters can also, perhaps more through curiosity that hunger, be

LEVER & POST VARIATIONS

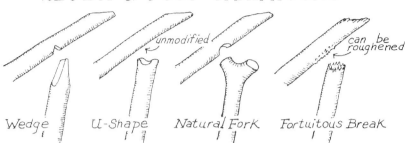

Wedge　　U-Shape　　Natural Fork　　Fortuitous Break

attracted to meat, including grasshoppers, fish innards, jerky, etc., and these baits can attract other potential quarry such as raccoons and opossums.

Woodrats, especially, can be enamored by items other than actual food (see below). In most primitive living, even survival, situations one frequently has on hand some pre-gathered or brought-with foodstuffs. You then must decide whether you're better off this yourself or to gambling on expending some for bait to potentially catch something greater.

Whatever your bait, affix it solidly to the bait stick. If the bait is not strong enough to thread onto the stick and stay there, wrap and tie it on with cordage, plant fibers or even a couple of your own hairs (harder for survivalist skinheads). Your chances of success will increase the farther under the rock you can set the bait. Use the lowest possible angle, rock-to-ground, that still allows room for the quarry's head to reach the bait. When tripped, the contact between the falling rock and the most vulnerable anatomy of the quarry is almost immediate and immobilizing and the quarry has almost no time to react and pull away.

Setting the Trap

When you attempt to set your first Paiute deadfall, you may question my labeling it as simple. You may even scream loudly and profanely at the deadfall components (or at me!), especially after several aborted attempts in which the rock smashes your hands! Please persevere. It is a delicate trigger mechanism; familiarity and success require practice.

Since I am actually setting the deadfall when I determine the working length of the bait stick, I usually snap it with my teeth rather than cutting it because my left hand is already occupied in holding the trigger pin to the post to prevent the rock from falling. Then relocate the friction contact point with the tip of the bait stick, then very slowly allow the free end of the trigger pin to swing slightly forward until it contacts, and subsequently is apply all its pressure against, the butt end of the bait stick. If all goes well, the bait stick does not slip from the rock and the deadfall is set!

To prevent crushing your hands under your own deadfall (which can be serious with a heavy rock), place a fist-size rock under the deadfall rock but not obstructing the space where you'll position the bait stick. This will block the complete falling of the deadfall rock should it slip while you're setting it. Of course, remove the block once the deadfall is set. I offer thanks to the long-forgotten person who suggested this improvement. For years I just figured having a perennial case of "bloody deadfall knuckles" was part of the game!

Blocking, or fencing, the sides of the deadfall rock takes little time and can further insure success. The object is to guide or channel the quarry into the set from one side near the front so that when its head reaches the bait, most of its body is also under the rock. However, don't fence so completely that the critter is apt to bump the trigger pin or bait stick before reaching the bait. Use sticks, bark slabs, smaller flat rocks, etc., leaned against the sides of the deadfall gently enough not to trip it. Make sure the fencing materials are long enough to reach above or overlap the top side of the deadfall rock so they can't accidentally fall underneath and inhibit the rock when tripped.

Hopefully the following tips and troubleshootings will round out the previous descriptions and discussion and ease your initiation to *the* Paiute deadfall.

Tips and Troubleshooting
The most commonly encountered problem beginners face in setting the deadfall is the lever and the post wanting to swing or twist to one side. Counteract by:
1.   Making sure there is *no* wobble in the rock when the front is lifted to working height. Trim or shim if necessary.
2.   Reposition or reshape top end of the lever for more solid meshing/contact between it and the rock.
3.   Use a post with a forked or broader base instead of a dowel-shaped cylindrical base.

If the cordage and trigger pin want to slide up the post:
1.   Lightly rough up the post surface. A naturally weathered surface will grip the cord better than smooth bark or a cleanly peeled stick.
2.   Flatten the area of post and/or trigger pin where the two contact each other.
3.   Alter the angle that the lever and cord pull on the post by slanting the

post more (moving its base slightly further from rock), or try positioning the post more vertically and lowering the cord end of the lever.
4.   Ascertain if you possibly need a shorter or longer working length of
     either cordage or lever.

If the free end of the trigger pin (where it abuts the end of the bait
stick) wants to swing downward toward the ground, try:
1.   Flattening portions of the post and trigger pin to create more surface
     of contact between the two.
2.   Shortening the trigger pin.
3.   Abutting the end of the bait stick against the trigger pin closer to the
     post.
Note: These three most common problems are often interrelated; frequently one simple adjustment can eliminate all of them.

Don't forget where you set your traps! With only a handful, this is little
problem, but with a line of more than a dozen or so it's easy to do. Figure
out a system to mark or remember each and every set. Check traps at least
once a day; twice is better, although the most appropriate times can vary
according to the particular quarry's habits.

In hot weather, especially, you'll want to collect your catches as soon
as possible before bloating occurs, yellow jackets have carved away half
your meal, or you suddenly notice myriad vultures circling overhead! At
the same time, you don't want to check in the midst of the quarry's highest
activity period or so frequently that you alter their behavior patterns.

I normally make an early morning and a mid-to-late-afternoon round,
and vary that if circumstances warrant. One deadfall may catch a noc-
turnal woodrat overnight and, when reset early in the morning, catch a
diurnal squirrel later that same day. If nothing happens at some traps over
two whole days and nights they're probably not in lucrative spots and
should be moved. Always take down all traps before leaving an area; it is
irresponsible and unethical to leave baited deadfalls set if you'll not be
there to make use of the catch.

Knowing where to set traps and what kinds are most appropriate for
any particular critter or habitat grows with experience. You have to begin
somewhere. It's advantageous to read up on the animals and their habits
pertinent to any wild area you frequent. With that information as a base,
your best trapping successes will come from directly observing live animals
going about their repetitive daily patterns. Note their species, numbers,
sizes, times of activity, routes taken, habitual runways, foods eaten,
locations of burrows, nests or forms, interactions with each other, ad

infinitum. When animals remain unseen, investigate likely habitats for tracks, scat, food storage spots—any signs revealing their activities. The scope of this chapter can only minimally introduce some ways and means for learning animal habits, but an old adage sums up the goal worth striving towards: "The fundamental principle of successful trapping is to determine what the animal you wish to trap is going to do, and then catch him doing it!"

While a sprung and empty deadfall does not supply you with any meat, it can potentially supply you with some extremely useful information if you can learn to read what actually happened, then make necessary adjustments to the set. (If the ground surface around or near the deadfall is accommodating, I like to deliberately smooth over a patch of dirt just so I can see what tracks may appear.)

When you approach a downed deadfall but see no obvious catch, pause a moment, study the scenario and snap a mental photo. Note the position of the rock, other visible components, and any obvious tracks or signs. Then carefully lift the rock—often you will have been successful. A pancaked deermouse or chipmunk is not much, but it's food. Congratulations!

If nothing is there, your personal interpretive phase begins. Note the position and condition of the bait stick—does bait remain or is it gone? Any signs of hair, blood or a struggling animal? Did the rock fall in line or is it askew? The latter might indicate the quarry was bigger than the rock could handle. Any cattle tracks around? Any fencing material under the rock? Just a few "baited questions" here to get the aboriginal Sherlock Holmes in you activated!

In twenty years of teaching this trap to hundreds of people in field conditions, I've noted that beginner deadfalls found sprung but quarry-less the first few times have most commonly self-destructed due to inadequate strength, stability or positioning of components or they were set so tenuously the slightest breeze or raindrop could trip them. I close with a personal "what happened here?" vignette entitled:

A Packrat Tale
During the final living-with-the-land week in one of my Aboriginal Life Skills courses in Oregon's Wallowa Mountains, I had set a Paiute deadfall one afternoon along the sheltered base of a rimrock where woodrat tracks and scat were obvious in the dry dust—a sure catch I thought. It was baited with a fresh biscuitroot (Lomatium sp.) and the cordage portion of the trigger apparatus was two-ply dogbane (Apocynum cannabium) string. Upon checking it the next morning the deadfall was found to be sprung but empty, bait and bait stick still under the rock.

Strangely, the dogbane cord had been nibbled and frayed almost through in two places. It was a good set—I didn't understand how the critter was escaping. Not yet having really discerned the nature of the failure, I reset it with a new length of cord and same bait. The second morning the deadfall was again sprung, empty, bait stick under the rock as before, but the entire lever-cordage-trigger pin apparatus was completely gone.

After a couple of minutes of incomprehension, the cartoon light bulb (aboriginal hand drill burst into flame) brightened my mind. I had twice missed the rat because it was never under the deadfall rock when tripped, and the rat was not at all interested in the biscuitroot bait–it wanted the dogbane cordage! OK. This time I made a new lever and pin and substituted a thin buckskin thong for the cordage piece. I removed the biscuitroot from the bait stick and in its place tightly wrapped a generous length of dogbane cord.

Finally, by the third morning I had solidly caught that fat packrat! We feasted on three rats that day, as another participant's deadfall was successful and I had caught a second rat in a pole snare actually set for a chickaree (red squirrel). End of tale.

While my information is definitely not exhaustive, for some this may be more than you ever cared to read about the Paiute deadfall! Hopefully for others it will stimulate field application or even research into the physics of weight distribution throughout the trigger components. Except where otherwise credited, this article is presented as my own opinion, assessment and experience. To each his own. Me? Really, I'm glad I know how to catch a critter when I need one!

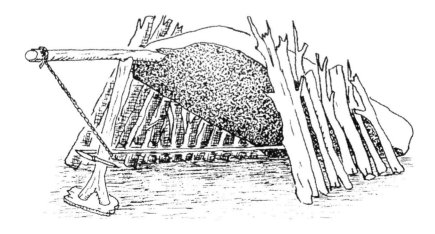

Paiute Deadfall Troubleshooting Comparisons

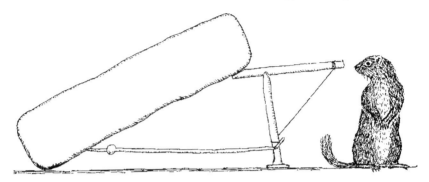

Low Rock Angle

+ Quick falling time when tripped. Rock-to-quarry contact almost immediate, with minimal reactionary escape time.
+ Quarry must be mostly under rock to reach bait, especially with adequate fencing.
+ Potentially broad and stable contact area between lever and rock.
+ Shorter fencing materials adequate.
- Bait stick normally must be longer, thus strong spine more critical, though I've not found this to be a problem.
- Friction contact between bait stick and rock can be more difficult to achieve.

Post positioned in front of rock

+ Rock cannot abort its fall by landing on top of upright post.
+ Rock nearly always flips lever and post beyond path of its fall.

Near-horizontal lever position *(Some variation up or down is OK)*

+ Specifically shaped coupling between top of post and underside of lever can be advantageous, but not imperative.
+ More solid, increases surface contact between top end of lever and rock.
- Cord may want to slide up post (Normally correctable by roughening post surface or slightly adjusting angles between lever, cord, and post.

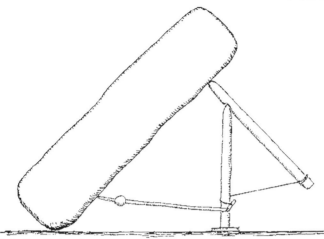

High Rock Angle

- Longer falling time when tripped, thus more time for quarry to react and possibly escape.
- Smaller percentage of quarry's body likely to be under rock.
- More tenuous, unstable contact between rock and lever.
- Taller fencing materials required.
+ Bait stick is shorter, choice and spine of suitable materials is broader.
+ Friction contact between bait stick and rock is potentially easier to achieve.

Post positioned under rock

- When tripped, rock can begin its fall but actually land atop lever and post (which did not receive sufficient speed or force to flip them out of the way) and remain upright.
- Tripped rock can begin to flip lever and post away but, because of its high angle and thus sluggish start, only knocks them over, often resulting in base of post remaining under front of rock thus blocking its complete fall.

Note: I used this style of deadfall set for several years with adequate success, but I also experienced the above two problems occurring more times than I can remember.

Diagonal "figure 4" lever position

- Requires a carved no-slip coupling between top of post and underside of lever.
- As mentioned above, high rock angle in conjunction with diagonal lever position creates less stable, less surface contact between lever and rock.
+ Cordage does not tend to slide up post.

Linda Jamison
with Larry Dean Olsen and Zeke Sanchez

Philosophy
of a Caveman
• •

"We just go out there and love the kids. The more you love

them, the faster they come around. We live with them,

experience everything with them. A student is never asked

to do anything an instructor isn't already doing."

Many people in our country have faced survival situations in the past. It seems certain that there will be more and perhaps even greater challenges to our way of life in the future. Those who possess the qualities of life most needed for survival will accept its rigors with the energy necessary to lead meaningful and productive lives no matter how many of our modern conveniences are lost to us and no matter how basic our existence becomes. They will know the odds, realize the blessings of simply living rather than groping for comforts and ease. They will possess the spiritual power necessary to raise themselves out of poverty, be it mental or physical, and lead a standard of life full of more meaning than gadgets.

Two such men are Larry Dean Olsen and Ezekiel (Zeke-Good Buffalo Eagle) Sanchez.

Larry Olsen, author of the best-selling book *Outdoor Survival Skills*, originated the award-winning "480" thirty-day survival trek at Brigham Young University and has been a pioneer in instituting primitive survival courses as an effective rehabilitation program in the United States.

Zeke Sanchez was a BYU student when Larry's program first started. His grades were faltering and he was dismissed because, in his words, "he paid more attention to the girls than the grades." From his youth, Zeke had lived in the desert with his family, practicing "survival" skills as a part of everyday life. When he was given the chance to join Larry's experimental program, he gladly enlisted. Because of his proficiency in outdoor skills,

225

his leadership ability and compassion for others during the expedition, he was asked to join the program's instructor team.

Larry and Zeke have been friends and trail companions for twenty-five years. They have endured the kinds of things that bind people together, like saving one another's life. Today they share in the management of "Anasazi," a youth rehabilitation program with headquarters in Mesa, Arizona. Anasazi's instructors take troubled youth into the desert and teach them to live a stone-age existence for forty to fifty days. Both Larry and Zeke agree that many of the experiences shared on the trail have provided some of life's greatest lessons.

Zeke tells of one such experience. "It was 1970, on a BYU program in southern Utah. I had just driven all day from California where we were doing some presentations and promotional things for the survival program, and that night, as I came in late, we had an instructor meeting. Some of the students were still coming into camp after repelling in the Circle Cliffs area. They had been out there all day trying to find their way down. It is quite a dry place to be, so some of them were in need of water. One particular girl, Beth Rasmussen, had a medical problem that she had overlooked on the health questionnaire, and so we were not aware of it. Anyway, someone shouted that a student had collapsed by the fire. By the time we got there, Beth's heart had stopped and they were doing CPR, trying to revive her. We moved the crowd aside to give her some air, and by that time Mack Smith already had his hands on her head to give her a healing blessing, so we both laid our hands on her head and blessed her to recover.

"We didn't have any backup vehicles on that trip and two of us decided we would go out and get one of the vehicles we had left in Boulder. I selected someone to go with me, and he was a big fellow so I knew if I didn't make it, he would.

"His name was Val Snow, he was a ball player for the NY Mets. I was already tired from traveling all day and hardly getting any sleep, but we headed out on the Burr Trail at the Water Pocket Fold that night under the light of a full moon. It was up and down, up and down all night. And it was a long night.

"When we finally got to Deer Creek, we had to stop for water. As soon as I bent down, my legs cramped and I couldn't move and I fell into the stream. Water was running into my nose. I couldn't breath and I couldn't get up. I never felt such pain. I was crippled up like a pretzel. Val lifted me out of the stream.

"He set me on the bank and tried to talk with me. I told him to go on without me, but he wouldn't leave me. I was concerned about the girl and getting the vehicle because we didn't know how she was at that point.

Larry Olsen, left, and Zeke (Good Buffalo Eagle) Sanchez have been trail partners since the early days of BYU's "480" program (photos by Linda Jamison).

"At that time I was kind of ornery," Zeke confided. "I'm not so ornery now. Anyway, I tried to get up and walk around a little and found that I could drag my feet some. So I decided that I would drag myself but when he saw how painful it was for me he put his arm around me and practically carried me all the way to Boulder. That was a long way.

"When we finally got to the vehicle, he had to lift me into it because my legs wouldn't move. He drove all the way back. The sun hadn't come up yet and I had him drop me off about a quarter of a mile back because I was embarrassed, you know, big macho Zeke. Like I said, I was ornery then. I didn't want anyone to know I had been hurt. So pretty soon here comes Larry and he pampered me a little and they took care of me.

"Well, we found that Beth was alright, and she hiked all the rest of the way to the sand dunes, then on to Lake Powell and across the lake. I hiked with her and the rest of the group as they finished the trip. She is happily married today and has several children, in fact she became an instructor and married one of the instructors who worked with her."

But that wasn't the whole story. Larry, relates what happened before Zeke arrived that night.

"We started out at Capital Reef National Monument and hiked down the Water Pocket Fold. The first night a snow storm blew in. We were headed for a cave and everyone had hiked until they were exhausted. Beth had been in the lead group and had moved back and forth to the slower ones, helping some of the others that were dragging behind. By the time we got within a couple of miles of the cave everyone was really straggling.

"She forged ahead with some of the other instructors and her group started a fire and she began making ash cakes (wheat and water cakes that are cooked in the ashes). She worked all night patting out ash cakes to feed to the stragglers as they came into camp. So she was very exhausted the next day.

"Then we hiked all the next day to get down to the Burr Trail road and it was a very difficult trip. She had been up all night serving and helping others, then hiked all day. That night when she collapsed, she was making ash cakes for other people again. And when she collapsed, she almost fell into the fire.

"That was the only time in the twenty-five years we have been running trips that we felt we were in danger of losing someone, but she was brought back to health as a result of the blessing she was given. As a matter of fact, she still tells the story quite often. She is quite a woman."

In the early days of the BYU Youth Leadership 480 Program, the average distance covered was 300 miles in 26 days. "But there were a lot of activities along the way," said Larry. "On the very first trips, I think what we didn't know was to our advantage.

"We just went out and lived with the students and loved them, and taught them. Then later, when it became popular, other groups took a look at what we were doing and said, 'oh yes, this looks like a good thing and we're going to make it work better.' So they brought in therapists and various different perspectives like the psychological "T grouping" and "circles" and that kind of thing and made it seem like that was necessary for success."

For a few years Larry also experimented with those kinds of programs, but found them to be ineffective. "We've come full circle and now we're back to the way it was when we first started out," he explains. "We just go out there and love the kids. The more you love them, the faster they come around. We live with them, experience everything with them. A student is never asked to do anything an instructor isn't already doing."

"And we don't have separate instructor camps like other programs do, where the students and instructors camp separately and they have extra food and party all night," Zeke contends. "We don't do that. This is important because we have to build relationships of trust."

Obviously this formula works. The following comments from students that completed Larry and Zeke's program testify to their growth as a result of this approach:

"Perhaps the most important element in my rebirth is that which Larry Olsen defines as 'relationship of important to essential.' In the wilderness it was obviously more essential to have water than anything else..."

"One of the greatest things I've learned is that there is no simple way out of anything. Simple, primitive man had a very complex life in my estimation. He had to acquire the training and skills of a dozen tradesmen of our day. And he was beset with as many problems as we have today."

"About midway through the course I came to the realization that I was not going to be taught by the common method of teaching, nor was I going to learn the things I came out expecting to learn. For example, the day when we found Tim. The wind was quite strong and I was quite tired–a combination that brought out a continual flow of foul language to relieve the tension from a situation over which I had no control. When I finally finished cooking, in spite of the wind, Larry called everyone over and told us a story of how the wind recorded everything that everyone said. A thousand hours of lecture couldn't have done a better job than that one story. I felt very small and ashamed of my immaturity, but at the same time I was very glad that it had taken place because I realized that what I had done wasn't really necessary, and it was only my own immaturity that made me do it."

In today's uncertain world, the wisdom these two men have garnered and continue to pass along to those they teach is invaluable. But Larry sums it up best with his own philosophy.

"I have lived life at its most basic level from a cave-dweller existence to the wandering life of a stone-age hunter without any shelter at all. I have lived in shacks, cabins, middle-class cracker boxes, and in mansions. I have experienced almost every level of material existence so that I might learn the qualities necessary for survival. It has been my business to teach those qualities to others and so I had to know.

"Perhaps the most significant observations of all my experience has been that no matter what a man (or woman) possesses materially, his survival depends solely on the quality of his personal life–nothing else. I call this the Philosophy of a Caveman."

Richard Jamison

Living with Nature
Shelter and Insulation

● ●

Two-hundred-fifty centuries ago man learned the most

basic concepts of shelter-building by trial and error. The

knowledge was passed down from generation to genera-

tion, from continent to continent, or learned indepen-

dently by different people all over the world..and still

retained thousands of years later by late-bloomers on the

North American Continent.

Remove the average American from his thermostatically controlled home and office and insulated underwear and what will become of
him? Of course, no one can make a blanket prediction, but the fact remains
that whenever so-called civilized people journey from their artificial
environment, they are immediately "out of sync" with their surroundings.
    Too often, reference to "the elements" is negative. The elements are
not an enemy to be reckoned with, the elements are our natural surroundings. Yet many people are so far removed from the unaffected environment, they no longer know the meaning of natural as it relates to the
human experience. Thus, their greatest concern often becomes how to
protect themselves from nature, rather than to unite and co-exist with it.
But once we understand our relationship to our natural surroundings, and
our own limitations, we can live almost anywhere, from the frozen Arctic
to the Sahara.
    But it is not reasonable to assume that a person, simply because he or
she has the skill necessary to live in a particular environment, can do so
without some preparation. I've had students look around the classroom

and say, "O.K., if we were stranded here for a week, how would we survive?"

"Well," I tell them, "we could certainly stay warm and dry, but we'd be very hungry and thirsty by the end of the experiment."

By the same token, a person caught unprepared in sub-zero temperatures in a tee shirt, sandals and shorts would likely die from exposure before he had a chance to protect himself, even if he knew how to find shelter.

More often than not, it is stupid mistakes, not Mother Nature that causes people to die from exposure. She is not cruel; we are often simply neophytes when it comes to existing in her realm. We should recognize and respect the irony of Mother Nature's law—she provides the supplies to build a shelter, but she holds the awesome power to bring it down.

What it really takes to live comfortably in any weather and terrain is a lot of study into what has worked before, what can be learned from modern research and technology, combined with basic "abo" logic. Stir that information up in your brain and you will be better prepared to live with the elements than any generation since humans first left their caves.

Ice Age Adaptability

Before the advent of man-made fibers, people pretty much had to rely on their imagination and what was available to them to keep warm. In fact, it was not unusual for a chilly Neanderthal to settle down for the night under the stars in a pile of dry leaves. This crude method of insulation did not last long, however, before man decided to turn over a new leaf.

If you say "Neanderthal" to friends and ask for their first association, you'll probably get "cave-man." While most excavated Neanderthal remains do come from caves, that's because open-air sites would be eroded much more quickly. Neanderthals must have constructed some type of shelter against the cold climate in which they lived, but those shelters must have been crude. All that remain are post-holes and a few piles of stones.

But we know that the Ice Age hunter became pretty good at adapting to his weather-driven life because he survived three 100,000 year periods of freezing and warming. Life was obviously hard and most people died young. It is estimated at least half the Neanderthal population perished in childhood, and less than 5% lived past the age of 40, partly due to exposure.

Cave-dwelling Paleolithic people were often desperately hungry. Because of the blizzards outside their caves, they were forced to hunt within them. And there, by a stroke of luck they found just what they needed—a big hibernating beast whose meat and fat were delicious and whose pelt made the best kind of cold-weather garment. This animal, now extinct, was the cave bear, which weighed over 1,000 pounds at maturity. Cave bears were so prolific in the Austrian Alps that the bones of 50,000 of them were found in a single cave.

So animal pelts and fur replaced leaves and became all the rage in insulated apparel. Entire families were outfitted in this newest line of outerwear. And, although this was somewhat more sophisticated than foliage insulation, the cold still got under their skins.

Around 75,000 B.C. when the fourth glacial advances refrigerated Europe, man stayed in the north and developed new skills simply through the effort to keep warm.

The human economy of the Old Stone Age was based entirely on hunting, which not only gave man his food but provided raw materials, such as hide, sinew and bone. During the winter, large-scale mammoth hunts were organized in what is now Russia and other parts of the north. After the mammoths were eaten, their bones were used to make tools and weapons and their tusks were used to anchor the skin coverings of dwellings dug out of the frozen ground. Undoubtedly, one wooly mammoth, the largest land-dwelling animal that man has ever encountered, would have provided warm protection against the cold for a number of people.

By 35,000-28,000 B.C. descendants of Neanderthals had special tools for dressing animal skins and had figured out how to increase the effectiveness of skin-and-fur insulation by lacing their clothes together with thongs. (It took another 14,000 years to develop the first bone needles with eyes which equipped women to stitch leather clothing.)

The Big Melt-down
Then, about 20,000 years ago, Europe became gradually warmer and man emerged from the protection of his caves and began a life in the open. Late Cro-Magnon clans built dwellings from wood, stone, bone or skins or lived in natural rock shelters and spent much of the year in cozy base camps, complete with hearths and cobblestone floors which provided insulation in the winter. And, in an ingenious piece of interior design, they heated the cobblestones before placing them on the frozen mud. The stones melted the hard ground, settled in snugly and made sturdy, dry floors.

They also established seasonal camps–the Paleolithic equivalent of summer condos. Built on rises, these shelters provided a good view of migrating herds. Seventy-five percent of the sites were found to face south, indicating that the builders took advantage of solar heat. Nothing has really changed, has it? Even in our own time, southern exposure adds value to a home.

This less sedentary lifestyle required temporary shelter that could be moved or abandoned and rebuilt as the people followed the herds.

Prehistoric sheep with dark hairy coats that caught on branches or simply fell off their bodies in heavy clumps every spring also roamed Europe. It is likely that early people took advantage of the matted wool for warmth, but this is only speculation since wool, like other natural fibers, is biodegradable and rarely part of archaeological finds.

Man almost certainly discovered the food value of sheep first, but when he began to fashion garments to protect his body from hot or freezing temperatures, he learned that sheep could be worth more alive than dead.

About 12,000 years ago, when man realized that with sheep he could roam and prosper on the windswept mountains and plains, a cooperative relationship developed–man protected the sheep from predators, sheep provided man with food and clothing. Wool clothing also allowed nomadic tribes to expand into extremes of terrain and climate. The Bedouin still use wool for their tents and wear wool clothing as insulation in the desert.

"Felting" compacts wool, making it less permeable, warmer, studier, and more water resistant. Magdalenian shepherds probably stumbled onto felt when they put loose wool in their sandals for comfort on a long journey and the moisture, movement, and warmth transformed the wool into felt. In fact, wool was so popular in the lives of Asian nomads that in the fourth century B.C. the Chinese called their territory "the land of felt." Man, whose body is least suited of all the animals to live in inhospitable climates, has made use of the natural material ever since.

Modern-day Insulation
But modern man is probably less well adapted for living in extremes than his ancient ancestors who were toughened and acclimated to a degree of heat and cold exposure which modern man has been clever enough to avoid. In today's jet age we can travel to extreme variations of climate in mere hours.

It takes an average person who works in a controlled atmosphere approximately two weeks to become acclimated to an new environment. My own experience has shown this to be true. When leading a trip, I find it is easier to sleep on the fifth and sixth day than the first four days because I have come from a controlled environment. I generally try to acclimate myself prior to a trip by opening the windows and sleeping without blankets.

Yet people who work in the outdoors and are continually subjected to the cold or heat can still maintain dexterity under these conditions. For instance, fishermen, loggers, and construction workers suffer few effects from being exposure to the weather to which they are accustomed; but they also dress suitably for their exposure.

I experienced this acclimation in the Bitterroot valley of Montana during one particularly cold winter. From late winter to spring temperatures were well below zero. At first I bundled up when I went to the wood pile. With each successive week the extremes seemed more bearable, until after a month of this activity I found myself checking the thermometer because it felt warmer than it actually was. By April, when it warmed up to 10° F. I was in my shirt sleeves.

Lacking the time to acclimate, the answer is insulation. According to the *Oxford American Dictionary*, to insulate is: 1) to cover or protect with a substance or device that prevents the...loss of heat; 2) to isolate from influences that might affect it. The key word being "affect."

Try this experiment next time you play couch potato: lay a single open sheet of newspaper over you. Within seconds you can feel the warmth generated from your body. You can easily see that doesn't take much insulation to stay warm if it is the 'right' insulation (remember, paper is a 'natural' product). Actually, anything in nature that works can be used as insulation: in addition to the down from birds, wool, and animal fur there is plant seed "down" (the fluffy seed pods of various plants), bark, grass, leaves and plant stalks.

We humans can take a lesson from the animal world as we see small creatures insulate their burrows with grass and fur. Birds use fibers and feathers to soften their nests before laying eggs, and insects build elaborate habitats with mud and bits of grass. What makes them so effective is that wool, fur, feathers and down, have a wonderful loft–they trap great quantities of air which in turn capture and retain body heat. Today, the modern search for a better insulation is driven by the attempt to "out-loft" nature.

But there is no insulation–natural or man-made–that is lighter, warmer, or softer than down. Down is the soft, shaftless clusters culled from the breasts and underbellies of geese and ducks. Each cluster is shaped like a ball, composed of thousands of fibers growing out of a central point. Feathers have shafts and are curved. Both feathers and down create a natural protective shield from the elements. They keep ducks and geese warm, even in the coldest climates by creating pockets of trapped air which insulate the birds. The colder it is, the harder your body works to produce heat, therefore more heat is trapped by the clusters of down, keeping you toasty warm.

Granted, down looses its loft when it gets wet, and some people believe that it also loses its insulating power when it is wet. Yet it takes down longer to get saturated than it does synthetics; its natural oils shed water and act as a built-in repellent. The main problem is quick drying: down simply does not give up water as easily and quickly as man-made fibers. However, in giving up water slowly, it preserves important body heat and energy.

So what do today's manufacturers of insulative material try to duplicate? According to a report by Dr. Fred Fortess, director of apparel research at the Philadelphia College of Textiles and Science, a single gram of wool gives off 27 calories of heat when it goes from dry to wet; as wool absorbs moisture from the air, the fibers liberate heat. This is a characteristic of wool that scientists have been trying to improve in synthetic fibers.

Du Pont claims their Micro-loft insulation offers "down-like" comfort. All manufacturers show charts and graphics that compare their products to the insulating ability of down and most fall short of achieving the fill power of down. (Fill power is a rating of down's quality as measured by its lofting ability. One ounce lofts to a maximum of 700 cubic inches.)

It is a difficult challenge: cut the wind and retain the warmth without getting all steamed up inside. Add to the challenge by wanting maximum performance and minimum weight. Yet nature's miracle insulators can meet many of these requirements.

The most common and profuse types of seed down come from cattails, thistles, milkweed and cottonwood. And, since some species of these plants grow all over the continent, I'm sure you can find at least one of them in your area. Other plants also yield seed "fluff" but it takes longer to collect in quantity, therefore is less energy effective. One disadvantage of seed down to duck or goose down is that it is seasonal.

Milkweed, thistle and cattail seeds ripen in late summer. Occasionally you can find cattail seed heads during the winter months that are still intact, and sometimes even into the following spring. But the wind, rain and snow generally strip thistle seeds by early fall and the dry pods of milkweed open completely to release their seeds to the ground. You can generally find large clumps of cottonwood seed pods on the ground in the early summer, but rain quickly flattens them, destroying the insulating properties.

The good thing about cattails and milkweed pods is that you can collect and store the entire seed head or seed pods before they explode and have a good supply all winter. Just remember...these are seeds and stored seed heads and pods attract critters looking for food.

Because it is easy to collect and often abundant, cattail down can be very useful in a variety of ways. First, it provides everything you need for a cozy bed. But don't sleep directly on the down because it gets into your mouth and nose and activates allergies. Instead, contain it between layers of cattail leaves, grass or bark. The insulation above you keeps it's loft, that below you gets compressed, so add extra layers between you and the ground where you intend to sleep.

You can also stuff seed down into socks, pant legs, gloves, or wrap some in a bandanna and use it for a headband or hat. But remember, too much of a good thing isn't always better. If you compact the down into your clothing, it restricts air flow and actually reduces the insulating effect. Your goal should be to provide a loose layer of insulation to trap body heat.

Unless your shoes or boots are exceptionally large, the best way to take advantage of seed down to warm your feet is to make a "bootie" by filling the space between two socks. Booties are great to wear around camp, for sleeping or for intermittent periods to warm feet on the trail.

I once made a cattail down vest from two shirts sewn together with yucca fiber and stuffed with approximately 17 cattail heads. It was comparable to a duck down garment for warmth and only slightly heavier in weight. We also made our son a cattail-down sleeping bag from his wool survival blanket and he used it for many moons, even after the down went flat. But that is the main problem with seed down, it is not as resilient as bird down–after a few weeks of use it should be replaced. Of course it can't be washed without destroying the loft, and it tends to "mat" if it gets wet.

The most comfortable sleeping comes when you have plenty of insulation beneath you. In fact, about 4 inches of dry grass laid criss-cross is a good mattress. Since most of your body heat escapes downward, about 70% of your insulation should go beneath you. It is normal for people to pile on the top layer to try to stay warm, but if you keep in mind the 70% rule, you will sleep far warmer and consequently, more comfortably.

Long strips of dead bark from cottonwood, juniper, sage, aspen or basswood trees, grass, and dry leaves all make excellent bedding or insulation. Gather as much as you can justify. In other words, if it is scarce take just enough to provide the warmth and insulation you need; if abundant, make yourself comfortable. The thicker your bedding, the warmer you will sleep and the more rest you will get for your effort. A good night's sleep helps your mind function at its utmost with new ideas and problem solving. It is pretty obvious if you spend the night shivering and shaking in the dirt you won't be your best the next morning.

Dry fallen pine needles also supply great (although sometimes piercing) comfort and insulation. The layer of needles piled up nearest the trunk of evergreen trees are usually dry, especially at lower elevations. The best thing about pine needles is their ability to "fill gaps." If you scatter a quantity of them on the floor of your shelter you won't have to be so careful about removing roots, rocks and filling in holes. The result is a "springy" cushion that can be covered with other less prickley bedding. It makes your shelter smell great, too. (See "A Soft Bed in the Woods" by Ernest Wilkinson, *The Best of Woodsmoke*. Horizon Publishers, 1983. p. 77.)

I emphasize dry pine needles because damp or wet bedding saps the heat from your body like wet clothes. Wet clothes cause heat loss at a rate 25 times faster than normal, and if the wind is blowing, the damp cloth acts as a wick that conducts body heat away much faster than it can be produced.

Not to mention the fact that your body is constantly perspiring, even when the weather is cold. If your clothes let this moisture accumulate, they can lose as much as 90% of their insulating properties. Any moisture that accumulates in your clothing acts as a direct pathway for heat to escape.

This is the reason I council my students to gather wood early in the afternoon: to avoid stumbling around in the dark, but also because they tend to put all their clothing on in the evening chill, then work up a sweat dragging in a wood supply. The resulting perspiration causes chilling which is hard to overcome in the night air. Besides, exercise in the cold uses up more fat than exercise in the heat.

Cattail stalks and reed grass are more rigid than cattail leaves or rushes, but they can easily be worked into mats by gathering several stalks into a bundle and tying them together. Keep in mind that not only does a sleeping mat provide insulation from the ground, but it also provides comfort. The body needs to be relaxed for much needed sleep and give energy under stress. A good sleeping mat provides warmth while it takes bumps and holes out of the hard ground.

Mats are most easily made with rushes, cattail leaves or long strips of dead bark. If you take the time to weave sleeping mats, you may as well take time to prepare your materials properly so the finished product will last as long as possible. Rushes and cattail leaves have to be dried first, then dampened a little to make them pliable enough to weave without breaking. Otherwise the leaves will shrink as they dry and your mat will fall apart. A simple over-under weave is the fastest method, gathering large clumps into each section. Seed down, grass or other material can be sandwiched in as you weave, or you can make two mats and put extra insulation between them. For a stationary camp this works great. In the morning, sleeping mats should be picked up to keep them from being walked on, and to prevent uninvited bedfellows.

Mats have several uses, not the least of which is to contain natural plant fibers. If you plan to occupy your camp for a month or more, consider the value of making shelter liners of mats similar to canvas tepee liners. You can also use grass, cattail or bulrush leaves sewn together and used to encircle the shelter. A few reeds or cattail leaves, bark or grass spread on the ground provides quickie insulation and keeps your sleeping area clean. Take it out in the morning and "fluff" it up and shake out small uninvited guests.

There are some things so perfect man can never hope to improve them, and snow is a prime example of one of Mother Nature's ideal insulators from, ironically, cold–one of the greatest challenges that can be faced by the body.

I once made a cozy (32-36°) snow cave shelter with pine boughs to insulate me from the melting snow, and rested dry and comfortable while a blizzard raged outside. In the winter, such protection is often a life or death factor, especially due to the possibility of excessive heat loss caused by wind chill. But "shelter" involves much more than building a refuge or crawling into a snow shelter or cave; insulation means protecting all parts of your frail body.

According to scientists, extreme cold is comparable to the effects of fear, rage, pain, asphyxia, or extreme heavy labor. So it is crucial to note that we enter the "very cold" range of wind-chill when the temperature is a mild +40° and the wind blowing only 25 mph. Thus, the necessity of protection for the body either by shelter insulation or directly insulating the exposed areas of the body becomes more evident with the increasing velocity of the wind.

Any shelter is good insulation if it provides protection from rain, snow, and particularly, wind. In cold weather the very activity of building a shelter or gathering insulating material can help generate body heat. Although excessive movement can cause dangerous perspiration, light activity helps generate body heat. Not to mention the fact that several people can be made safe and comfortable in one shelter and huddle together for additional warmth.

Two hundred fifty centuries ago, man learned the most basic concepts of shelter-building by trial and error. The knowledge was passed down from generation to generation, from continent to continent, or learned independently by different people all over the world..and still retained thousands of years later by late-bloomers on the North American Continent.

Before the Christian era, the earliest Basketmaker culture (hunter-gatherers) built domed structures over saucer shaped depressions. These shelters lacked one feature that Cro-Magnon people considered essential–an interior fireplace. Presumably, their heating system consisted of stones warmed in an outdoor fire and then laid in a pit dug in the house floor.

Much like the sweat lodges which were popular much later in history and are still used today.

A likely explanation of the outside fire pit is that the pit houses were covered with flammable brush and grass, making an interior fire dangerous. But whatever the reason, later inhabitants of the area, the Anasazi, built more conventional houses with a central fire pit, and a hole in the roof for smoke to escape.

A few hundred years later these people started to plant corn and squash and became a little more settled. They built more permanent homes of circular layers of logs laid in a sort of rail-fence arrangement and cemented with mud mortar.

Still later, the Basketmakers settled into slab-lined pit houses and planted beans, which required more attention than corn and squash, started using the bow and arrow, and began making pottery.

Then, about 900 A.D. pit houses went out of style and small pueblos, or cliff houses appeared. At first, they were just rows of joined masonry rooms one or two stories high, usually with an associated kiva, a circular chamber used for ceremonial purposes.

From there, the dwellings became more and more sophisticated and entire communities were built in large stone conclaves, like the famous dwellings in Mesa Verde, Colorado.

By studying these and other early dwellings, we can learn basic, time-proven principles that can be applied to any shelter construction today. Early people combined their human needs and ingenuity with the natural resources around them to develop shelter most suited to their lifestyles, within their natural environment. Many natural shelters can be found that can be as comfortable and weatherproof as a man-made construction.

For instance, the natural sheltering abilities of hollow-based trees, upturned roots, large logs or boulders will protect against the elements in a pinch. And a huge sage or juniper with it's umbrella-like branches can provide a dry shelter.

Dirt banks, rock shelters and caves can be improved with the addition of a few poles and some bark or other material piled against it, to keep out wind and rain.

A good campsite provides several things: protection from the wind, storms or flooding; level ground; an abundance of firewood; and food and water sources. Consider the need for mobility or permanence. If you plan to settle into a base camp for several days, it is important to have a good water source nearby for cooking and drinking. I like a flat area near water, but not too close. Everyone likes the relaxing sound of rushing water, but remember that insects are drawn to water and the air is more humid and cooler in the canyon floor and near the stream.

Improvised shelter can be found in rock overhangs or caves and improved with the addition of a few dead limbs or brush (Photo by Linda Jamison).

Next, choose an area where materials are close at hand. Large rocks are handy to bank a fire for warmth at night and to make cooking easy. A good supply of wood that can be broken up for firewood should be nearby as well as plenty of willows and large cottonwood trees to use as building and bedding materials.

The type of shelter I prefer to build in the desert environment is called a "wickiup." All wickiups seem to have two features in common: a frame or skeleton of poles, and some sort of covering. It is a spontaneous shelter that is time-tested and remains open for improvement by anyone.

Naturally, the size and materials used vary greatly with environment and culture. For instance, Apache wickiups were often thatched with grass, while Ojibwa wickiups were pole domes covered with sheets of birch or other bark. Plains Indians used animal hides to cover their rendition of a mobile home, which was warm, secure and easy to move as they migrated with their game. (For information on wickiup construction see 'The Wickiup' by Jim Riggs, *The Best of Woodsmoke*, Horizon Publishers, 1982. p. 22.)

Regardless of what shape or type of shelter you build, some factors should always be considered. For instance, build shelter that is sturdy enough to withstand the worst weather you plan to encounter and you will never worry about having it collapse in the middle of the night during a storm.

Determine the size of your shelter before you start. A little pre-planning can make all the difference in how well your shelter protects you from cold or heat, which is why you are building it in the first place. Especially in cold weather when you need to heat the interior, don't make it bigger than necessary. But do allow room to stow your gear and some dry firewood inside the shelter in case of rain or snow.

Whenever possible, face the opening of your shelter to the morning sun and keep the prevailing night wind at it's back. A large doorway left open can capture reflected heat from the night fire, yet provide shade and allow plenty of air to circulate during hot afternoons. If rain threatens, the doorway can be closed by a thatched grid, or a pre-fabricated panel can be used as a moveable closure and windbreak.

A small fire pit can be used inside an enclosed shelter as long as you leave an opening in the top for smoke to escape (like a tepee), burn non-resinous wood and keep the flames low. It's pretty obvious why you shouldn't use resinous woods that spark like Juniper or pine in an enclosed shelter. Soft woods like cottonwood or sage are good for a quick start up, then add some hardwoods like oak or maple for long-burning coals.

Spark reflectors are made with a few upright stakes or by piling up a few green pine boughs about six inches high around the fire pit to catch flying sparks and prevent burning up your dry bedding or your entire shelter for that matter. Bedding should be kept at least a foot away from your fire pit or reflector fire.

Shelters are relatively easy to build in a rich forest environment. That's why building one in the desert where marginal materials are available is a real test of ingenuity. But forested areas provide their own unique challenges. The main concern is moisture from both the ground and from above in the form of rain or snow, so it's important to insulate well. Moisture also indicates a fire within the shelter for warmth. So, you must build your shelter large enough that a sleeping fire will not set it on fire, yet not so large that you will lose valuable heat.

Among the many types of shelters that are quick and easy to build, the "A" frame takes the least amount of work and materials: Three forked stakes are wedged together or lashed to form a tripod, a long pole is stretched backward and rested on the ground, then logs and snags are leaned against the main pole to enclose the sides. The end can be closed or left open as you like, depending on the weather. Add a layer of insulation to the outside, then dry pine needles for bedding and you are finished. In heavy snow areas the snow will eventually pack to form insulation over the shelter.

A quickie shelter can also be built against a rock for added protection from wind and rain and the rock base holds heat from your reflected fire.

Another common mountain shelter is a lean-to. It is similar to the "A" frame but can be enlarged for more people. I like the lean-to because the design allows me to have a sleeping fire the length of my body. A lean-to is especially vulnerable to wind when one side is left open, but it is easy to enclose quickly in case of a storm. It is also inclined to collect winter snow drifts, so be sure to face your shelter so that the prevailing winds blow crosswise rather than directly into or behind it. If you plan to stay in an area for a week or more, excavate the floor a few inches and use the dirt to pile up around the outside for better insulation.

Obviously, the rule to building an adequate shelter is improvise, improvise, and improvise. Each geographical location will demand different structure and materials, each season of the year will mean more or less insulation.

You can use your own ingenuity to devise various types of shelters suitable for the circumstances at hand, but a good shelter is like a work of art, it should be built with pride in workmanship and an eye to utility.

The majority of my trips take place in the desert, a strange country where you can shiver all night in the cold and swelter in the heat of day, all in the same 24 hour period. And the first night is generally the worst for most students, probably because they don't know what to expect. Most of them wake up several times during the night. I can almost set my watch by it.

In an open wickiup, the fire is built just outside the opening of the shelter, not inside, and banked with rocks or logs to reflect heat into the shelter. Once you get a good bed of coals going, you can add a log about as long as the shelter doorway. The reflected heat keeps you warm most of the night. And you can keep a few extra pieces of wood within arm's reach to add in the coldest hours of early morning. A good pit fire surrounded with stones ashes over rather quickly and can remain alive for many hours to provide relatively safe heat.

I recall one particular morning, about 2 a.m., I heard some rustling and one of the younger girls crying. She was sleeping about 5 feet from the fire, her wood pile was too far away to reach and she was using her wool sweater for a pillow. We made a few adjustments, I put some warm rocks from the fire trench into the bottom of her blanket to warm her feet, and we both got a good night's rest.

Most of us sleep with all our clothes on, including our boots for maximum insulation. This keeps us warm, but it can also create problems. Soles have actually burned right off the bottoms of boots while the wearer snores contentedly. Hair can also catch a spark if your head is too near the fire, so the best and safest way to sleep is lengthwise to the trench. Of course, this necessitates one fire for every couple of people, so we have

The wickiup is a spontaneous shelter that has two two common components: a frame and some sort of covering (Photo by Richard Jamison).

devised other ways of maximizing our heat in really cold months. We huddle up on draft beds. But that's another entire chapter (see "Primitive Comfort–The Hot Draft Bed", *Primitive Outdoor Skills*, p. 131).

On the trail, everyone begins with equal advantage: blanket, knife, the clothes they are wearing, extra socks, a hat and a jacket. They don't always end that way, as was the case for one careless fellow. It was early spring and the weather was unpredictable with fluctuating cold nights and warm days. Each morning he shed his jacket and shirt and just left them where he took them off–generally scattered all over camp. I took him aside and explained that, since his clothing was about all he had in the world on this trip, he should take better care of it. Peeling off a layer in the heat is one thing, whipping up a sage bark robe before the evening chill is quite another.

To some, sound advice lasts a lifetime, to others it disappears in the wind. The weather was mild until about the fifth day when I noticed gathering black clouds that signaled a possible front coming in. By the time storm clouds loomed on the horizon and darkness rushed in to close the day, temperatures fell rapidly and it was too late to build shelter from the bitter winds and cold. I suggested that we move our camp to an area with better shelter options, just in case. After the move we settled in, started new fires, staked out our sleeping positions and commenced to find firewood and set new traps for our meal the next day.

The temperature dropped and we put on our jackets and wrapped up in our blankets. Everyone except, you guessed it... We all began to search. "What does it look like," we asked.

"A quilted Levi jacket," he answered.

"Maybe you dropped it on the trail when we were moving," someone suggested.

"No, I left it right here on this rock by the fire," he assured us.

"Maybe this is it," replied my son, as he fished five metal Levi buttons out of the ashes of the fire. The guy was devastated.

The next morning we woke up to three inches of unexpected snow.

Mature cattail seed heads offer profuse amounts of fluff that can be easily collected in quantity and used for insulation. (Photo: Richard Jamison)

Notes and References

Our Human Family

Notes:

1. Charles P. Mountford, *Brown Men and Red Sand*, (Melbourne: Robertson and Mullens, 1948).
2. Brian M. Fagan, *The Journey from Eden: The Peopling of Our World*, (London: Thames and Hudson, Ltd., 1990): 9.
3. Jared Diamond, "The Great Leap Forward," *Discover* (May 1989): 57.
4. *Epic of Man*, Courtlandt Canby, ed., (New York: Time Incorporated, Book Div., 1961): 39-40.
5. Jared Diamond: 57.
6. Brian Fagan: 23-41.
7. Sharon Begley with Fiona Gliezes, "My Grandad Neanderthal?" *Newsweek*, (16 October 1989): 70-71.
8. *Epic of Man*: 18-23.
9. Robert Redfield, "The Folk Society," *American Journal of Sociology*, 52 (January 1947): 299.
10. "The Search for Our Ancestors," Kenneth Weaver, ed., *National Geographic* (November 1985): 614.

The Ultimate Weapon

Notes:

1. Gilbert Blue (Catawba), personal communication, 1979; Bill Brescia (Choctaw), personal communication, 1985; Richard Crowe (Cherokee), personal communication, 1980.
2. Tom Underwood, personal communication, 1988.
3. Claude Medford, interview with author, 1988.
4. Hayes Lossiah (Cherokee), personal communication, 1980.
5. Medford, 1988.
6. Blue, 1979.
7. Bonnie Wyatt, personal communication, 1989.
8. Roger McDaniel, personal communication, 1988.
9. Underwood, 1988.
10. Richard Crowe, personal communication, 1985.

References:

Bossu, Jean Bernard. *Nouveaux Voyages Aux Indes Occidentales*. Paris, 1768.

Kroeber, A.L. *Anthropology*. New York: Harcourt Brace, 1948.

Nash, Charles H. "Choctaw Blowguns." *Ten Years of Tennessee Archaeologist, 1954-1963. Vol. II.* 1963.

Romans, Bernard "A Concise Natural History of East and West Florida." *NewYork* Vol I. (1775).

Speck, Frank G. "The Creek Indians of Taskigi Town," *Mem. American Anthropological Association.* 2:1 (1907).

"Ethnology of the Yuchi Indians," *Anthropological Publications of the University Museum: University of Pennsylvania.* 1:1 (1909).

"The Cane Blowgun In Catawba and Southeastern Ethnology," *American Anthropologist.* 40 (1938).

Swanton, John R. "The Indians of the Southeastern United States." *Bureau of American Ethnology. Bulletin 137.* 1946.

Timberlake, Lieut. Henry. *The Memoirs of Lieut. Henry Timberlake (who accompanied the three Cherokee Indians to England in the year 1762) containing...an accurate map of their Over-hill Settlement.* London, 1765.

Primitive Process Pottery

Brian, Wayne. *Primitive Pottery Processes: Workshop Guide for Students.* Mesa: Wayne Brian, 1990.

Fewkes, Jesse Walter. *Archaeological Expedition to Arizona.* U.S. Government Printing Office, 1897.

Harlow, Francis H. *Historic Pueblo Indian Pottery.* Museum of New Mexico Press, 1970.

Hartt, Fred. *Notes on the Manufacture of Pottery.* Rio De Janeiro: Office of South American Mail, 1875.

Lambert, David. *The Field Guide to Geology.* New York: Facts on File, Inc., 1988.

Lambert, Marjorie F. *Pueblo Indian Pottery.* Museum of New Mexico Press, 1970.

Read, H.H., and Janet Watson. *Beginning Geology.* New York: The Macmillan and Company, Ltd., 1966.

Societe d'Exploitation. *Ancient American Pottery.* Paris: Les Editions Du Chene, 1950.

Stacey, Joseph, ed. *Southwestern Pottery Today; Special Edition.* Arizona Highways, Vol. 50:5 (May 1974).

Stiles, Helen E. *Pottery of the American Indians.* New York: E.P. Dutton & Co., Inc., 1939.

Stone Survival Tools

Fisher, Donald B. "Stone Tools for Survival." *Dirt Times* (Summer 1989).
Hellweg, Paul. *Flintknapping: The Art of Making Stone Tools.* Canoga Park: Canyon Publishing Co., 1984.
Hellweg, Paul. "Grinding Arrowheads." *Flintknapping Digest* (October 1984).

Yucca

Harrington, H. D. *Edible Native Plants of the Rocky Mountains.* Albuquerque: The University of New Mexico Press, 1970.
Rose, J. N. *Notes on Useful Plants of Mexico.* U.S. National Museum, Contribution to United States National Herbarium 5 (1899): 209-259.
Saunders, C. F. "The Yucca and the Indian." *The American Botanist 17* (February 1911): 1-3.
Stanley, Paul C. "Some Useful Plants of New Mexico." *Annual Report of the Smithsonian Institute.* Government Printing Office, Washington D.C.: 1912: 447-462.
Tanner, Clara Lee. *Prehistoric Southwestern Craft Arts.* Tucson: University of Arizona Press, 1976.
Tate, Joyce L. *Cactus Cook Book.* Arcadia, California: Cactus and Succulent Society of America, Inc., 1978.
Wheat, Margaret M. *Survival Arts of the Primitive Paiutes.* Reno: University of Nevada Press, 1967.

Traditional Basketry Materials

Adovasio, J. M. *Prehistoric North American Basketry* Carson City: Nevada State Museum Papers. Vol. 16:5 (1974).
——*Basketry Technology: A guide to Identification and Analysis* Chicago: Aldine. 1977.
Barrows, David P. *Ethno-botany of the Coahuilla Indians of Southern California* Chicago: Univ. of Chicago Press, 1900.
Bates, Craig. "Yosemite Miwok/Paiute Basketry: A Study in Cultural Change." *American Indian Basketry* 2:4 (1982): 3-22.
——"Lucy Telles: A Supreme Weaver of the Miwok/Paiute." *American Indian Basketry* 2:4 (1982): 23-29.
——"Traditional Miwok Basketry." *American Indian Basketry* 4(1) 1984: 3-15.
Berenstein, Bruce. "Panamint Shoshone Coiled Basketry: A Definition of Style." *American Indian Art* 4:4 (1979): 69-74.

Emmons, G.T. *The Basketry of the Tlingit. Bulletin 3.* New York: American Museum of Natural History, 1903.

Harrington, John P. "Chainfern and Maidenhair Adornment Materials of Northwestern California Basketry." in *So Live the Works of Men.* Fred Harvey and Donald D. Brand eds. Albuquerque: UNM Press, 1939.

Heizer, Robert F. "One of the Oldest known California Indian Baskets." *Masterkey* 40 (1968): 70-74.

Kroeber, A.L. *Handbook of the Indians of California.* Bureau of American Ethnology 78. Washington DC: Smithsonian, 1925.

Hart, Merriam C. *Studies of California Indians.* Berkeley: UC Press, 1955.

——*Indian Names for Plants and Animals among Californian and Other Western North American Tribes.* R. F. Heizer ed. Socorro, NM: Ballena Press, 1979.

Merrill, Ruth M. *Plants Used in Basketry by the California Indians.* Ramona: Acoma Books, 1970.

Moser, Chris L. *Native American Basketry of Central California.* Riverside: Riverside Museum Press, 1986.

Newman, S.C. *Indian Basket Making: How to Weave Pomo, Yurok, Pima and Navaho Baskets.* Flagstaff: Northland Press, 1974.

Peri, David W. and Scott M. Patterson. "The Basket is in the Roots, That's Where it Begins." *Journal of California Anthropology* 3:2 (1976): 17-32.

Rozaire, Charles E. *Analysis of Woven Materials From Seven Caves in the Lake Winnemucca Area,* Pershing County, Nevada. Carson City: Nevada State Museum Papers 16:4 (1974).

Tuohy, Donald R. *A Cache of Fin Coiled, Feathered, and Decorated Baskets from Western Nevada.* Carson City: Nevada State Museum Papers 16:4 (1974).

Wolpert, Cheri Rae. "Pomo Indian Baskets." *California Scenic* 1:1 (1987).

——"Karuk Basketry." *California Scenic* 2:1 (1988).

A Paleo Prescription

Notes:
1. Brian M. Fagan, *The Journey from Eden: The Peopling of Our World,* (London: Thames and Hudson, Ltd., 1990): 76.
2. Fagan: 61.
3. Fagan: 42-43.
4. Boyd Eaton and Marjorie Shostak, "Fat Tooth Blues," *Natural History* (July 1986): 6-13.
5. Melvin Konner, "What Our Ancestors Ate," *New York Times Magazine* (5 June 1988): 54-55.

6. Francine Hermline, "The Food-Stress Link," *Working Woman* (May 1993): 92.
7. Arlene Stadd, "Why We Crave," *Weight Watcher's Magazine* (November 1992): 54-56.
8. Reuben, *The Save Your Life Diet,* (New York: Random House, 1975): 4-10.
9. "The Search for Our Ancestors," Kenneth Weaver, ed., *National Geographic* (November 1985): 623.

An Introduction to the Atlatl

References:
Allely, Steve. "Great Basin Atlatls: Notes from the N.W. Corner." *Bulletin of Primitive Technology.* 1:4 (1992).
Baker, Tim. "Thong-thrown Arrows and Spears." *Bulletin of Primitive Technology.* 1:4 (1992).
Brian, Wayne. "Guiness World Record - Distance Record Holder." Personal Conversations. 1992.
Cahill, Tim. "The Atlatl, A Great Leap Backward." *Mother Earth News,* 1987.
Callahan, Errett. *The Cahokia Pit House Project: A Case Study In Reconstructive Archaeology.* Unpublished Draft, 1988.
Collins, Wilkie. "About Atlatls." *Homochito Replications Catalog,* 1988.
Comstock, Paul. "Throwing Darts With The Baton de Commandment." *Bulletin of Primitive Technology* 1:4 (1992).
Frison, George. "Elephant Hunting." *The Mammoth Trumpet.* 2:3.
Harwood, Ray. "The Atlatl." *Flintknappers Digest.* 2:3.
Miles, Charles. *Indian and Eskimo Artifacts of North America.* American Legacy Press, 1979.
Hunter, Wryley. "Reconstructing A Generic Basketmaker Atlatl." *Bulletin of Primitive Technology.* 1:4 (1992).
Olsen, Larry Dean. *Outdoor Survival Skills.* BYU Press, 1981.
Perkins, William R. and Paul Leininger. "The Weighted Atlatl and Dart: A Deceptively Complicated Mechanical System." *The ATLATL.* 2:2; 2:3; 3:1 (1989).
——*Instructions for the Mammoth Hunter Atlatl and Dart System.* BPS Engineering.
Ratzat, Craig. "ATLATLS: Throwing for Distance." *Bulletin of Primitive Technology.* 1:4 (1992).
Raymond, Anan. "Experiments in the function and performance of the weighted atlatl." *World Archaeology: Weaponry and Warfare.* 18:2 (1986).

Stokes, John, Director of The Tracking Project. Personal Conversations, 1987.

Stanford, Dennis. "Bison Kill By Ice Age Hunters." *National Geographic* 155:1 (1979).

Tate, Marcia. *The Atlatl Story: An Ice Age Hunting Weapon.* Tate Enterprises, 1987.

——*The Atlatl Newsletter of the World Atlatl Association.* Edited by William Tate. Multiple Volumes.

Tate, Bill. *Survival With the Atlatl: The Ancient Weapon of the Ice Age Hunter.* Tate Enterprises, 1987.

Webb, William S. "The Development of the Spear Thrower." *Occasional Papers in Anthropology* (University of Kentucky) 2 (1957).

Wescott, David. "An Introduction to the Atlatl." *Backwoodsman Magazine.* (November/December 1988).

The Paiute Deadfall

Notes:
1. John McPherson, *Making Meat: II,* (Randolph, Kansas: McPherson, 1988): 21-22.

References

Cressman, Luther S. *Prehistory Of The Far West, Homes of Vanished People,* Salt Lake City: University of Utah Press, 1977: 108.

Dalley, Gardiner F. "Swallow Shelter and Associated Sites," *University of Utah Anthropological Papers,* 114, Salt Lake City: Univ. of Utah Press, 1976: 62-63.

Fowler, Catherine S., Comp. and ed. "Willard Z. Park's Ethnographic Notes On The Northern Paiute Of Western Nevada, 1933-1944, Vol. I," *University of Utah Anthropological Papers,* 96, Salt Lake City: Univ. of Utah Press, 1989: 23-24.

Olsen, Larry. "Deadfall Trapping." In *The Best of Woodsmoke,* compiled by Richard L. Jamison, 71-76. Bountiful, Utah: Horizon Publishers, 1982.

Jennings, Jesse D. "Prehistory Of Utah And The Eastern Great Basin," *University of Utah Anthropological Papers,* 98, Salt Lake City: Univ. of Utah Press, 1978: 47.

Kelly, Isabel T. "Ethnography Of The Surprise Valley Paiute," *University of California Publications in American Archaeology & Ethnology,* 31 (1932): 87-88.

Loud, Llewellyn L., and M. R. Harrington. "Lovelock Cave," *University of California Publications in American Archaeology & Ethnology*, 25:1 (1929): 154-155.

Lowie, Robert H. "Note On Shoshonian Ethnography," *Anthropological Papers Of The American Museum Of Natural History*, 20:3. American Museum Press, 1924: 199.

McPherson, John *Making Meat II*. Randolph: Kansas: McPherson, 1988: 21-22. (Available at P.O. Box 96, Randolph, KS 66394.

Olsen, Larry Dean *Outdoor Survival Skills*. 4th ed., Provo, Utah: Brigham Young University Press, 1973: 78-79.

Steward, Julian H. "Ethnography Of The Owens Valley Paiute," *University of California Publications in American Archaeology & Ethnology*, 33, (1933): 254.

Wheat, Margaret M. *Survival Arts of the Primitive Paiutes*. Reno: University of Nevada Press, 1967: 72-73.

Index

A

Aboriginal lifestyle 3
Africa 5, 13
Anasazi Indians 192-193
Animal tracking. *See Tracking*
Archery 189
Arrowheads 54, 57-58
Ash Cooking 116-117, 228
Atlatl 177-190
    darts 185-187
    manufacture 187-188
    use 180-183, 186, 188
Axe, hand 54, 57

B

Badger 196-197
Basketry
    bark 89-92, 149-161
    decorative materials 95-98
    juniper 88, 149-161
    leaves and grasses 93-94
    materials 85-98
    pine needle 199-208
    roots 87-89
    seed pods 92-93
    shoots 86-87, 121-136
    vines 92
    willow 86-87, 121-136
    wood splints 94-95
Blowgun, Southeastern 15-24
    darts 22-23
    history 16-17
    manufacture 17-22
BYU Youth Leadership
    480 Program 225, 228

C

Catawba Indians 15-17, 20, 22, 24
Cattails 238
Cherokee Indians 15-18, 22-23
Choctaw Indians 15-17, 20
Clay 35, 37-42
    collection 37-38
    modeling 42
    preparation 39-40
Cooking 109-120
    ash 116-117
    boiling 120
    fires 110-111
    grilling 113-115
    pit 109, 117-120
    skewering 111-112
    spit 112-113
    stone oven 115-116
Cordage 66-67, 68
Cro-Magnon 11, 147, 233, 239

D

Deadfall. *See Paiute deadfall*

F

Finland 25-34
    fishing 29-34
    hunting 25-29
Fire Piston 163-175
    discovery 166-170
    manufacture 172-174
    origins 170-172
    use 174-175
Fishing 29-34
Flintknapping 54-59
    ethics 58-59

Food 75-76, 137-147
    cooking. See *Cooking*
    nutritional value of
        wild foods 140-141
    nutritional value of
        wild game 144-145
    yucca 75-76

H
Hertzian Cone 54
Hide Glue 77-84
    care 83-84
    manufacturing 80-83
Homo Sapiens 5, 9-10, 138
Hunter-gatherer 8-9, 53, 137, 142
Hunting 25-29

I
Insulation 234-239
Ishi 26

J
Juniper-bark baskets.
    See also basketry 149-161
    aboriginal examples 151
    manufacture 155-161
    removing bark 153-154
    tools 150, 152

K
Kiddles 33-34
Knife, stone 54

L
Leadership 8
Lean-to. See *Shelter* 242-243

N
Native American culture and
    tradition 2, 11, 13, 85
Neanderthals 4, 6-11, 232-233
Nettles 23

O
Oven. See *Cooking, stone oven*

P
Paiute deadfall 209-223
    components 213-217
    setting 217-218
    troubleshooting 218-223
Paiute Indians 192-193, 210
Pine needle baskets. See *Basketry*
    199-208
Pit Cooking. See *Cooking, pit*
Possibles Bag 61, 193, 197
Pottery 3, 35-52
    clay 35, 37
    coil and scrape technique 43
    color 46
    decoration 45-46
    designs 49, 51
    glossary 51-52
    firing 48-49
    form 40
    history 36-37
    modeling 42
    painting 46
    polishing 45
    slips 45
    tools 41
Ptarmigan, snaring 25, 28

R
Raffia 202
Rivercane. See *Blowgun,*
    Southeastern

S

Sandals, Yucca 72-73
Search-and-Rescue. *See Tracking, man*
Shelter 231-232, 239-245
Snow Cave 239
Spit Cooking 112-113
Steam Pit, 117-120
Stone tools. *See Tools*
Stone Oven 115-116
Survival 106-108, 225

T

Tachypyrion. *See Fire Piston*
Thistle 22, 23
Tools 53-59
Tracking 99-108
    animals 95-102
    man 102-106
Tracking stick 104
Trail marking 106-107
Traps. *See Paiute deadfall*

W

Wickiups, *see also shelter* 241, 244
Wild Foods 137-147
Willow Baskets. *See also Basketry*
    86-87, 121-135
    finishing 131-135
    harvesting willow 124-125
    materials 123-124
    shaping 131
    splicing 128-129
    spokes 129-131
    tools 125
    twining 128
    weaving 125-126

Y

Yucca 4, 61-76
    bags 74
    basketry 69
    brushes 76
    cordage 66-67, 68
    firestarter 74-75
    food 75-76
    identification 61-64
    needle and thread 71
    sandles 71-74
    soap 76
    uses 64-76
    weaving 69-71